Text Analytics

Text Analytics
An Introduction to the Science and Applications of Unstructured Information Analysis

John Atkinson-Abutridy

CRC Press
Taylor & Francis Group
Boca Raton London New York

CRC Press is an imprint of the
Taylor & Francis Group, an **informa** business

A CHAPMAN & HALL BOOK

First edition published 2022
by CRC Press
6000 Broken Sound Parkway NW, Suite 300, Boca Raton, FL 33487-2742

and by CRC Press
4 Park Square, Milton Park, Abingdon, Oxon, OX14 4RN

CRC Press is an imprint of Taylor & Francis Group, LLC

© 2022 John Atkinson-Abutridy

Library of Congress Cataloging-in-Publication Data
Names: Atkinson-Abutridy, John, author.
Title: Text analytics : an introduction to the science and applications of unstructured information analysis / John Atkinson-Abutridy.
Description: First edition. | Boca Raton : CRC Press, 2022. |
Includes bibliographical references and index.
Identifiers: LCCN 2021056159 | ISBN 9781032249797 (hardback) |
ISBN 9781032245263 (paperback) | ISBN 9781003280996 (ebook)
Subjects: LCSH: Text data mining. | Natural language processing (Computer science) |
Semantics—Data processing. | Document clustering.
Classification: LCC QA76.9.D343 A85 2022 | DDC 006.3/12—dc23/eng/20220105
LC record available at https://lccn.loc.gov/2021056159

ISBN: 978-1-032-24979-7 (hbk)
ISBN: 978-1-032-24526-3 (pbk)
ISBN: 978-1-003-28099-6 (ebk)

DOI: 10.1201/9781003280996

Typeset in Minion
by codeMantra

eResources are available for download at https://www.routledge.com/Atkinson-Abutridy/p/book/9781032249797

To Ivana, my wife and my light

Contents

List of Figures

List of Tables

Preface

WHEN I THOUGHT ABOUT WRITING THIS BOOK, I WASN'T CLEAR ENOUGH where to start, as there are many related topics that could be addressed. However, it was clear to me that I wanted to share knowledge in the simplest possible way, so that professionals with basic knowledge could not only understand the theoretical and practical topics related to text analytics but also perceive their applications and impact in a cross-sectional way in many areas.

The challenge wasn't simple, because despite my experience as an academic, I'm used to writing specialized scientific articles (papers) and technical books, giving technical conferences to scientific audiences and directing scientific-technological projects evaluated by experts, etc. that is, activities aimed at professionals/scientists who are able to understand complex issues. But this isn't the case for common professionals and specialists in general; in other words, accessible and understandable formal literature was required for them to understand the fundamentals in a simple way as well as the applications.

There were several alternatives to address the above, such as theoretical books, which are already available. However, these are usually focused toward more advanced professionals and/or postgraduate students leaving aside practical and applied aspects. On the other hand, there are several practical books focused on programming aspects; however, they're usually highly biased to the author's own conception of the subject. Furthermore, in my experience as an academic teaching text analytics and text mining courses for many years, both within and outside Chile, I've been able to verify how the students, professionals, or technicians who rely on such books simply don't understand what they're doing, not being able to compare/analyze methods or models, being unable to go beyond what's written. This is mainly because they're over-focused on coding in specific languages, where, unfortunately, many functionalities are arranged as "black boxes", that is, hiding all the technical details, making it hard to replicate their experiences using other computational methods or tools.

The book's nature was clear then. This should be an introductory book combining the basic theoretical foundations of the different paradigms and methods of textual analytics, with practical aspects, accompanied by examples in some programming language, which would allow us to fully understand the background and logic of computational methods, but at the same time, being flexible enough to use and implement them in other languages or computational tools.

I should take advantage of my academic experience to help professionals better understand computational concepts and methods. For more than 25 years, I've taught undergraduate and postgraduate courses related to text analytics, text mining, natural-language processing, and artificial intelligence at several national and foreign universities. While doing this, I learned a lot from students and professionals alike, understanding what was easier or difficult for them to understand, their questioning of what was established, their ways of taking something complex and simplifying it, etc.

On the other hand, my extensive experience as a scientific researcher and consultant, developing and leading scientific projects, and transferring technologies to the public and private sectors, should also have something to say in the way I'm focusing this book. Indeed, much of what the book conveys had to do not only with the basis behind computational methods but also with the challenges and considerations involved in the study, use and design of computational methods in real practical problems. Thus, the book is the result of both types of experiences, which allows us to understand not only the *how* but also the *why*.

After all these years doing this, why am I creating this text analytics book now? Globally, this is a long-standing topic, and we started seeing this in the mid-1990s in Chile, at the academy. However, in many ways, society and industry weren't prepared, and, up to a certain extent, many didn't see the need to be prepared, considering it to be something abstract and, therefore, impractical, taking into account not only the small amount of data available for them in that period but also performing several analytical tasks manually, like the old days.

However, the access and size of data sources, and in particular unstructured ones such as texts and documents, have experienced exponential growth in the last 10 years. This led to important scientific advances in both new and improved methods of text analytics as well as a greater need for companies, not only to analyze structured information automatically per se but to generate insights from it, improving their decision-making and business productivity.

Nor is it fortuitous that the writing of this book went through two major local and international crises. First, there was the unprecedented social crisis that affected Chile in October 2019. Then, since the end of 2019, the world has been affected by a gigantic global pandemic of the COVID-19 disease, and, even now, when finishing this book, when it will come to an end is still uncertain. But what do these two recent events have in common?

In addition to the already increasing information overload, in the case of Chile, the social crisis generated an enormous flow of information, especially related to social media information, whose analysis was key to making strategic decisions in terms of discovering links in informal textual information. On the other hand, in the case of the pandemic, there has been a large accumulation of scientific literature (i.e., formal textual information), around the investigations that shed light on various factors related to COVID-19, and that, due to its dimension (more than 45,000 articles) and complexity, it's necessary to have advanced textual analytics methods that can automatically extract and discover relevant knowledge that allows research to progress, a task that clearly cannot be performed manually by human experts.

The above shows once again not only the technological, critical, and strategic relevance of text analytics but also the need of a book capable of introducing this technology as a powerful decision-making tool.

Crises bring opportunities, and this book was written in the midst of a crisis.

ABOUT THIS BOOK

This is an introductory book to the science and applications of text analytics or text mining, which enables automatic knowledge discovery from unstructured information sources. With this purpose, the book introduces the main concepts, models, and computational techniques that allow solving several real decision-making problems coming from textual and/or documentary sources.

Audience

If you have textual data sources that you need to understand, this is the right book for you. If you want to obtain textual data and want to take advantage of it to discover and/or detect important knowledge, this is also the right book for you. If you want to understand the paradigms and computational methods to perform textual analytics, this book then is a must for you. If you are looking to understand the basic theoretical and practical aspects to teach a course in text analytics, this is definitely a suitable guide for you.

Although this book is introductory, it would help if you are familiar with the following aspects:

- Basic knowledge of linear algebra, statistics, and probabilities.

- Basic concepts of *Machine Learning*.

- Some knowledge of Python. If you don't know how to use it, it's not a problem since it's really easy to learn. In particular, it would be useful if you're familiar with the definition of functions, handling of storage structures (i.e., tables, lists, matrices, data frames, dictionaries, and files), and some basic visualization libraries.

Organization of the Book

This book has nine chapters, each of which contains two parts: (1) An introductory part that teaches the main concepts, paradigms and methods, models; and (2) a second part showing practical exercises in Python on everything that was studied in the chapter. On the other hand, for the reader's familiarity and as complementary literature, each chapter will end with the basic terminology used internationally.

Chapter 1: Text Analytics

This chapter introduces the main concepts, approaches, and applications for the automatic analysis of unstructured information (i.e., texts) known as textual analytics. In addition, the textual analytics process, tasks, and main challenges are described.

Chapter 2: Natural-Language Processing

This chapter introduces the basic concepts and computational and linguistic techniques that make it possible for a computer to process natural language. In addition, the main techniques and the way in which they address different problems associated with language processing in texts written by humans are described (i.e., morphological analysis, syntactic analysis, semantic analysis, discourse analysis).

Chapter 3: Information Extraction

This chapter introduces the concepts and some methodologies for the identification and extraction of specific information from the document body, using NLP techniques (i.e., relation extraction, named-entity recognition). In addition, the main problems and how they can be solved to support the tasks of text analytics are also described.

Chapter 4: Document Representation

This chapter introduces the different concepts, approaches, and models to computationally characterize and represent textual information in the form of documents so that they can be used in textual analytic tasks. Typical approaches based on indexing methods and space model vector for documents are described (i.e., term frequency models, inverse document frequency models).

Chapter 5: Association Rules Mining

This chapter introduces the main concepts, methods, and problems associated with the patterns extraction from documents, in the form of association rules. The main approaches and metrics for evaluating the quality of the discovered patterns are described (i.e., APRIORI algorithm).

Chapter 6: Corpus-based Semantic Analysis

This chapter explores the fundamentals of different techniques and models, allowing readers to study and model the meaning of words and documents. For this, different approaches are described for the automatic generation of low-dimensional distributed representation or word embeddings (i.e., LSA, Word2Vec) that allow one to efficiently capture the meaning of words and documents in context from the training corpus.

Chapter 7: Document Clustering

This chapter describes computational concepts and methods for performing document clustering. Modern grouping principles, metrics, and algorithms (i.e., K-means, self-organizing maps) are introduced to find hidden patterns in the document corpus.

Chapter 8: Topic Modeling

This chapter introduces the main concepts and methods for grouping documents based on latent topics within those documents. The main approaches for the automatic generation of topics based on probabilistic models (i.e., pLSA, LDA) are discussed.

Chapter 9: Document Categorization

This chapter describes the main concepts, models, and techniques for performing automatic text categorization. Different probabilistic and stochastic methods are described to predict the category to which the documents belong from a training corpus (i.e., Naïve Bayes classifier, Maximum entropy classifier).

Exercises

Each chapter has an exercise section that shows examples and simple practical applications written in *Python* of the different models and methods described. Each chapter introduces concepts that are cumulative, so your hands-on exercises also reuse code functionality from previous chapters. The sample programs are divided by chapter, and there's also a functions library defined in all chapters common to various exercises called "utils.py". All this, together with all the text documents used in each exercise, are available on the book site: https://www.routledge.com/Atkinson-Abutridy/p/book/9781032249797

Everything is programmed in *Python 3.7* in the *Spyder* environment for *Windows*, under the *Anaconda*[1] distribution. In addition, we use methods and functions that are available in two libraries:

- NLTK[2]: The *Natural-Language Toolkit* (NLTK) was created by academics and researchers as a tool to create complex natural-language processing (NLP) functions and algorithms for multiple human languages using *Python*. In addition to libraries for different NLP tasks, NLTK includes sample datasets and graphical demos to explain the principles of NLP tasks.

- SpaCY[3]: This is an NLP library in Python and Cython designed to build industrial systems. SpaCY includes several pretrained machine learning and statistical models for more than 50 languages.

---

[1] https://www.anaconda.com/products/individual
[2] https://www.nltk.org/
[3] https://spacy.io/

Both provide functionality for similar tasks. However, NLTK is more aimed at scientists/researchers who want to build and experiment with more complex algorithms, while SpaCY is oriented toward application development, providing access to tasks with the best results, but not allowing for practical deep experimentation compared to NLTK.

In order to have the facilities provided by both tools, some packages must be installed through the Anaconda command console:

pip install spacy

pip install --user -U nltk

In addition, a pretrained language model for English[4] must be installed in SpaCY, which is based on a news corpus (en_core_news_sm):

python -m spacy download en_core_news_sm

On the other hand, sample documents in the form of short news, and those used in the exercises of each chapter are available in the corpus folder on the book site. This contains a sample of international news summaries divided in three subdirectories: music (22 summaries), sports (10 summaries), and coronavirus (16 summaries). In addition, for some exercises, data sets available in three CSV format files will be used: "training.csv" (data for model training), "testing.csv" (data for model testing), and "new.csv" (data for model application).

John Atkinson-Abutridy
Santiago, Chile

---

[4] https://spacy.io/models/en

Acknowledgments

I THANK ALL THOSE WHO HELPED WITH THE READING AND REVISION of the draft of this book in its different stages, providing comments, corrections, and invaluable feedback: Graciela Mardones, Margarita Hantke, Mabel Vega, Diego Palma, Eladio Lisboa, Diego Reyes, Victor Toledo, Rodolfo Abanto, Gonzalo Gómez, Carlos Parrá, and Francisco Pallauta. Special thanks to Andrés Morales who made a wonderful front cover design.

I want to thank my wife Ivana, who always supported and urged me to write this book. I owe her a lot for all the time she sacrificed so I could move forward and finish this book.

Author

John Atkinson-Abutridy earned a PhD in Artificial Intelligence from the University of Edinburgh, UK. He is currently a full-time professor at the Faculty of Engineering and Sciences of the Adolfo Ibañez University (Santiago, Chile) and has been a full-time professor at other Chilean universities such as the Technical University Federico Santa María (Valparaíso) and the University of Concepción (Concepción), as well as visiting professor and researcher at various European, North American, and Asian universities. His main research areas include natural-language processing, text analytics, artificial intelligence, and bio-inspired computing, on which he has published more than 90 scientific articles. In the last 24 years, Dr. Atkinson-Abutridy has directed several scientific and technological projects at national and international levels and has been a visiting researcher at several universities and research centers in the USA, Europe, Asia, and South America. As a business consultant, he has led the implementation of advanced technological projects in artificial intelligence, as well as transferred and commercialized intelligent systems for multiple productive sectors. He is a professional member of the AAAI (Association for the Advancement of Artificial Intelligence) and a senior member of the ACM (Association for Computing Machinery).

CHAPTER 1

Text Analytics

1.1 INTRODUCTION

There are thousands of scientific articles in the world on viruses and diseases that human specialists aren't able to read or analyze. How could computers process such documents and be able to make discoveries and/or detect patterns of interest so that humans can make decisions about new treatments, drugs, and interactions between bio-components? A company receives hundreds of complaints or inquiries from customers daily through its website or emails. How could this company analyze those complaints to study and determine common behaviors and customer profiles in order to offer them a better service? An Internet news outlet receives hundreds of national and international news reports weekly. How could this medium synthesize, group, or characterize them to provide more filtered and digested information to readers seeking specific data? As a result of several national events, various public bodies receive thousands of opinion messages through social networks such as *Twitter*. How could these messages be analyzed in order to determine trends and/or preferences of users regarding those events?

Clearly, in the last decades, we've experienced a gigantic growth of the data available in various electronic media. The information overload is such that it becomes very difficult to take advantage of such data using conventional technologies, so new abilities are required for its efficient

DOI: 10.1201/9781003280996-1

analysis. This will depend on the nature of the information, which in general can be divided into two large groups:

- *Structured data*: Corresponds to data that have been organized in repositories such as a database, so that its elements can be accessed by effective analysis and processing methods (i.e., an SQL table).

- *Non-Structured data*: Corresponds to data that don't have a predefined structure or model or that's not organized in a predefined way, making them hard to understand using traditional computational methods (i.e., news and customer complaints).

Depending on the nature of the data, we can perform two types of tasks on them: *search* and *discovery*, as shown in Figure 1.1.

A *search* task is goal-oriented, which means that you must provide a clear criterion to receive the results that you need (i.e., a condition that must be met by the data attributes). In this scenario, we're not looking for anything new, we're only reducing the information overload, retrieving only data which satisfy certain conditions (Zhai & Massung, 2016). Then,

- *If data are structured*: We must specify some condition, key or characteristic, of the data we want to search. For example, you want to retrieve the information of all the clients that were registered in a company in 2018 from a SQL database. For this, there are usually database engines capable of efficiently accessing, query and retrieve data from a previously specified combination of attributes (i.e., a structured *query*).

- *If data are not structured*: We must then search for documents relevant to a *query*, consisting of a list of keywords. For example, you want to

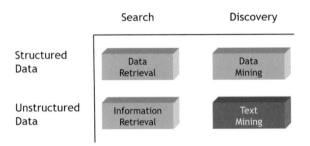

FIGURE 1.1   Search versus data discovery.

search documents online that contain the terms rent and houses. For this, *information retrieval (IR) technologies* (Büttcher et al., 2010) are usually available in the form of web search engines such as Google and Yahoo or specialized search systems (i.e., MEDLINE medical literature search engines[1]).

Unlike *search*, a *discovery* task is by nature opportunistic, that is, you don't know what you want to search for, so data hypotheses are automatically explored to discover new opportunities in the form of *data hidden patterns* (or *latent*), which can be interesting and novel. Then,

- *If data are structured:* We must have some *discovery* task in mind so that later, *some Data Mining technology* (Tan et al., 2018) can mine the data to discover or extract *hidden patterns* that are *actionable*, that is, having the ability to act regarding some kind of process that produces real results. For example, given a database of purchase transactions made by customers in a supermarket, we would like to know if there's any behavior pattern which allows us to understand how these purchases are associated with each other, to make recommendations, create better promotions, adjust the product layout, etc.

- *If data are not structured*: We must have some discovery task in mind about textual data, so that later, some *Text Mining* or *Textual Analytics Technology* can automatically discover hidden patterns in texts that support decision-making. For example, given a set of documents that describe complaints from clients of a company, we would like to find patterns that allow characterizing these complaints, finding nonobvious connections between them, and grouping them to generate recommendations.

The nature of unstructured data and the complexity of its analysis have generated a growing need for technologies that allow it to be analyzed and automatically discover *insights* (i.e., hidden aspects regarding how users/clients act, which can generate opportunities for new products/services, strategies, etc.). This becomes even more latent at the business level, considering that unstructured information represents more than 85% of the data handled by corporations. Hence, this has impacted practically all

---

[1] https://www.nlm.nih.gov/bsd/medline.html.

industrial, public, scientific, and technological areas in a transversal way. Thus, we can find different types of textual information, including emails, insurance claims statements, news pages, scientific articles, innovation patents descriptions, customer complaints, business contracts, and opinions on forums and/or social networks, among others.

Clearly, it's not possible to analyze this kind of data with known *Data Mining* techniques, due to its linguistic nature, and therefore the unstructured and free way to express human knowledge. For this, computational techniques are required to discover *patterns of interest* in those textual information sets.

1.2 TEXT MINING AND TEXT ANALYTICS

Text mining and *text analytics* are highly interchangeable terms. Text mining is the automated process of examining large collections of documents or corpora to discover patterns or insights that may be interesting and useful (Ignatow & Mihalcea, 2017; Struhl, 2015; Zhai & Massung, 2016). For this, text mining identifies facts, relationships, and patterns that would otherwise be buried in textual data (Atkinson & Pérez, 2013). This information can be converted to a structured form that can be later analyzed and integrated with other types of systems (i.e., business intelligence, databases, and data warehouses). On the other hand, text analytics synthesizes the results of text mining so that they can be quantified and visualized in a way that supports decision-making, producing actionable *insights*, so text mining encompasses broader aspects than text analytics.

The applications of *text analytics* in industrial and business areas are many, including document clustering, text categorization, information extraction to populate databases, text generation, association discovery, etc. However, since the goal is to automatically analyze textual information sources that are written in natural language by humans, computational methods (Jurafsky et al., 2014) must be able to address three key linguistic problems:

1. *Ambiguity*: Natural language is by nature a communication mode characterized by inherent ambiguity. In linguistics, this ambiguity originates when some linguistic object has multiple interpretations or meanings. Thus, this ambiguity can be lexical (i.e., a single word with more than one meaning), syntactic (i.e., a single sentence that has several possible grammatical structures), semantic (i.e., a sentence with several possible interpretations), and pragmatic (i.e., a

sentence with several possible contexts to determine its intention). To understand why this is relevant to text mining, consider the following two sentences extracted from informal texts, when searching for the word *nail*:

The nails of the installation are rusty.

Her nails are split after falling out.

Assume the desired task was to *group* phrases like these to determine common patterns. In this case, if we take few words to compare these sentences, a *group* with both sentences would be created. However, you know that this isn't right, because both sentences refer to very different topics since it's the same word that has two interpretations.

2. *Dimensionality*: Given the lexical ambiguity of the previous example, if you try to compare both sentences that have a simple syntactic structure and just a few words, you could surely compare them out without much difficulty, but even so, with quite limited analysis. However, the reality is much more complex, since a text written in natural language is highly dimensional, that is, it has many characteristics or dimensions that can describe it. Each dimension could be a word, a term (i.e., "San Francisco"), or a phrase, etc.; so, if you consider collections of many texts or documents, clearly, using conventional data analysis methods is not enough. For example, the dimensions of a *Twitter* message are all the words and symbols it contains, and if thousands or millions of messages are considered, clearly the dimensions begin to increase enormously, increasing the difficulty of some analysis tasks.

3. *Linguistic Knowledge:* For a human reader, the previous example sentences are relatively simple to understand for further analysis. However, for a computational method to be able to understand them, there should be a lot of lexical (i.e., Do I know the word?), syntactic (i.e., Is the phrase well formed?), semantic (i.e., What's the meaning of the phrase?), and pragmatic (i.e., What's the text trying to communicate as a whole?) knowledge.

For example, consider the following opinion taken from a social network: "*I didn't like your customer service*". Suppose we want to automatically determine if it expresses a positive or negative emotion about a product or service. Clearly, for this to be effective, a computational method should have or infer lexical (i.e., Are the words known and relevant?), syntactic (i.e., Is the sentence well written?), and semantic (i.e., What's the literal meaning of the phrase?) knowledge. However, the analysis is not enough, as pragmatic knowledge is also required (To whom is this opinion referring in the context? What is it trying to communicate?), which allows reasoning about the implicit intentions of that statement and that can feed further analysis tasks. Otherwise, the answer will still be pending: didn't like customer service, but from "whom?"

To address these insight discovery aspects in textual information, text mining combines three areas: *Natural-Language Processing, Machine Learning, and IR*, as shown in Figure 1.2.

Natural-Language Processing (NLP) provides theories, models, and methods so that a computer can understand natural language (written or spoken) at different linguistic levels (i.e., phonetic, morphological, lexicon, syntactic, semantic, discursive, and pragmatic). In practice, NLP techniques focus on creating systems that process textual information in order to make it accessible to other computer applications. Usually, many of these require retrieving information from specific unstructured data sources (i.e., texts, images, and videos), in which an analysis based on some measure of relevance (i.e., importance) is key with respect to a certain input query in order to make them available to other tasks and applications. To this end, *information retrieval (IR)* methods and models can be used (Büttcher et al., 2010) in which NLP plays a fundamental role in characterizing and "understanding" some elements of the information (i.e., documents) that's retrieved. Many NLP tasks can be solved by using traditional rule-based approaches and probabilistic methods.

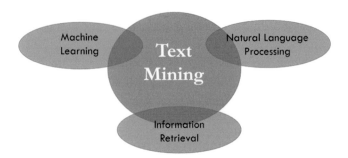

FIGURE 1.2   The scope of text mining.

However, in many language comprehension and textual analytical tasks, problems are complex and non-deterministic in nature, so there are no efficient algorithmic methods to address them. In those cases, *machine learning* (ML) is applied, an AI area that provides computational techniques allowing a computer to *learn* how to perform a task based on experience (Wilmott, 2020; Mohri et al., 2018). Thus, an ML system improves its performance with experience, without the need to write explicit rules or models. Models automatically created by ML are thus capable of generalizing behaviors for unknown cases, improving the performance of certain tasks.

1.3 TASKS AND APPLICATIONS

Depending on the *textual analytics* question you want to answer or the discovery task you have in mind, virtually all kinds of textual information can be analyzed clearly at different levels of linguistic and analytical complexity. Although specific problems and tasks are described in detail throughout this book, it's important to provide an overview to understand some of the typical tasks. For this, let's assume the following:

- You have a collection of documents (i.e., news, reviews, articles, tweets, etc.).

- For simplicity, each document is represented as a list of two real-valued features, which results in a 2-dimensional numeric vector.

- For visualization purposes, each document will simply be represented as a data point in a 2-dimensional space.

Then some tasks could include:

- *Text Clustering*: Suppose that you want to group written customer complaints, according to some mathematical measure of closeness (i.e., cosine similarity), which allows understanding how such information is related. For example, Figure 1.3 shows black data points representing such complaints (i.e., documents) according to two characteristics, which have been grouped by some method so we have two complain groups (i.e., red circles) that could express certain "hidden" patterns in the complaints contained in the documents, which might aid in business decision-making.

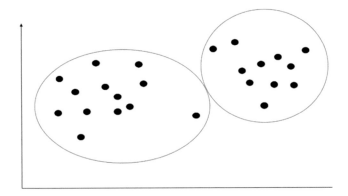

FIGURE 1.3   Document clustering.

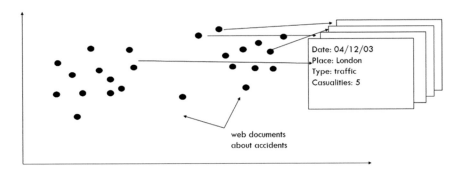

FIGURE 1.4   Information extraction.

- *Information extraction*: Suppose you have a large collection of documents describing traffic accidents, from which you want to extract specific pieces of information to feed other applications (i.e., *Date, Place, Type of Accident, City*). Figure 1.4 shows data points representing these documents, from which specific information can be extracted to further fill out some template or transfer them to an SQL database.

- *Text Categorization*: Suppose you receive many messages from social networks like *Twitter* and want to automatically separate them depending on whether they express a positive or negative emotion about your products and services. Figure 1.5 shows data points representing different types of opinions. For this, *categorization* methods can be applied, which automatically classify new opinions received,

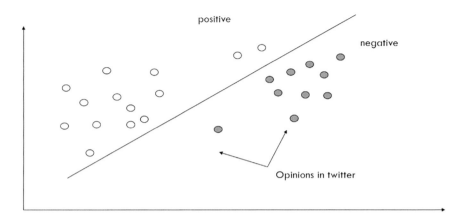

FIGURE 1.5   Text categorization.

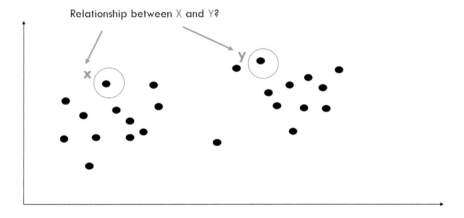

FIGURE 1.6   Relationship inference.

from models built with experience. This should allow separating positive polarity views (i.e., yellow data points) from those expressing negative sentiments (i.e., blue data points).

- *Relationship Inference*: Suppose that you suspect that complaints about a product/service (i.e., broadband) from your company are closely associated with complaints about a certain staff and from that company. However, the specific link between the two is unknown, so you want to explore the information to find out more details about the possible link. Figure 1.6 shows that, once both products are identified in a collection of complaint documents, a textual analysis method could be used to identify some semantic references between them. Next, this method could identify specific relationships that account for this link to make future decisions.

1.4 THE TEXT ANALYTICS PROCESS

In a perfect world, tasks such as those described above could be carried out using some textual analysis computational method (Bengfort & Bilbro, 2018; Ignatow & Mihalcea, 2017; Aggarwal, 2018), assuming that the textual data of input are ready to be processed and that the results are always the best. However, this assumption is quite far from reality, and it's required to carry out several activities before carrying out the analytical task itself.

The process starts from a collection of texts automatically extracted from a repository (i.e., website, document database) or available directly in some electronic media. Linguistically speaking, a collection of documents on some subject, topic, genre, etc., is usually called a *Corpus*, and can usually contain pure text or text with some specific purpose annotations, made by humans for further analysis.

As shown in Figure 1.7, the following activities of the *text mining* process are carried out:

- *Text Pre-processing*: This stage transforms an input text into a more "digestible" form for computers. Usually, this involves performing tasks such as *tokenization, normalization,* and *noise removal. Tokenization* separates text strings into smaller pieces called tokens.

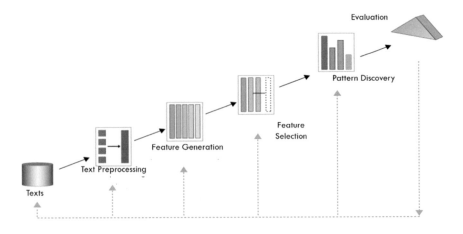

FIGURE 1.7 The text mining process.

For example, paragraphs can be tokenized into sentences, and sentences can be tokenized into words. On the other hand, *normalization* standardizes all text (i.e., convert characters to lowercase), while *noise removal* cleanses text, for example, removing extra whitespace, removing irrelevant characters, or reducing variability in the form of the words (i.e., the reduced form infect is the same for the word infected). Note that noise could also be reduced by removing many words that don't contribute to the analysis of a text such as some articles, prepositions, etc., usually known as *stopwords*.

The approaches to doing this stage are discussed in Chapters 2 and 3.

- *Feature Generation*: At this stage, relevant *features* must be extracted from textual data, which can be used later to build textual analysis models. This stage is critical since we need to convert free text into some numerical representation that can be understood by further analysis methods (Kuhn & Johnson, 2019). These features can usually be words, short sequences of words, phrases, etc. As a text can have many features or dimensions, the usual representation of a document is based on vector models of the features and their importance.

  The approaches to doing this stage are discussed in Chapters 3 and 4.

- *Feature Selection*: Eventually, the previous activity could extract too many features representing a document. However, not all of them could be relevant. This high dimensionality can make not only inefficient further tasks (i.e., computation time and memory space required) but also generate too much noise in the data, making it difficult to understand and therefore to discover patterns of interest. For textual information, we need to evaluate and weigh the characteristics in order to select the most relevant to represent the texts, a process usually known as *indexing* (Büttcher et al., 2010). For example, the most important words or phrases could be the characteristics of a text; however, in an opinion analysis task, types of words such as adjectives and names could be the important characteristics, as they allow to discriminate one type of opinion expressing a positive sentiment from other expressing a negative sentiment. Usually, the features selection for *indexing* purposes can be based on statistical methods, information theory, ML models, linguistic taxonomies, etc. (Kendall & McGuinness, 2019).

  Approaches to doing this stage are discussed in Chapter 4.

- *Pattern Discovery*: Once the best features are extracted and selected to represent textual data, several textual analytical tasks can be performed, depending on whether our focus is on the *patterns* we want to discover or the result that can be generated from those *patterns*:

  - *Patterns as the focus of discovery*: This considers relationship extraction tasks, which explain specific links or associations between document elements.

  - *Result as focus of discovery*: This considers tasks in which some analytical method tries to discover implicit patterns that are used to make decisions. This includes document classification tasks, document clustering, an analysis of similarity between texts, etc.

    Approaches to doing this stage are discussed in the Chapters 5–9.

- *Pattern Evaluation and Interpretation*: As in the previous stage, the interpretation or evaluation of the *patterns* discovered by each task will depend on whether the focus is on the *patterns* or the *results*. This aims, on the one hand, to generate patterns that are ideally useful, actionable, and novel, and, on the other hand, to feed back the previous stages of the process in case it's required to improve the quality of those patterns. For example, the evaluation of a textual categorization task can be seen as the *accuracy* of the classification of previously unseen documents; the evaluation of a pattern discovery system can be seen as the degree of *novelty* or the degree of understanding that the detected relationship represents; the quality of a document *clustering* task can be determined as the degree of novelty that represents the groups discovered or learned by the method; the evaluation of an analysis association task between document items can be determined as the level of relevance and correlation represented by the associations, and thus, with other analysis methods.

  Approaches to doing this stage are discussed in Chapters 5–9.

1.5 SUMMARY

Text analytics is the science that is based on examining and discovering interesting and ideally actionable patterns from large collections of documents (corpuses) written in natural language. To make this possible, text analytics combines techniques and models from NLP, ML, and IR. This combination allows performing tasks such as document categorization, text clustering, specific information extraction from documents, association discovery, topic detection, etc. These tasks are the basis for cross-cutting applications in all domains, both in the private and public spheres, from scientific applications to industrial and business applications.

1.6 QUESTIONS

In this section, some questions are proposed for discussion around tasks and applications of text analytics:

1. What are the main differences between a text analytics application and a NLP application?

2. What difficulties does linguistic ambiguity cause in a text analytics or text mining task?

3. List two differences between analyzing informal texts on social media and analyzing formal news texts.

4. How does the dimensionality of documents affect the performance of a text analytics task?

5. Describe two problems that can arise when analyzing documents using only lexical analysis, that is, at the word level.

6. Suppose two applications that involve the handling of textual information: One that allows hotel reservations to be made through natural language and the other that allows the detection of names of personalities in news texts. In which of them is it necessary to use NLP tools and in which is it required to use a textual analysis method?

7. How can a ML method help a text analytics task?

8. You should automatically group all news reaching your email and then store it in specific folders. What analysis methodology would you use, a clustering method or a categorization method?

9. What's the fundamental difference between an IR task and an information extraction task?

10. What type of *features* could be selected as input to a text mining or text analytics task?

11. In the text mining process, the evaluation of patterns discovered by some analysis task is essential. In what ways could these patterns be evaluated in order to generate insights?

12. Describe two types of patterns that can be discovered in text analytic tasks.

13. In a textual analysis task, such as the sentiment classification on social networks, you could simply use keywords such as *features*, so that an automatic classifier can determine whether an opinion expresses positive or negative sentiments. What's the problem that we'll encounter if such an application uses only such a type of *features*?

14. State which of the following applications use NLP models and which use text analytics approaches:

    - Simple document search engine

    - Keyword-based sentiment classifier

    - Rules-based spam filter

    - Virtual tutor that helps a child understand math

    - Assess quality of texts written by job applicants

    - Classify medical diagnoses

15. You know there is an important link between an organization X and a person Y in a set of news articles. What text analytics approach would you take to determine the specific link that exists?

16. A service company receives many written complaints (no more than 2–3 paragraphs) through its web portal. What kind of analysis method would you use to generate statistics about the client's complaints for a given date?

17. You have a large database of invention patent descriptions and want to determine whether a new patent "application" that comes to you is similar to one that you already have in your database. What text analytics and/or NLP approach would you use to address this problem?

CHAPTER 2

Natural-Language Processing

2.1 INTRODUCTION

The following news excerpt was published in an international newspaper:

UK Prime Minister Boris Johnson has entered the Intensive Care Unit at St. Thomas Hospital in London tonight as the symptoms of his coronavirus worsen, acknowledged a Downing Street spokesman.

Johnson was admitted to the hospital on Sunday and until Monday afternoon "took the reins of the government", according to Foreign Secretary Dominic Raab, who may be forced to temporarily assume the leadership of the cabinet.

Once you've carefully read this text, try to answer the following questions:

1. What's Boris Johnson?

2. Why Boris Johnson was admitted into St. Thomas?

3. What's the role of Dominic Raab?

4. What's the relationship between the first and second paragraph?

With some ease you can recognize that Boris Johnson is a two-word term that forms the name of a person (and not a thing) in question (1), that there's a verbal relationship (i.e., "…has entered") indicating that Boris Johnson was admitted to a hospital called St. Thomas in question (2), that

DOI: 10.1201/9781003280996-2

the term Dominic Raab is the name of a person whose words around him indicate that he's a secretary of foreign relations in question (3), and that the second paragraph explains a consequence of what's described in the first paragraph, and furthermore, with all these information, you could even infer the objective of communicating this news.

As humans, answering the above seems relatively straightforward. However, cognitively speaking, our brains had to carry out multiple language processing tasks, which aren't only complex but require access to a lot of linguistic knowledge, which we have acquired over the years, almost without realizing it.

- Perhaps we had never seen the sentences in the example news. However, we were able to generalize structures and/or "rules" regarding the words used and the sentence formation.

- Every time we tried to answer some of the questions, we had to understand the way the words are structured in the text and their functions in it, the way they connect to form sentences, the meaning of those words and sentences, how these sentences logically connect to create a meaningful text, and, finally, in which way they're expressed to provide the communicative objective of the message.

- For this to be possible, we had to access several internal linguistic resources acquired over the years: dictionaries, grammar rules, previous knowledge about the meaning of those words and sentences, etc.

Now suppose that we want to carry out these natural-language comprehension tasks on longer texts than the example, such as the complete news item that appears every week in the media. Even with lots of experience, training and infinite time, it wouldn't be feasible to perform such tasks manually. Hence, we clearly need efficient computational methods that allow us to process language automatically and efficiently to understand human written texts and infer important knowledge that allow us to make decisions.

2.2 THE SCOPE OF NATURAL-LANGUAGE PROCESSING

Natural-Language Processing (*NLP*) is the area of *Artificial Intelligence* (AI) that allows computers to understand human language to perform complex tasks on different linguistic objects (i.e., speech, words, phrases, meaning).

By using these capabilities, computers can understand and make sense of unstructured data that enables them to acquire knowledge that's implicit in language (Bird et al., 2009; Eisenstein, 2019; Ghosh & Gunning, 2019). For this, NLP combines models from linguistics, computer science, AI, and cognitive sciences, in order to create intelligent systems capable of understanding, analyzing, and extracting meaning from written (text) or spoken human language (Jurafsky et al., 2014).

There are many examples of NLP capabilities in current technologies, such as:

- Systems that automatically create answers to questions written or spoken (as in Apple's SIRI) in natural language (Atkinson & Andrade, 2013).

- Automatic summarization from one or more documents (Atkinson & Munoz, 2013).

- Automatic dialogues in human–computer interaction (Atkinson, 2007a; Wu et al., 2019).

- Self-service systems in contact centers (Sankar et al., 2019).

- Spam categorization.

- Sentiment analysis on opinions or reviews coming from products and services.

- Information extraction from online documents in order to populate databases (Atkinson et al., 2014).

- Grammar checkers and autofill prediction in word processors (like MS Word).

- Many others.

Clearly, the problems faced by these applications aren't only complex but also involve the handling of enormous amounts of textual information that's generated every second everywhere in the world: texts on social networks, emails, web searches, complaints from clients, news in electronic media, scientific articles, etc.

To perform the above tasks, NLP uses a combination of theories, models, and techniques from different disciplines. Thus, *linguistics* is used to understand the structure and meaning of a text, analyzing different aspects such as word formation (i.e., morphology), lexicon, syntax, semantics, discourse, and pragmatics. Then, *computer science* and AI techniques use such *linguistic knowledge* as techniques to solve specific language-related problems in certain analysis tasks.

2.3 NLP LEVELS AND TASKS

When humans try to understand language, we aren't aware of the specific aspects or processing level we're focusing on; therefore, we intuitively see this phenomenon as a large "black box" in which many cognitive activities take place in thousandths of a second, allowing us to identify, associate and understand what we're reading or hearing (Bermúdez, 2020). However, if we could see all the details of our internal processing, we would notice that we're doing basic tasks of a language analysis, which later allows us to understand it as a whole.

In this way, we try to identify sounds or phonemes (*phonetics*) to convert them into character sequences in order to form words (*morphology*); we then try to determine the function of these words, so, if they're valid (*lexicon*), we connect those words according to their roles to form sentences (*syntax*); we try to determine the literal meaning of words and sentences (*semantics*); we relate these sentences to form a global meaning and identify the communicative intention behind the spoken or written text (*discourse*); and finally, we try to connect and associate language with actions in reality (*pragmatic*) (Gillon, 2019; Jurafsky et al., 2014). These actions not only allow us to change the state of the world but also update our internal and emotional beliefs. As a result, this processing involves not only our linguistic–cognitive abilities but also emotional abilities. For example, imagine what would you think if your boss told you: "*You're fired*!!", and then, when you do the *pragmatic* analysis, look at the changes you're experiencing in terms of your beliefs (i.e., "*Oh, I thought that my boss trusted me or that I was his best worker...*") and your feelings (i.e., "*I feel terrible, I never thought this would happen to me, I wasn't expecting it...*").

Although the different levels of linguistic processing appear to be *sequential*, where one level is a "prerequisite" for the next, cognitive processing is carried out in *parallel* most of the time. Furthermore, in certain complex processing tasks, we may even need to "roll back" to previous processing levels to be able to solve some pending ambiguity. For example, imagine that someone is speaking to you and you didn't hear one of the first words well, you will surely keep moving forward until you hear other sounds, words, and sentences in order to have the necessary context to identify what you didn't hear at the beginning. On the other hand, in other interactions that show some ambiguity, this resolution isn't enough, so you require to use different input interaction sources, usually combining linguistic and visual means (i.e., you didn't understand something that you heard or read, but when you see some of the *speaker's* movements or gestures, you can go back to the beginning and solve this ambiguity).

As computational methods are required to perform the various NLP tasks, we must assume that we're operating under a sequential computation model; so the full flow of NLP can be seen as a *pipeline* of levels and associated tasks as shown in Figure 2.1. Depending on the language task to be addressed, only some levels and processing methods can be used. However, many applications involve the full flow in that *pipeline* (i.e., automated, voice-activated airfare reservation systems). On the other hand, the *pipeline* can pass through several stages at its right if we want the computer to understand the input language, or to the left, if we want the computer to produce an output language (i.e., give an answer to a client). For example, in an automated translation application, the computer receives and processes some input text, going through all the stages and then, it generates an output text, that, in this case, would be the translation of the original text.

NLP follows a multilevel *pipeline*. Note that for textual analytical purposes, several of them are usually not necessary (i.e., phonology, pragmatics). However, it's important in those cases to at least understand its general principles to put them in context, in several applications.

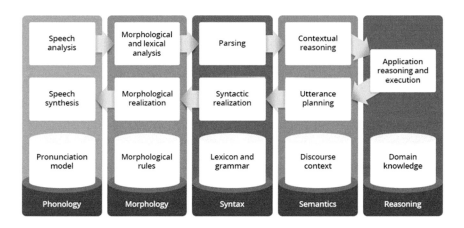

FIGURE 2.1   Levels, tasks, and linguistic resources in NLP.

2.3.1 Phonology

The phonological analysis level must interpret the acoustic signals of a person, interpret individual units or *phonemes*, and convert them into word sequences. Note that communication with a *speaker* (sender) transmitting a *message* to a *listener* (receiver) uses a noisy communication channel. As a consequence, the message emitted by the *speaker* through the medium doesn't reach the *listener* in the same way, so it's necessary to decode the message to obtain the most probable phonemes and words (Rabiner & Schafer, 2011). For this, stochastic and/or machine learning methods are usually required to generate some *language model* (i.e., for pronunciation) that allows them to learn to recognize phonemes and words from sound samples (i.e., waves or acoustic signals).

2.3.2 Morphology

The level of morphological analysis determines how words are constructed from their smallest significant units called *morphemes*. The analysis of morphology is necessary because a text can use different forms of a word (i.e., infect, infected, etc.), which could produce too much linguistic variability and, therefore, increase the dimensionality of a text, obfuscating the real meaning of the individual word (Bohnet et al., 2018).

For example, we could know the meaning of the word *infect* and we couldn't really know about the word *infected*; however, if we analyze the form of the latter we could determine that it's a form variation of the former, that is, a morphological variation. This type of analysis is essential in many applications where reducing morphological variability is key: Imagine that you're searching online for documents talking about infection, there're only documents about those infected. If the search engine doesn't carry out such a morphological analysis, it won't really know that they're actually talking about the same concept. However, in other applications, this variation is necessary. For example, imagine a self-service system for customers through natural language in your bank where you could make one of the following queries: "I want to know the balance I have in my checking account..." or "I want to know the balance I had in my checking account...". In this case, the variation in the verb form (i.e., have/had) will clearly generate different responses.

To accomplish this, morphology must try to find the morphemes for each word, which usually consists of a *stem* and an *affix*. The *stem* represents the meaning of the core of the unit while the *affix* represents the piece that adheres to the *stem*, changing its linguistic function or *inflection*. For example, suppose the following words:

1. *Doctors* can generate the morpheme *doctor*+s, which indicates the plural form (+s) of the word.

2. *Retrieved* can generate the morpheme *retriev*+ed, which indicates the general *stem* and the plural past tense variation (+ed) of the word, which is common to generate other variations (i.e., *retrieve, retrieval*).

In general, forms can take a noun (singular or plural), a verb (different tenses), and so on. However, you may have noticed in previous inflections that, although in both cases a word is reduced to its base unit, the type of stem is different: in the first case, the stem is an existing word, whereas in the second case the stem wouldn't exist in a dictionary, but it's powerful enough to generate a wide variety of word forms.

These inflections can be generated automatically using two types of morphological analysis:

- **Lemmatization**: Reduces the words to their canonical form in the dictionary, better known as their *lemma*. For this, it's required to know the *grammatical function* (i.e., verb, noun, adjective) of the word to solve the inflection. Because of this, it's sometimes a bit more difficult to create a *lemmatizer* for a new language, since knowledge of the specific language structure is required. For this purpose, various stemming algorithms use lexical databases such as *WordNet*,[1] which stores not only word taxonomies but the specific relationships that connect them.

- **Stemming**: Reduces words to their *stems*, which don't need to have the same root as those existing in a dictionary. Hence, the *stem* can be an equal or shorter form of the word, so stemming becomes a reduction method, which can generally be addressed with algorithms based on morphological and/or heuristic rules, which must verify multiple conditions to determine how to perform the reduction. For example, in English, regular verbs have suffixes like *ed* and *ing* that can be useful to transform words such as infected or infecting, which can generate the same root, infect, which in this case exists in the

---

[1] http://wordnetweb.princeton.edu/perl/webwn.

dictionary. The usual methods available are based on rules and dictionaries and include the *Porter* algorithm and improved versions like *Snowball* and others that also allow incorporating new rules such as the *Lancaster* algorithm. However, when forms aren't regular (i.e., go vs. went), slightly more complex methods based on probabilistic models and machine learning are required (Bird et al., 2009; Flach, 2012).

As a whole, both methods of morphological analysis significantly improve the result in textual analysis applications, since they allow reducing the noise caused by linguistic variability and therefore allow a significant reduction in vocabulary size. Technically, developing a *stemmer* is much simpler than building a *lemmatizer*, since in the latter, a lot of linguistic knowledge is required to create dictionaries that allow searching for the appropriate form of the word. However, the *lemmatization* generates a greater reduction since stems are smaller (i.e., more general), being able to cover a greater number of variations.

2.3.3 Lexicon

The level of lexical analysis tries to understand the linguistic roles or functions of words, usually known as their part-of-speech (POS). For this, a lexicon is usually used containing the basic units or lexemes and their individual senses. For example, the word book can take the form of a verb (i.e., "to book a flight") or a noun (i.e., "to read a book"). However, its lexical role or POS can only be determined when its use within a context is observed in some sentence.

A basic requirement for lexical analysis is that the words of a text must be properly separated. For this, a set of words must go through a task called tokenization, which breaks them down into individual useful units or tokens. Usually this is done both to separate those words (i.e., word tokenization) and to separate sentences within a text (i.e., sentence tokenization) using methods based on separation rules or some automatic classification technique, which allows a tokenizer to infer the limits of words or sentences.

The task seems trivial, as the words can be separated by punctuation and the sentences by points. However, there are many situations in which such a separation isn't so evident. For example, if you want to perform the tokenization of sentences in the text "The current account balance is $100.784 as of August 4, 2019", clearly the use of the point as a token separator will generate an incorrect tokenization (i.e., there will be two tokens "$100" and "784"), hence more robust methods are required to classify the limits. For example, the tokenization of the sentence "The customer service cannot be better" should produce the token list: ["The","customer","service", "cannot", "be", "better"].

Once the input text is tokenized, we need methods that automatically determine the roles or POS of each word in context. This role assignment task can be seen as the problem of assigning POS tags to each of the words in a text, commonly known as the POS tagging problem. Examples of POS-type tags include N (noun), V (verb), DET (determiner), ART (article), P (preposition), etc. Generally, the total tagset to be used depends on each language and granularity level, since in certain applications, only the general tags for each word (i.e., name) would suffice while in others, greater specificity may be required, such as the tagset available in the Penn Treebank[2] with 26 types of tags.

For example, for the sentence "The visitor infected a person in the office", the POS tagging task should assign the best tag that corresponds to each word. So, in this case the best POS tag assignment for the phrase would be:

The	visitor	infected	a	person	in	The	Office
DET	N	V	ART	N	P	DET	N

Thus, the POS tagging task can be seen as the classification problem, in which a method should automatically assign the best POS tag to each word from a predefined set of POS tags. For this, two aspects must be addressed:

- A word could have multiple linguistic functions, and therefore, multiple possible POS tags depending on the context. In the example, the word sick can be associated with the N (Name), V (verb), or ADJ (adjective) tags, but in this context, the best candidate was the N (Name) tag.

- By assigning each role or POS tag, you're also identifying important relationships between words (i.e., there's a relationship between sick and infected), which will later help you understand the meaning of the whole sentence.

---

[2] https://www.ling.upenn.edu/courses/Fall_2003/ling001/penn_treebank_pos.html.

In general, there are four computational approaches to POS tagging:

1. Rule-based methods: These use expert-defined rules to perform the tagging (i.e., "IF the current tag is DET and... THEN the tag of the next word is N..."). Although the method doesn't require training samples (i.e., annotated text samples with the correct labels), it's not a robust method, because rules can change depending on the context, making it difficult to maintain and scale.

2. Statistical methods: These are supervised approaches that require training texts, from which the label probabilities for each word are estimated. This method can be easily scaled. However, it doesn't take into account the context of the words in sentences, so it will always assign the same tag, with the highest probability to a word, regardless of the context (Bengfort & Bilbro, 2018).

3. Stochastic methods: These use supervised sequence prediction models based on Bayesian probabilistic inference approaches. Usual techniques include Hidden Markov Models (HMM) and a generalization called Conditional Random Fields (CRF). From an input text, and a set of training texts, the method can generate the most likely sequence of POS tags associated with the words in that text (Baron, 2019).

4. Machine-learning-based methods: These correspond to sequence models that use supervised learning techniques from a collection of training texts annotated with the correct labels to then predict the best sequence of labels for an input text. Unlike stochastic methods that assume that there's some probability distribution, these approaches learn to model input sequences (i.e., words) that are transformed into output sequences (i.e., POS tags). In general, the usual methods are based on recurrent artificial neural networks and LSTM (Long Short Term Memory) methods, which allow capturing the context surrounding a word to make predictions of POS roles (Aggarwal, 2018).

Stochastic POS Tagging

A popular stochastic POS tagging method is based on HMM. An HMM is basically a probabilistic transition machine that allows to perform prediction and classification tasks, and whose states can be observable or unobservable (hidden). A Markov model represents a system where future states depend only on the current state (Markov assumption). For the purposes of POS tagging, it's assumed that we can represent a Markov model by using a finite-state machine, which incorporates probabilistic estimates.

Each of the nodes in the machine represents one or multiple states and each blue arrow represents a possible transition from that state to another state. Furthermore, there's a probability that a certain transition will reach a current state. For this, it must be satisfied that the probability of the transitions originating from a given state always amounts to 1.

In the machine of Figure 2.2, each state is observable and emits (generates) an output called unobservable or hidden state (black arrows). Thus, we can see how frequently the flu state emits fever after the coronavirus state emits cough. However, what would happen if both coronavirus and flu caused cough or fever? Furthermore, let's assume that we've the coronavirus and flu states and we want to predict the fever and cough sequence from these states. In this case, we can only observe coronavirus and flu, but we need to predict fever and cough, that are the hidden states that are coming next.

In our transition machine representing the HMM, the black arrows represent emissions coming from the hidden states, fever and cough. Next, we need to estimate the probabilities of both transition and emission.

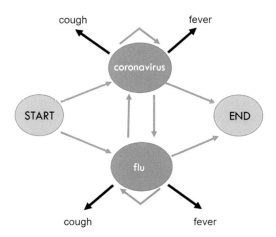

FIGURE 2.2   A simple Markov model.

The probability of transition from a state s_{i-1} to a state s_i can be calculated using a Maximum Likelihood Estimate (MLE) (Baron, 2019) as follows:

$$P\left(s_i \mid s_{i-1}\right) = \frac{C\left(s_i, s_{i-1}\right)}{C\left(s_{i-1}\right)}$$

where $C(s_i, s_{i-1})$ is the total number of times (counter) that we observe the s_{i-1} state in a transition to the state s_i and $C(s_{i-1})$ is the total number of times that we observe the state s_{i-1}.

For example, suppose the following two-state sequences:

coronavirus flu flu

coronavirus coronavirus coronavirus

We can see that the sequences always start with coronavirus. So, we're in the initial state twice and both lead to coronaviruses and never to flu. From there, we could say that P(coronavirus | START)=1 and P(flu | START)=0. On the other hand, to calculate the transition probability to go from the coronavirus state to the end state, we see that coronavirus only goes through the end state once. In addition, there are four observed instances of coronavirus, so P(END|coronavirus)=0.25, and so on with the procedure for other transition probabilities.

On the other hand, the emission probabilities can also be calculated using MLE. Thus, the probability that a s_i state emits a t_i tag can be estimated as:

$$P\left(t_i \mid s_i\right) = \frac{C\left(t_i, s_i\right)}{C\left(s_i\right)}$$

where $C(t_i, s_i)$ is the number of times (i.e., counter) where the s_i estate emits the t_i tag and $C(s_i)$ is the total number of times where we observe the s_i state. For example, let's estimate the probability that the coronavirus state will emit the cough output given the following emissions for our two-state sequences:

cough, cough, fever

fever, cough, cough

For the first sequence, coronavirus emits cough, then flu emits cough, and finally flu produces fever. Then coronavirus is observed four times

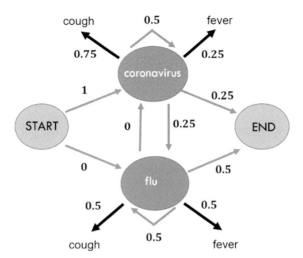

FIGURE 2.3 Hidden Markov Models (HMM) with transition and emission probabilities.

and emits cough three times. Therefore, the probability of cough emission given that we're in the coronavirus state is 0.75, and so on with the procedure for the other emission probabilities. Figure 2.3 shows the complete machine with the estimated probabilities.

For our POS tagging task, the objective of an HMM is to find the best sequence of T tags given a sequence of W words, that is:

$$T = \arg\max_{T'} P(T'|W)$$

Since label emissions are not observable in an HMM, we can apply Bayes rule to transform this probability into an equation that we can calculate efficiently, using MLE:

$$T = \arg\max_{T'} P(T'|W) = \arg\max_{T'} \frac{P(W|T')P(T')}{P(W)} \approx \arg\mathrm{m}$$

where

- $P(W|T)$ is the probability of obtaining a sequence W of n words given a sequence T of labels. To estimate this, we can assume that the probability of occurrence of a w_i word depends only on its own t_i label.

In other words, the word doesn't depend on neighboring labels or words, therefore:

$$P(W|T') \approx \prod_{i=1}^{n} P(w_i|t_i$$

- $P(T)$ is the probability of obtaining the sequence of T labels. To estimate this, we can assume that the probability of obtaining a label t_i depends only on the previous label t_{i-1}, usually known as the bi-gram assumption, therefore:

$$P(T) \approx \prod_{i=1}^{n} P(t_i|t_{i-1}$$

Note that in the previous transformation of T, $P(W)$ is a constant, so its probability value doesn't change, and the final formula can be estimated simply by removing it.

Finally, the best tag sequence can be determined by calculating:

$$T \approx \arg\max_{T'} \prod_{i=1}^{n} P(w_i|t_i) P(t_i|t_{i-1}$$

where $P(w_i|t_i)$ corresponds to the emission probability and $P(t_i|t_{i-1})$ corresponds to the transition probability.

Given a training sentences corpus labeled with their corresponding POS tags, training the HMM is simple: We must calculate all emission and transition probabilities. Thus, the basic idea is to account for the values required by the MLE during training. Then the model must calculate the probabilities during the test for new input text.

Note that the HMM estimates probabilities. However, we want to obtain the label sequence. For this, algorithms are required to provide us with the maximum probability label sequence associated with a sequence of words. There are several search methods for this purpose, but some methods aren't efficient, providing suboptimal solutions (i.e., once a tag is chosen for a word, the possible tags for the following words may be limited). One of the classic efficient methods is known as the Viterbi algorithm, which uses dynamic programming, allowing the search of probable sequences and "recording" the path traveled, so there's no need to explore the entire search space (Russell & Norvig, 2016; Rabiner & Schafer, 2011).

2.3.4 Syntax

The syntactic analysis level tries to determine the structure and roles connecting words in a sentence (i.e., *grams*) in order to generate a model for the complete sentence. This relationship usually takes the form of a *grammatical* or syntactic structure of the sentence, following certain language *rules* called a *grammar*. Intuitively, the lexical level already provides a preamble to the grammatical functions of words. At the syntactic level, we must determine how words and their roles account for grammatical relationships.

As shown in Figure 2.4, the parsing task is performed by a computational method called a *parser*. This takes an input text and a set of grammar rules (i.e., grammar) and determines if there's a valid language structure for that text. Otherwise, it's determined that the entry doesn't have a *valid structure*, so it's not recognized as part of the language. However, grammar's nature can be *ambiguous*, so there can be more than one valid syntactic structure for the same input text, hence the parser must find the best valid structure.

In general, there are two types of analysis that a parser can perform: *full (in-depth) analysis* and *partial analysis*, both of which produce different types of structure:

a. *Full Parsing*: the parser takes a grammar and generates a syntax tree or parse tree structure, which attempts to detect all relationships that match the grammatical rules for the entire text of entry. A usual type

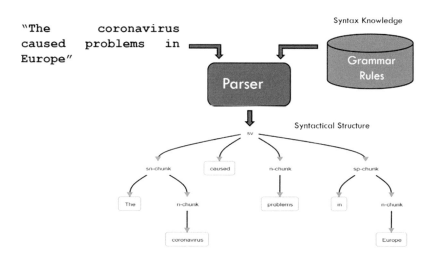

FIGURE 2.4   Syntactic analysis task.

of grammar is called a *Phrase Structure Grammar* (PSG) whose focus is on grammatical or constituent groups, whose role is to group word sequences that fulfill a certain function. Then, a set of rewriting rules defines how these constituents must connect to each other to form more complex structures. For example, a Noun Phrase (NP) is one where a name acts as a word that acts as the head of the group, and at the same time, FN acts as a subject or object of a verb, in the form of a Verbal Phrase (VP), and so with other constituents. A simple PSG could be made up of the rules shown in Figure 2.5.

A typical type of PSG is called a *Context-Independent Grammar* (CFG) that contains a set of production rules of the form:

$$A \rightarrow B$$

where the left side (A) represents a generator symbol that's re-rewritten or produces the symbols on the right side (B). The right side of a rule specifies how different symbols should be combined (i.e., words, tokens, constituents). In the case of the example, the initial rule is **O**, which is formed by an NP followed by a VP.

In the simplest case, the *parser* should start with the initial rule, successively applying rules that can produce other rules or input tokens until it reaches a point where the application of the rules covers all the input tokens.

The successive application of these rules generates a syntactic tree structure (i.e., *parse tree*) in which the upper levels represent generating symbols (i.e., nonterminal) while the last level (i.e., tree leaves) represents the symbols or words in a vocabulary (i.e., terminals) that must match the entry. For the example, since the entire input sequence is covered by the grammar rules, we can not only confirm

O	➜	NP VP
NP	➜	Det NOMINAL
NOMINAL	➜	Noun
VP	➜	Verb
Det	➜	a
Det	➜	the
Noun	➜	flight
Verb	➜	arrived
Verb	➜	landed

FIGURE 2.5   Context-Independent Grammar (CFG) rules.

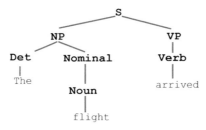

FIGURE 2.6   Parse tree for the sentence "The flight arrived".

that the input is valid but also that the parser generates the structure or syntactic model as shown in Figure 2.6.

There are several constituent parsing techniques for this type of grammar, including CKY, Earley, probabilistic parsers, etc. However, parsers are highly dependent on the type of grammar used to model syntactic knowledge. Another type of grammar popular in many NLP applications is called *Dependency Grammar* (DG). Unlike a PSG that's based on the relationship between constituents, a DG is based on directed one-to-one dependency relationships between each word of a sentence (*head*) and its *dependents*. The only word that has no dependency is the root of the sentence. For example, in many cases, the verb is taken as the stem root of a sentence, so the other words are directly or indirectly connected to the root verb, having a *dependency* relationship.

Each of these dependency relationships has its own meaning and is part of a predefined set of universal dependency types.[3] The DG parser tries to find these dependencies in the form of a directed graph. For example, Figure 2.7 shows the result of dependency parsing for the sentence *the flight arrived without problems* from the words and their POS roles.

Some of the dependencies in the example aren't that difficult to understand: the dependency relation **nsubj** acts as the subject or agent in the sentence (i.e., *arrived → flight*), the dependency relation **det** holds between a nominal head and its determiner (i.e., *flight → the*), and so on.

  b. *Shallow Analysis (Chunking):* A major feature of the previous parsing task is that the structure search process is carried out for the entire

---

[3] https://universaldependencies.org/u/dep/index.html.

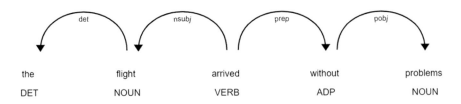

FIGURE 2.7 Dependency grammar for "The flight arrived without problems".

text, and, therefore, an attempt is made to find a recursive structure in-depth that covers the entire entry, that is, a *full parsing*. However, analyzing complex texts can take a high computational time. On the other hand, for many applications, it's not always required to produce the complete structure. For example, if we wanted to extract only the actions from a text (i.e., verbal relationships) and the organization names that are mentioned, we would only need to detect groups such as VP and NP, respectively, regardless of the rest of the syntactic tree structures.

For this type of task, superficial analysis methods or a *shallow parser* is required to detect syntactic segments or *chunks* that don't overlap, that is, without considering the complete tree structure. Because of this, the parsing task is more efficient and results in detecting only the *chunks* relevant to the problem. Thus, if we want to find only NP, we require chunking the NP type. In practice, this can be seen as a *classification* problem, in which the chunks of some interest group, to which each word of a sentence belongs, must be efficiently detected. In other words, a shallow parser must identify the words that are at the beginning of a chunk (**B***egin* label), those that are inside a chunk (**I***nside*) and those that are outside the chunk and/or that belong to another chunk of interest (**O***utside*). Hence, the classification problem must determine the most probable **BIO** type label for each of the words in a text.

For example, consider the sentence *The flight arrived without problems* and that we only want to extract the chunks from NP, the chunking task produces the sequence of tags: [BEGIN, INSIDE, OUTSIDE, OUTSIDE, BEGIN], detecting two NPs: [the, flight] and [problems]. Another way to visualize this is through a simple two-level tree, where one level contains the POS words and roles and the other contains the chunks, generated for a sentence (S):

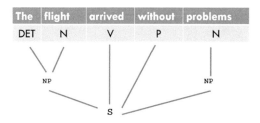

2.3.5 Semantics

The level of semantic analysis determines the literal *meaning* of a word or sentence. For this, semantics tries to identify the interactions between individual meanings (words) in contexts given in a sentence. As with the other linguistic levels, a semantic analysis must also solve ambiguity problems as words or sentences can have multiple possible interpretations or meanings.

Semantic analysis can help to understand a text from its constituent parts. For this, we need to perform the semantic analysis from three perspectives: that is, lexical semantics (of words), sentence semantics, and complete text semantics (i.e., discourse):

1. *Lexical Semantics*: This consists of determining the meaning of the individual words. Usually, the meaning can be extracted from electronic dictionaries and/or conceptual hierarchies (i.e., taxonomies, ontologies). Using electronic linguistic resources, such as *WordNet* or methods to construct semantic graphs (Kendall & McGuinness, 2019), it's possible to explore and extract the meaning based on the semantic relationships of a word with others. For example, Figure 2.8 shows a network of meanings or semantic graph for the sentence: *The flight arrived without problems*, similar to a dependency path.

    However, these sources of linguistic knowledge aren't always available for any domain, although very powerful resources exist in areas such as medicine. (i.e., UMLS[4]) and agronomy (i.e., AGRIS[5]), among others. When these electronic resources aren't available, the meaning could be extracted from the contexts in text samples. Since a word can have more than one meaning, an automatic disambiguation method for possible senses (*Word Sense Disambiguation*) should

---

[4] https://www.nlm.nih.gov/research/umls/index.html.
[5] https://agris.fao.org/agris-search/index.do,

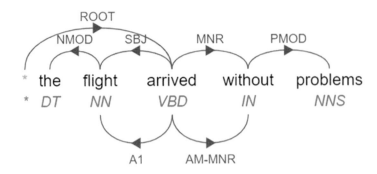

FIGURE 2.8 Semantic graph for the sentence "The flight arrived without problems".

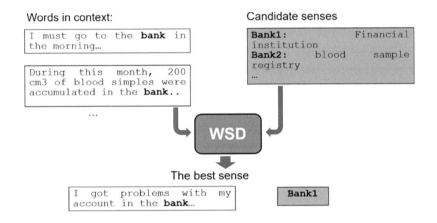

FIGURE 2.9 The task of Word Sense Disambiguation (WSD).

be used. For example, if you take the word *bank*, you could have the following contexts of possible uses and, therefore, possible meanings:

1. *The client entered the **bank** to obtain his balance.*

2. *The river **bank** was full of plastics.*

3. *The blood **bank** didn't have enough supplies.*

Clearly, obtaining the *best* meaning will depend on the ability of a classification method to select the best senses from samples.

The general approach (Figure 2.9) usually requires some supervised learning method that uses a corpus of *training* examples that contains context-tagged words with their meaning. Then a classifier is trained, who learns to label the meaning of a word in a new context. Some of these methods for determining meaning, and therefore semantic similarity between words and texts, include corpus-based methods such as *Latent Semantic Analysis* (LSA), Word Embeddings techniques such as Word2Vec and BERT among others (Landauer et al., 2014; Devlin et al., 2019).

2. *Sentence Semantics*: The meaning of the words alone doesn't allow us to understand the meaning of a complete sentence, so we need ways to combine individual meanings to generate the meaning of a sentence. Suppose the following sentences from clients who want to check their bank information:

   a. *Until my checking want to know the account of yesterday balance.*

   b. *I want to know the balance of my checking account until yesterday.*

   If you consider sentence (a), although you can understand the meaning of individual words, you'll probably have a hard time understanding it as a whole because it has an invalid syntactic structure. However, if you read sentence (b), combining the meaning of the individual words with the relationship that connects them can help you determine the meaning of the complete sentence, commonly called *Compositional Semantics.*

   A common approach to representing the meaning of sentences is based on the *First-Order Logic* (FOL) models and their variants (i.e., Lambda calculus, situational logic). There are other approaches to distributed representations such as LSA and techniques based on artificial neural networks such as *Sentence2vec*, LSTM, and BERT, among others (Graves, 2012; Bokka et al., 2019; Goldberg, 2017). The latter can produce good results in terms of representing efficient vectors that represent the meaning of words or sentences. However, they cannot account for language understanding or composition of meaning yet, since they correspond to *predictive* methods that allow generating the best representation only in certain contexts given a large number of training texts.

FOL approaches are geared toward generating formal semantic representations of sentences, which then allow us to reason about them. Hence, if we determine the logical truth of an expression (i.e., true or false), we can then understand this sentence, and, therefore, we could answer a question.

To achieve the above, the semantic representation must be produced from the previously generated lexical and syntactic knowledge. This facilitates the composition of meanings since it starts from the meaning of the words to then connect them to each other (through syntax) to finally compose the complete sentence meaning.

Suppose we want to represent the meaning of the sentence "Each of the infected traveled in January". To produce the complete representation, we must formulate semantic relationships using FOL (De Swart, 2015). For this, we first need to define some variables: X that represents a person and F that represents a certain date. Then we need to establish the individual semantic relationships:

General Form	Relation
Someone got infected	infected (X)
Someone travels on a certain date	travel (X, F)

Then, using the language of quantifiers and predicate logic (Gillon, 2019), we can generate the candidate representation of the complete sentence:

$$\forall x \exists f \left(\text{infected}(x) \Rightarrow \text{travels}(x, f) \right)$$

Keep in mind that the sentence can have different representations that are reflected if the order of quantification of the variables **x** and **f** were changed. To generalize the previous step, a Compositional Semantics Method (De Swart, 2015) should follow these steps:

1. Define individual semantic representations.

2. Generate the syntactic structure of the sentence with a parser.

3. Use the parser search to compose individual results.

4. Finish when the tree is built.

3. *Text or Discourse Semantics:* Keep in mind that the representation above refers to the literal meaning of a sentence. When you have a complete text that involves several connected sentences or statements, the individual literal meaning isn't enough to understand the meaning of a complete text. For example, consider that a *speaker* has a communicative goal in mind, for which he wrote a text consisting of the following sentences (or sentences):

S1: The government announced an increase in the number of infected.

S2: Additional quarantine will be declared in several cities of the country.

We can perform the interpretation of each of the sentences S1 and S2. However, understanding the full text requires detecting some coherent relationship between these statements. Thus, intuitively, you'll realize that the statement expressed by S2 is a *consequence* of the statement expressed by S1. Then, remember that the *speaker* had a (communicative) goal when producing that text, so it's not hard to imagine that to communicate the underlying message, the *speaker* had to express and connect the ideas he wanted to produce and then realize them in word meanings and sentences. A simple analogy to understand this process is to think that you need to put together a puzzle in such a way that finally not only all the pieces fit together but that you can "discover" the completely assembled image. In our case, the pieces of this "puzzle" are the statements or sentences, the connections between the pieces are our relationships, and the coherently finished puzzle corresponds to the message we wanted to detect. The structure formed between our statements and the relations that connect them is usually called a *discourse* structure, so the relations become discourse or rhetorical relations (Stede, 2011). For example, suppose the following sentences from a text:

S1: John went to the bank to deposit his check.

S2: He then took a taxi and went to Peter's car dealer.

S3: He needed to buy a car.

S4: The company where he currently works isn't near to any public transport.

S5: He also wanted to talk with Peter about his family problems.

A computational method could determine the meaning of each statement and then identify the discourse relationships, as shown in the structure in Figure 2.10.

For example, the connection between the statement S1 and S2 assumes that we've resolved the correspondence of the pronoun *He* in S2, because that will determine the similarity that will allows us to determine the

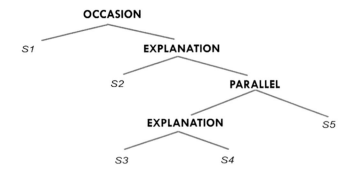

FIGURE 2.10   Structure of rhetorical relationships for an example text.

relationship and so on with much information implicit in the text (i.e., intentions, types of relationships, etc.).

2.3.6 Reasoning and Pragmatics

To interpret a discourse structure, a *hearer* must usually be able to recognize the communicative goal of the *speaker*; however, this objective isn't explicit. Then, through the structure of the discourse of statements, we must try to discover what the speaker is trying to say with its words or intentions (Gillon, 2019; De Swart, 2015). The task that makes it possible to connect statements with world or domain changes, and, therefore, reason about it is called *Pragmatic Analysis*. Its aim is to infer the (implicit) actions associated with discourse or *Speech Acts*. For this, a computational method must model and reason on the structure of the text. In order to discover all the *Speech Acts* and resolve all the implicit information (i.e., regarding the discourse, anaphoric relationships, etc.) to understand the intention of the message and be able to reason or answer questions.

The *speech act* is an action that a *speaker* performs (aka. *Performative*) when producing a statement and that we want to *imply* with language. Thus, in the previously given example, we could determine, with some ease, that the *speech act* involves a "health policy change declaration". To achieve this, computational methods require intensive knowledge, not only of the discourse but of the beliefs and intentions described in a text or automated dialogue. Thus, in the example previously given, we could determine with some ease that the speech act involves a *declaration of a change in a health policy*. To achieve this, computational methods require intensive knowledge not only of discourse but also of the *beliefs* and intentions described in a text or automated dialogue.

2.4 SUMMARY

NLP provides theories, techniques, and models that allow computers to understand written and spoken human language. Language is inherently ambiguous, so different levels and language processing methods must explore many candidate solutions efficiently for more complex tasks. This allows us to provide practical computational analysis methods at the phonetic, lexical, syntactic, semantic, discourse, and pragmatic levels. For this reason, the scope for the application of NLP technologies is wide in any domain where there's textual information, so as when analyzing scientific literature, customer sentiments on social networks, when extracting customer complains information, when categorizing insurance claims or with customer self-service systems, etc.

2.5 EXERCISES

This section shows practical examples of some of the NLP tasks used in text analytics applications. In particular, these exercises will review programs for morphological analysis, lexical analysis through POS tagging, and dependency parsing.

2.5.1 Morphological Analysis

For this exercise, you must download the example program that performs morphological analysis "morfo.py" from the book site. The program shows two types of analysis: Stemming and Lemmatization. The code is built with a first part that contains all the necessary functions for this and other examples, where you can do individual tests. For the second part, you'll have the code that basically invokes the previous functions and generates the results.

To begin, we must import some methods and variables available in different libraries: stemming methods (SnowballStemmer), language models (en_core_news_sm), list of *stopwords* in English, RE methods, and variables that allow defining punctuations within texts:

```
from nltk.stem import SnowballStemmer
import en_core_web_sm
from spacy.lang.en.stop_words import STOP_WORDS
from string import punctuation
import regex
```

The program must read some input document, extract its sentences, preprocess them (i.e., remove stopwords and punctuations), and perform the morphological analysis (i.e., Stemming or Lemmatization). For this example, we will use only one document from the corpus. However, as we'll see later, the functions are easily modifiable to analyze the entire corpus.

First, we must build a function to read a text:

```
def ReadText(FileName):
    f = open(FileName, 'r')
    text = f.read().split('.')
    f.close()
    return(text)
```

This function reads a text file from a certain given file name (FileName). All the read text is automatically separated when the function encounters a punctuation symbol ("."), returning a list that contains the different sentences. Then, we must define the function that performs preprocessing:

```
def PreProcessing(texts):
    cleanText = []
    for text in texts:
        text = RemoveStopwords(text.lower())
        text = RemoveNumbers_Puntuactions(text)
        if len(text)!=0:
            text = regex.sub(' +', ' ', text)
            cleanText.append(text)
    return(cleanText)
```

It takes a list of sentences extracted from a document. For each sentence, two cleaning tasks are performed: *stopwords* and special character removal, creating a new list of sentences or clean texts.

Stopwords removal takes a sentence, separates it into tokens (i.e., tokenization), and then determines if any of the tokens belongs to the *stopswords* list (STOP_WORD). For this, a filtered list is created from the sentence that contains words that weren't *stopwords*. This list is finally converted into a string and returned to the user at the end. The removal of the punctuation symbols just takes a sentence and replaces all special characters and numbers by null. From this string, you can search those characters belonging to a predefined punctuation list.

```
def RemoveStopwords(sentence):
    Tokens = Tokenize(sentence)
    FilteredSent =[]
    for t in Tokens:
        if t not in STOP_WORDS:
            cleanWord = t.rstrip()
            if len(cleanWord)!=0:
                FilteredSent.append(cleanWord)
    return(List_to_Sentence(FilteredSent))

def RemoveNumbers_Puntuactions(sentence):
    number_string = regex.sub(r'[\"\"\¿\°\d+]','', sentence)
    return ''.join(c for c in number_string if c not in punctuation)

def Tokenize(sentence):
    doc = nlp(sentence)
    tokens = [word.text for word in doc]
    return(tokens)
```

To *tokenize* a text, we use the nlp function from SpaCY. This takes a text or string from the entries and returns a docker, that is, a compartment that contains a result list of the several available tasks from an entry string: text that represents each word (token), lemma, POS label, NER label, etc. For our case, for now we'll only use the text that correspond to each word (word.text) contained in the docker to build and return a list of tokens.

The functions to carry out the morpholocical analysis are of two types: *Stemming and Lemmatization*. We've defined the functions for both in order for you to see different behaviors for the same text. Because of this, you should use one that best suits you. The stemming function takes an input sentence or string to perform the analysis using the nlp function, which delivers the lemma of each token. With these lemmas, we create a list that we'll finally turn into a string using our List_to_Sentence(..) function, which simply takes every element in a list and merges them into a string with (join(..)), separating them by a blank space. In the case of the function to perform *stemming*, the SpaCY docker doesn't provide this type of analysis, so we'll use the stemmer.stem method of NLTK. The reduce(..) function takes an input sentence, performs its tokenization and then forms a list with the *stem* of each token, returning a list converted into a string.

```
def Lematize(sentence):
    doc = nlp(sentence)
    lemmas = [token.lemma_ for token in doc]
    return(List_to_Sentence(lemmas))

def Stemmer(sentence):
    tokens = Tokenize(sentence)
    stems = [stemmer.stem(word) for word in tokens]
    return(List_to_Sentence(stems))
```

```
def List_to_Sentence(List):
    return(" ".join(List))
```

Finally, the main program that invokes the above functions is as follows:

```
FILENAME='E:/JOHN/BOOK/ENGLISH/TextAnalytics-Examples/CORPUS/sports/d1.txt'

nlp          = en_core_web_sm.load()
stemmer      = SnowballStemmer('english')
sentences    = ReadText(FILENAME)
cleanSentences = PreProcessing(sentences)

lemmas = [Lematize(sent) for sent in cleanSentences]
stems  = [Stemmer(sent)  for sent in cleanSentences]
```

First, the NLP method is initialized, loading the analysis models for SpaCY (en_core_web_sm.load()), and then the NLTK stemming method (SnowballStemmer[6]). Functions are then invoked to read the text and pre-process the sentences that were read. You must adjust the FILENAME variable with the location and name of the text file to use. Then, each sentence from the list generated in the preprocessing is lemmatized and a list is created with the result of each lemmatized sentence. The same process is applied to text stemming.

Once the program is run, you can display the content of the original content variables (sentences) and those pre-processed from the texts (cleanSentences):

```
Terminal 1/A

In [9]: sentences
Out[9]:
['The Jack Leslie campaign hopes to raise Â£100,000 ($124,000) for a statue
to honor Leslie, a striker for English club Plymouth Argyle in the 1920s and
1930s',
 " Former England international Gary Lineker has described Leslie's story as
extrordinary",
 '\nLeslie was picked to play for England in 1925, according to the National
Football Museum, but the call-up was later rescinded',
 '\nVisit CNN',
 'com/sport for more news, videos and features\n"They [the selection
committee] must have forgotten I was a colored boy," Leslie said years after
the incident',
 '\n"There was a bit of an uproar in the papers',
 ' Folks in the town [Plymouth] were very upset',
 " No one ever told me official like but that had to be the reason; me mum
was English but me daddy was black as the 'Ace of Spades",
 '\'\n"There wasn\'t any other reason for taking my cap away',
 '"\nWere he to have played internationally, Leslie, who had Jamaican
parentage, would have been England\'s first black footballer',
 '\nInstead, it is Viv Anderson who gained that title in 1978 -- more than
half a century after Leslie was in line to make his debut',
```

```
In [10]: cleanSentences
Out[10]:
['jack leslie campaign hopes raise â£ statue honor leslie striker english
club plymouth argyle s s',
 'england international gary lineker described leslie story extrordinary',
 'leslie picked play england according national football museum later
rescinded',
 'visit cnn',
 'com sport news videos features selection committee forgotten colored boy
leslie said years incident',
 ' bit uproar papers',
 'folks town plymouth upset',
 'told official like reason mum english daddy black ace spades',
 ' reason taking cap away',
 ' played internationally leslie jamaican parentage england black
footballer',
 'instead viv anderson gained title half century leslie line debut',
 'read years ahead time says driver shattered motorsport color barrier read
new study reveals evident racial bias tv football commentary leslie passed
away having scored goals appearances argyle earned promotion tier english
football ',
 'campaign build statue far raised â£ supported english football association
luke pollard member parliament plymouth sutton devonport',
 ' jack leslie black player appear england shirt dropped selected colour
skin pollard wrote twitter']
```

These correspond to lists of strings for both variables. However, you may notice the differences between the original text and the sentences from the already processed text. Then we can display the content of the variables that keep the lemmatized texts (lemmatized_text) and reduced texts (reduced_text):

```
Terminal 1/A

In [12]: lemmas
Out[12]:
['jack leslie campaign hope raise â£ statue honor leslie striker english
club plymouth argyle s s',
 'england international gary lineker describe leslie story extrordinary',
 'leslie pick play england accord national football museum later rescind',
 'visit cnn',
 'com sport news videos feature selection committee forget color boy leslie
say years incident',
 ' bit uproar paper',
 'folk town plymouth upset',
 'tell official like reason mum english daddy black ace spade',
 ' reason take cap away',
 ' play internationally leslie jamaican parentage england black
footballer',
 'instead viv anderson gain title half century leslie line debut',
 'read year ahead time say driver shatter motorsport color barrier read new
study reveal evident racial bias tv football commentary leslie pass away
have score goal appearance argyle earn promotion tier english football',
 'campaign build statue far raise â£ support english football association
luke pollard member parliament plymouth sutton devonport',
 ' jack leslie black player appear england shirt drop select colour skin
pollard write twitter']
```

```
In [13]: stems
Out[13]:
['jack lesli campaign hope rais â£ statu honor lesli striker english club
plymouth argyl s s',
 'england intern gari linek describ lesli stori extrordinari',
 'lesli pick play england accord nation footbal museum later rescind',
 'visit cnn',
 'com sport news video featur select committe forgotten color boy lesli said
year incid',
 ' bit uproar paper',
 'folk town plymouth upset',
 'told offici like reason mum english daddi black ace spade',
 ' reason take cap away',
 ' play intern lesli jamaican parentag england black footbal',
 'instead viv anderson gain titl half centuri lesli line debut',
 'read year ahead time say driver shatter motorsport color barrier read new
studi reveal evid racial bias tv footbal commentari lesli pass away have
score goal appear argyl earn promot tier english footbal',
 'campaign build statu far rais â£ support english footbal associ luke
pollard member parliament plymouth sutton devonport',
 ' jack lesli black player appear england shirt drop select colour skin
pollard wrote twitter']
```

You may clearly notice that the stemming process produces a greater reduction in the words form, which could make the further analysis methods more efficient. However, the word *stems* are a bit incomprehensible at first glance, so it might be more reasonable, in certain cases, to use lemmatized texts. In any case, in many applications that used reduced texts, this problem can be solved simply by creating a "parallel" table containing the reduced word and the original word, so that it can be retrieved when it's required in some analysis task.

2.5.2 Lexical Analysis

Here we'll work with a single program that performs a lexical analysis using POS tagging, called "POS_tagging.py", which can be downloaded from the book site. First, we must define a simple function that performs POS tagging for a text and returns a list of pairs (word and POS tag):

```
def POS_tagger(text):
    doc = nlp(text)
    TaggedText = ''.join(t.text+"/"+t.pos_+" " for t in doc)
    return(TaggedText.rstrip())
```

Again, the nlp function takes an input text or string and returns a docker. In this exercise, we only use the text that corresponds to each word (t.text) and its corresponding POS tag (t.pos_) to build a list of pairs. Then, the main program loads the language model, reads a text file with the name in FILENAME, and then invokes our function which performs the tagging:

```
FILENAME='E:/JOHN/BOOK/ENGLISH/TextAnalytics-Examples/CORPUS/sports/d10.txt'

nlp = en_core_web_sm.load()

text = open(FILENAME, 'r').read()
tagged_text = POS_tagger(text)
print(tagged_text)
```

Unlike the morphological analysis exercise, POS tagging needs to be conducted on the original text with no preprocessing as the language model has been trained on a full natural-language corpus. However, depending on the subsequent tags, you could remove the *stopwords* or perform morphological analysis using the functions described in the previous example.

Once the program is executed, you can see the following output for a read input text.

```
In [18]: tagged_text
Out[18]: 'Flamengo/PROPN trailed/VERB Rio/PROPN de/PROPN Janeiro/PROPN
rivals/VERB Fluminense/PROPN 2/NUM -/SYM 0/NUM in/ADP a/DET Brazilian/ADJ
league/NOUN game/NOUN played/VERB on/ADP a/DET warm/ADJ afternoon/NOUN ,/
PUNCT 27/NUM May/PROPN 2010/NUM ./PUNCT \n\n/SPACE When/ADV a/DET free/ADJ
-/PUNCT kick/NOUN was/AUX given/VERB near/SCONJ the/DET opposition/NOUN box/
NOUN in/ADP the/DET 90th/ADJ minute/NOUN ,/PUNCT Flamengo/PROPN goalkeeper/
NOUN Bruno/PROPN Fernandes/PROPN de/PROPN Souza/PROPN fancied/VERB his/DET
chances/NOUN ./PUNCT \n\n/SPACE His/DET right/ADV -/PUNCT footed/ADJ shot/
NOUN curled/VERB over/ADP the/DET wall/NOUN and/CCONJ hit/VERB the/DET top/
ADJ -/PUNCT right/ADJ corner/NOUN of/ADP the/DET net/NOUN ./PUNCT It/PRON
was/AUX his/DET fourth/ADJ career/NOUN goal/NOUN ,/PUNCT but/CCONJ he/PRON
barely/ADV celebrated/VERB -/PUNCT and/CCONJ defending/VERB champions/NOUN
Flamengo/PROPN would/VERB still/ADV suffer/VERB defeat/NOUN ./PUNCT \n\n/
SPACE A/DET month/NOUN later/ADV ,/PUNCT it/PRON would/VERB all/ADV be/AUX
a/DET distant/ADJ memory/NOUN ./PUNCT \n\n/SPACE Bruno/PROPN would/VERB be/
AUX behind/ADP bars/NOUN ,/PUNCT accused/VERB of/ADP ordering/VERB the/DET
kidnapping/NOUN and/CCONJ barbaric/ADJ killing/NOUN of/ADP a/DET woman/NOUN
./PUNCT'
```

Note that the POS tags assigned to each word are based on the *Universal Part-of-Speech*[7] tagset. This tagset contains 19 types of universal tags, so they don't allow encoding all grammatical features.

2.5.3 Syntactic Analysis

For this simple parsing exercise, we'll work with examples from two techniques: dependency parsing (i.e., full parsing) and chunking (i.e., shallow

---

[7] https://spacy.io/api/annotation#pos-tagging.

parsing). For this, we'll use two programs called "dependency.py" and "chunking.py", respectively, which can be downloaded from the book site.

In the case of the dependency parser (dependency.py), we'll use some graphic SpaCY[8] libraries to display its result (DisplaCy), along with the language model libraries that we've previously used:

```
import en_core_web_sm

from spacy import displacy
from pathlib import Path
```

Then, we define a function that creates an output file with the image (.svg) of the analysis performed by the parser for an input text. Since the parser performs the analysis for each sentence separately, we need to create a folder that contains an image of the analysis for each sentence. For this, we create a file name with a correlative number of each i-th sentence of the type "File_i.svg", in which that image is stored, with the function open(..):

```
def CreateOutputFile(sentence_ID,image):
    file_name = "File_"+ str(sentence_ID) + ".svg"
    output_path = Path(DIR_IMAGES + file_name)
    output_path.open("w").write(image)
```

The main program loads the language model and reads an input text file through the previously defined ReadText (FileName) function:

```
FILENAME ='E:/JOHN/BOOK/ENGLISH/TextAnalytics-Examples/CORPUS/sports/d10.txt'
DIR_IMAGES = 'c:/Users/atkin/Desktop/images/'

nlp = en_core_web_sm.load()
sentences = ReadText(FILENAME)

doc = nlp("the flight arrived without problems")
dep = [d.dep_ for d in doc]
sentence_ID = 0
for sent in sentences:
    doc = nlp(sent)
    image = displacy.render(doc, style="dep", jupyter=False)
    CreateOutputFile(sentence_ID,image)
    sentence_ID +=1
```

For each of the sentences in the document, we use the docker generated by the NLP method analysis. In our case, we're now using the dependency path (dep_) generated by the docker for each sentence, through the

---

[8] https://spacy.io/usage/visualizers.

"display.render(..)" method, which returns the image of the result of the syntactic analysis. Then, we create the output file with the corresponding image. At the moment we execute the program, it will create a folder with the images of the dependency parser for each sentence. Below, there's an example of the result of the first sentence:

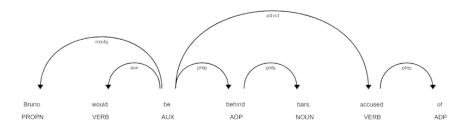

Note that the result considers both the dependency relationships of each of the words, depending on whether they're subjects or objects, along with their corresponding POS tags.

In the case of partial parsing ("chunking.py"), we use the docker that generates the NLP method. In the case of SpaCY, the chunking method has already been trained to recognize chunks of the NP, VP, and other groups, so we only need to specify the type of chunk we want to extract. For this example, we select the NP type chunks or noun_chunks, for which we define a function that performs the NP chunking, generating a list with all the recognized chunks (chunk.text):

```
import en_core_web_sm

def NP_Chunk(text):
    doc = nlp(text)
    NP_list = [chunk.text for chunk in doc.noun_chunks]
    return(NP_list)
```

Then the program loads the language model, reads an input text (without preprocessing), and invokes the chunk_NP(..) function to recognize all possible NPs:

```
FILENAME='E:/JOHN/BOOK/ENGLISH/TextAnalytics-Examples/CORPUS/sports/d10.txt'

nlp = en_core_web_sm.load()

text = open(FILENAME, 'r').read()
NP = NP_Chunk(text)
print(NP)
```

By running the program, we can display the contents of recognized NP chunks:

```
In [26]: NP
Out[26]:
['Flamengo',
 'Rio de Janeiro',
 'Fluminense',
 'a Brazilian league game',
 'a warm afternoon',
 'a free-kick',
 'the opposition box',
 'the 90th minute',
 'Flamengo goalkeeper Bruno Fernandes de Souza',
 'his chances',
 'His right-footed shot',
 'the wall',
 'the top-right corner',
 'the net',
 'It',
 'his fourth career goal',
 'he',
 'champions',
 'Flamengo',
 'defeat',
 'it',
 'a distant memory',
 'Bruno',
 'bars',
 'the kidnapping and barbaric killing',
 'a woman']
```

Note that the parser makes mistakes with some incomplete sentences (i.e., "Fluminense"). That's because the base elements for classifying the chunks are the words and their POS tags, so the POS tagger could have made incorrect predictions. On the other hand, the language model that SpaCY uses in its training doesn't necessarily cover the style of the texts that we're using as input, so it will eventually be possible to evaluate other pre-trained models.

CHAPTER 3

Information Extraction

3.1 INTRODUCTION

Suppose you have a corpus or a website, which contains many claims made by customers in a retail business, that we want to analyze. An example of an excerpt from one of these claims (informal and anonymous) is shown in Figure 3.1. Using a search engine, we could try to retrieve relevant complaints.

However, we still need to read and identify specific information from the texts. Imagine that, in order to populate a database and analyze customer profiles, you want to extract specific pieces of information from such complaints, for example, the date of the claim, the name of the company, and the products/services where users were complaining, or even more complex information, such as the specific relationship between multiple claims. In the example, it's relatively easy for a human reader to identify the date of the event (December 11), the company in question (Macy's), the product ("A Casio brand watch"), among other elements, using the appropriate context and extracting the correct information. If we had a large corpus of such texts, how could we automatically extract this kind of information?

For this, a textual analysis task called *Information Extraction* (IE) must be followed, which corresponds to the process of extracting prespecified information from textual sources. For this, IE combines Natural-Language Processing (NLP) and machine learning techniques to perform tasks such as answering questions in question-answer systems, extracting entity names that are mentioned, detecting events, extracting relationships between entities, etc. (Atkinson et al., 2014).

DOI: 10.1201/9781003280996-3

> Good afternoon. I want to say hello and present my
> claim for the following reason: I bought a Casio
> men's watch on December 11 through the website to
> use it as a Christmas gift and it arrived on date.
> The clock was checked and the time was adjusted,
> but it stopped working every so often. I called
> Macy's where they told me that I had to return the
> product to the supplier, since they weren't the

FIGURE 3.1   A complaint text.

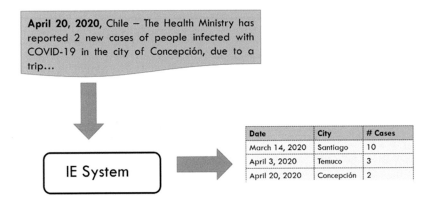

FIGURE 3.2   Relation extraction to feed a template.

Usually, in traditional IE the relationships to extract are predefined, so rule-based methods can be used to detect them. On the other hand, in *open* IE, relationships aren't predefined, so systems will extract any relationships detected from a corpus. In both cases, it's not required to analyze the language of the documents in an exhaustive way with NLP techniques, we only focus on analyzing and extracting information of interest to make it more efficient.

IE can be seen as the task of converting unstructured information into structured data as shown in Figure 3.2.

Although the IE task varies in complexity depending on the type of information you want to extract, in general there are three different approaches for it:

1. *Rule-Based Methods:* Based on human experience, a set of syntactic and semantic rules are manually coded to identify specific information of interest within texts. Then, a system uses these rules to extract information from those texts.

2. *Supervised Machine Learning Methods:* A machine learning model is trained with labeled examples about the type of information to be extracted (i.e., entities, relationships). The method can then detect this type of information on new documents. A drawback of this approach is that it requires a lot of tagged data to train an IE task.

3. *Semi-Supervised Machine Learning Methods:* When we don't have enough tagged data, we can use a set of *seed* examples to define high-precision patterns that can be used to extract more relationships from a corpus.

The general strategy for performing IE tasks follows the typical steps shown in Figure 3.3:

1. *Patterns Activation:* Sentences or fragments containing relevant information are located based on extraction patterns defined by rules or learned by a supervised machine learning method. For this, extraction patterns are generally used that must be triggered following the recognition phrases that contain the specific information. For example, consider the key terms that are triggered in the sentence "The service of <CompanyName> has been the worst..." to identify the name of the company (<CompanyName>) that someone gives

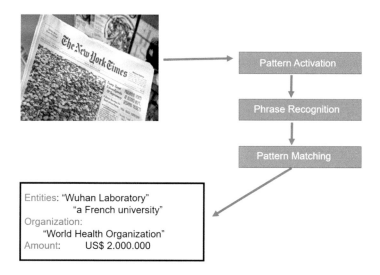

FIGURE 3.3   Steps in information extraction.

their opinion on. This can be used later to connect that entity with some relationship of interest.

2. *Phrase Recognition*: Phrases or syntactic structures that could contain the information to be extracted (i.e. entities, relationships) are detected. For example, linguistically, if a noun phrase (NP) is identified, the name of an entity (subject) performing an action in the text can be determined. On the other hand, if VPs are identified, the name of a verbal relationship can be determined, suggesting the specific action performed, and so on.

3. *Pattern Matching*: Using the extraction patterns of step (1), the triggering phrases of step (2) are detected to then generate the specific information defined in a *template*. In this way, simple patterns must be identified (i.e. "the service of <CompanyName>"), compound rules for the formation of this pattern based on words and their linguistic roles (i.e., "ART NN P NN *"), or specific relationships among them (i.e., "it was the worst…").

For example, consider the following text:

Peter Black will resign as CEO of Advanced Motors tomorrow. This London's company role will be taken by Jeffrey Stevenson.

Figure 3.4 shows different *templates* depending on the specific information that you want to extract from the text: simple entities names, binary relations, or any data record.

Single Entity	
Person	Peter Black
Person	Jeffrey Stevenson
Location	London

Binary Relationship	
Relation	Person-Position
Person	Peter Black
Position	CEO

N-ary Relationship	
Relation	Succession
Company	Advanced Motors
Position	CEO
Out	Peter Black
In	Jeffrey Stevenson

FIGURE 3.4   Simple and relational information extraction.

3.2 RULE-BASED INFORMATION EXTRACTION

The classic approach to IE is based on the use of *cascade* grammars and finite-state machines. Usually, it's designed having in mind a classic entity extraction task (i.e., person names, company names), extraction of relationships between such entities (i.e., *<Person Name> works for <Company Name>*), or to detect multiple mentions of the same entity.

IE systems are usually implemented using grammatical formalisms like those seen in Chapter 2. For this, the input text is seen as a sequence of *tokens,* and the rules are expressed as patterns based on *Regular Expressions* (RE) (Friedl, 2006) regarding the lexical properties of those *tokens.* To detect these patterns, there are several levels of processing, originating *cascaded* grammars, that is, they filter different linguistic elements from higher to lower levels of abstraction.

The information processing levels are adaptations of the NLP stages (Bengfort & Bilbro, 2018; Jurafsky et al., 2014): tokenization, morphological and lexical analysis, partial syntactic analysis, and discourse analysis. Typically, the upper levels of grammar analyze and *annotate* larger segments of texts.

An example of defining rules for a three-level *cascade* grammar can be seen in Figure 3.5. This allows you to recognize people's names and their titles. In a first level (level 0), a token sequence for the input text is generated; in the second level (level 1), rules are defined based on those tokens to identify different parts of the name; and then, in a third level (level 2), the previous rules are combined to identify and extract different ways of

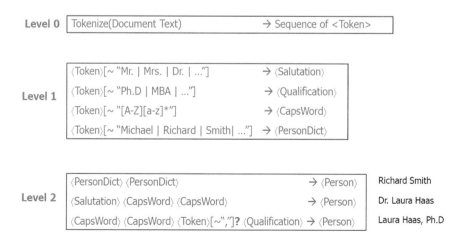

FIGURE 3.5   Example of extraction based on cascading rules.

expressing names and titles. This approach can be easily adapted to extract complex relationships.

The basic formalism for writing such rules at different levels of processing is called *RE*, which provide a concise and flexible way to search for instances of string patterns (i.e., *matches*) in a text (Friedl, 2006). An *RE* is written in a formal language that can be recognized by an interpreter, usually implemented as *finite-state machines* (Sipser, 2012). Virtually all modern programming languages have packages or libraries to handle RE.

In general, RE processing is conducted in two steps:

1. *Define an RE to search, using a language and available operators.*

2. *Search a match using the RE in some text.*

To define an RE, there are three types of operators and several special-purpose meta-symbols that combinedly allow the recognition of complex structures[1]. In addition, expressions with the symbols "(..)" can be "grouped" to refer to different groups of recognized expressions. An ER is a way of specifying a particular type of language called a regular language (type 0) in the Chomsky hierarchy (Sipser, 2012; Aho et al., 2013), so its implementation is simple since it's based on finite-state machines. Because of this, a RE can use the following *regular* text operators, like the one in Figure 3.4:

- *Union:* Allows to recognize one symbol or another by the use of "|". Example: "Mr.|Mrs." means that the expression "Mr." or "Mrs." can be recognized.

- *Concatenation*: Allows to join (concatenate) two expressions using the symbol ".". Example: "Mr. Johnson" means the expression "Mr." followed by the expression "Johnson".

- *Repetition:* Allows to repeat an expression with itself, zero or more times ("*"), or one or more times ("+"). Example: "(Name)*" means repeating the expression "Name" zero or more times.

3.3 NAMED-ENTITY RECOGNITION

Suppose you want to use the rule-based approach above to identify and extract entity names such as "Los Angeles", "Microsoft Corp", and

---

[1] https://docs.python.org/3/howto/regex.html.

"University of Tumbuntu" from a corpus. Surely, with some ease you could run a POS tagging task (Chapter 2) on the original text and define rules that combine certain lexical tags that identify an entity name. For example, defining the rule with the following sequence of POS tags to identify place names: "ADJ NOUN" would extract entities like "Long Beach". However, two problems could arise with this strategy:

1. As the size of the corpus increases, the variability of entity names, building, and updating rule-based extraction systems become less robust and extremely inefficient.

2. If information about entities is extracted, regardless of the context where they occur, the recognition accuracy can be significantly reduced. Consider, for example, the text "*He dreamed he was running in a long beach*" and the previously defined rule. The system would identify a place/location type entity (i.e., "long beach"); however, the context expresses a different entity.

Although such an approach could be used in restricted domains, generally more robust methods are required to recognize entities. One of these methods is known as *Named-Entity Recognition* (NER), which seeks to locate and classify named entities in texts, in predefined categories such as names of people, organizations, locations, amounts, time, monetary values, etc. NER is used in many NLP problems and can help answer many questions for several applications, such as:

- *What companies were mentioned in news articles?*
- *What named entities can characterize a document for further search?*
- *Were certain products mentioned in the complaints or comments?*
- *Does the tweet contain a person's name?*

For example, consider the following text: "Juan Sears complained 5 times during the year 2019". The result of the NER task would be:

Type	Value
PERSON	John Sears
Number	5
Date	2019

Before a method can recognize entities in a text, it should be able to automatically tag words with their POS roles. Then the method should *learn* to identify and classify sets of them. For this, there are several classification approaches:

- *Rule-Based Methods*: These create extraction rules to represent the word or label sequence structure that appear in sample texts. The named-entity type is assigned based on those rules.

- *Probabilistic Methods:* These model the probability of occurrence of a certain specific sequence of POS tags and assign the best-fitting entity type. Representative techniques include *Hidden Markov Models* (HMM), *Conditional Random Fields* (CRF), etc. In the case of an HMM, parts of the model could learn to identify/classify specific entity types (Flach, 2012).

- *Methods Based on Supervised Machine Learning:* These consider supervised machine learning methods to predict sequences of labels that form an entity. Usual methods include recurrent neural networks, LSTM networks, etc., which allow predicting the types of entities from the input token sequences (Wilmott, 2020; Goldberg, 2017; Sherstinsky, 2020).

Training a method to perform the NER task requires a large number of *annotated* corpuses, that is, texts that have been reliably labeled by humans with names and types of entities. Once the POS tags are identified, groups representing the named entities can be detected, using partial parsing or chunking methods, for NPs, VPs, etc. For this, the chunking task takes the tagged text as an input and produces segments or *chunks* that can indicate potential entities mentioned in a text.

Therefore, a usual mechanism is used to generate RE chunks, and in particular, segments that express NPs. For example, a rule could state that our NP chunk could be composed of a determinant (DT) followed by zero or more (*) adjectives (JJ), and then one or more (+) proper nouns (NNP). Thus, the RE that recognizes NP *chunks* can be defined as: "{<DT> <JJ>*<NNP>+ }"

The use of rules to identify chunks containing possible entities is much more powerful when considering the context. For example, consider the text "John Sears, leader of the No+Abuse movement". If an NP chunking is performed, two possible NP will be identified: "John Sears" and

"No+Abuse movement". However, these represent different types of entities: person and organization, respectively. One way to detect specific types is to define the second level of the *cascade*, specifying the context of the text sequence. In this case, this could correspond to the meta-rule: "<person>, in <charge> of <organization>", where a group of the form "<..>" represents any entity name that must be recognized by an RE at specific positions in the sequence.

3.3.1 N-Gram Models

One of the working assumptions of extracting entity names using rule-based systems or RE is that there's indeed a regularity in the word sequences and/or linguistic roles with which names are expressed. As a consequence of this, efficient deterministic algorithms can be implemented for this recognition task.

However, in many NER problems and in general in text analytics, many word sequences that determine names and phrases follow some statistical distribution, so it's not possible to define deterministic rules. In these cases, we need to move from rule-based language models to statistical language models (Jurafsky et al., 2014; Baron, 2019).

A *statistical language model* is basically a model that assigns probabilities to word sequences (or POS). This sequence could represent names of entities, parts, or constituents of a sentence that govern a grammar, etc. Each sequence is called an N-gram, where N is the length of the sequence. For example, look at the following phrases:

1. "San Francisco", is a 2-gram (bi-gram) or a sequence of two words.

2. "Infected by coronavirus", is a 3-gram (tri-gram).

3. "The infected people increased today", is a 5-gram.

Now, which of these three N-grams have you seen most frequently? Perhaps, "The infected people increased" and "infected by coronavirus". On the other hand, perhaps you hadn't seen "San Francisco" so frequently. Basically, the sequence "San Francisco" is an example of an N-gram that doesn't occur as frequently as the sentences in examples (2) and (3). Thus, we could assign a probability to the occurrence of an N-gram or the probability that a word occurs in next in a word sequence. This could be very useful not only for extracting N-grams but for predicting the next word in a sequence.

To model this type of sequences, $P(w|h)$ must be determined, the probability of a word w given some history (past) h. For example,

$$P\left(increased\,\middle|\,the\,infected\,people\right)$$

where

$w =$ "increased" and $h =$ "the infected people".

One way to estimate such a probability is using an approach that counts the relative frequency of words. For this, we can take a corpus and count the number of times the sequence "the infected people" appears and then count the number of times it's followed by increased. You may be asking yourself, why should I count this if it's already known that always after "infected people" comes "increased"? Precisely, therein lies the difficulty, since in a rule-based or deterministic approach, the sequence must be delimited *a priori*. However, in reality, the sequence follows a certain distribution, so after that sentence, other words could be used like increased, decreased, are, etc., hence we need to estimate the cases and then decide. With this we could even predict the most likely word to continue in that sentence.

In other words, the above probabilistic estimate is trying to answer the question:

*Of the total number of times we saw the story **h**, how many times did the word **w** follow it?*

Clearly, if the corpus is very large, it's not very feasible to make estimates to answer that question from the point of view of computational efficiency. However, this can be simplified using the *chain rule for probabilities*, as an intuitive way to generate the N-gram model. Instead of estimating the probability using the entire corpus, we could approximate it, using only a couple of historical words, that is, a *bi-gram* model.

A bi-gram model approximates the probability of a word given all previous words, using only the conditional probability of a word that precedes it. In our previous example, this would be estimated with the probability $P(increased|people)$. Thus, when a bi-gram model is used to predict the conditional probability of the next word, we're making the following approximation on a sequence of n words:

$$P\left(w_n\,\middle|\,w_1^{n-1}\right) \cong P\left(w_n\,\middle|\,w_{n-1}\right)$$

This assumption that the probability of a word only depends on the previous word is known as the Markov assumption (Baron, 2019). Thus, the probability model of a sequence can be seen simply as the multiplication of the probabilities of each bi-gram that forms it. Markov models are a probabilistic model that assumes that we can predict the probability of a future element without looking much into the past. With this approach, we can generalize the bi-gram model to a tri-gram model, which looks at three words in the past, and thus generalize to the *N-gram* model.

One of the ways to estimate the probability function of this type of model is by using the MLE estimator. To calculate the bi-gram probability of a word **y** given a previous word **x**, MLE simply counts the number of times the bi-gram **x-y** appears in the training corpus (C (x, y)) and normalizes it by the sum of all bi-grams that share the same first **x** word, $C(x)$, that is:

$$P(y|x) = C(x,y)/C(x)$$

For example, consider a corpus with four sentences:

1. He told me many thanks.

2. He went to San Pedro.

3. San Pedro has a beautiful climate.

4. It's raining in San Francisco.

Let's assume a bi-gram model, so we'll determine the probability of a word only based on those previous words. To estimate the probability of the word thanks to many, we can write it as:

$$P(\text{thanks}|\text{many}) = C(\text{many}, \text{thanks})/C(\text{many}) = 1/1 = 1$$

We can say without doubts that, wherever the phrase many occurs, it will be followed by the word thanks. Now let's calculate the probability of the word Pedro after San. We can determine P (Pedro|San), which means that we're trying to estimate the probability that the next word is Pedro given the word San:

$$P(\text{Pedro}|\text{San}) = C(\text{San}, \text{Pedro})/C(\text{San}) = 2/3 = 0.67$$

This is because in our corpus, one of three San words was followed by Francisco, so $P(\text{Francisco}|\text{San}) = 1/3$. In the corpus, only Pedro and Francisco occur after San having 2/3 and 1/3 of probabilities to appear, respectively.

If we want to create predictive software for the following word based on our corpus and a user types San, he'll receive two options: Pedro (first place) and Francisco (second place).

3.4 RELATION EXTRACTION

Imagine that we're exploring texts to find the specific link that exists between different types of entities. A first approach would be to use some distance measure (i.e. *cosine* between document vectors) to determine how distant or close such texts could be. However, this is usually not enough, since we still have no idea if there's any specific *relationship* that connects them. For example, consider that analyzing the occurrence of the terms, a statistical correlation has been found between a person and an organization as shown in Figure 3.6a. To identify a specific relationship, a computational method should analyze the texts where these entities are mentioned and then try to hypothesize the possible relationship between them. Figure 3.6b shows potential text snippets that could fit that relationship.

There are many types of relationships that are useful to detect when analyzing texts: cause–effect relationships between medications and pathologies, relationships between people and organizations, relationships between people and their emotions, among others. For example, Figure 3.6 shows instances of specific relationships extracted from texts in biochemistry articles, where you want to detect the relationships or interactions between proteins mentioned in a certain scientific article. From what's identified (i.e., protein names, in gray tone), it can be inferred that the CBF-A protein interacts with CBF-C and that the CBF-B protein is associated with the "CBF-A+CBF complex-C" (see Figure 3.7).

Then a *relationship extraction* method would attempt to extract semantic relationships from texts that usually occur between two or more named entities. As in the previous examples, relationships can be of different types and are characterized using *triplets* SVO (Gillon, 2019), that is (*Subject,*

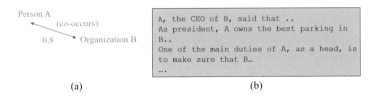

(a)   (b)

FIGURE 3.6   Association and search for specific relationships.

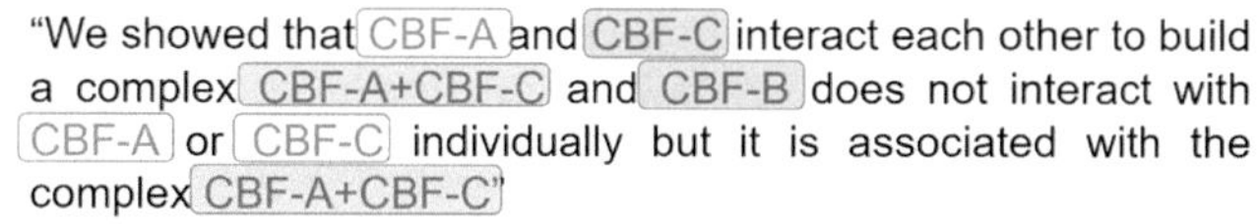

"We showed that CBF-A and CBF-C interact each other to build a complex CBF-A+CBF-C and CBF-B does not interact with CBF-A or CBF-C individually but it is associated with the complex CBF-A+CBF-C"

FIGURE 3.7   Extracting protein-protein interaction relationships.

Verb, Object), such as (John, complained, service) for the sentence "John complained about the service".

As in general-purpose IE, there are three approaches to extract this type of relationship:

1. *Rule-Based Methods*: Many types of relationships can be identified using manually defined extraction patterns, looking for SVO triplets in documents. However, just by looking at the keyword matches of a query, it's possible to retrieve many irrelevant documents. These can be filtered by tagging a text with POS tags and then instantiating a pattern matching some rule or RE. For example, suppose the phrase "Montevideo is in Uruguay" could be labeled generating the sequence "NNP VBZ IN NNP" (i.e., proper noun, verb, preposition, proper noun). Then, we can apply the rule "CITY is in COUNTRY", where CITY and COUNTRY are groups that should fit with NNP sequences, obtaining the values: CITY = Montevideo and COUNTRY = Uruguay.

   Unfortunately, these types of extraction rules aren't able to handle larger range patterns or sequences with greater complexity than syntactic groups (i.e., "Richard and Anne got married"). To address this, we can use the dependency paths generated by a *dependency parser* to determine all words with a grammatical dependency role on others. This can significantly increase the coverage of the extraction rule.

   An advantage of this approach is that humans can define patterns that can be highly accurate and tailored to specific domains. However, these patterns usually have low coverage power due to the variability in the use of the language, being also very demanding in coding time since all the possible rules must be made for each type of relationship to extract.

2. *Supervised-Learning-Based Methods*: This type of technique requires a training corpus that contains annotated texts (i.e., POS tags, dependency paths, NER tags) with their respective relationships.

Furthermore, these are used to train a binary classifier that determines if there's a specific relationship between two entities and if they require annotated input text characteristics. Usually, all steps followed to *train* the classification models are the following:

a. Manually tag texts, depending on whether a sentence is relevant to a specific relationship type or not. For example, for the relationship "CEO", the sentence "Apple CEO, Steve Jobs, told Bill Gates", is relevant while "Charles, fan of cakes, told Bill Gates" isn't.

b. Manually label the relevant sentences as positive/negative if they express the type of relationship sought. For example, for the sentence "Apple CEO, Steve Jobs, told Bill Gates", the triplet (Steve Jobs, CEO, Apple) is positive, while the triplet (Bill Gates, CEO, Apple) is negative.

c. Train a classifier on sentences to determine if a sentence is relevant to the type of relationship.

d. Train a classifier on the relevant sentences to determine if the sentence expresses the relationship or not.

e. Use the classifiers of (c) and (d) to detect relationships in new texts.

We can even use a variation of this type of approach to extract more complex semantic relationships such as *hyperonyms* (i.e., words whose meaning encompasses the meaning of other words - generalization relationship) to infer relationships. For example, *vegetable* is a hyperonym of *lettuce*, *sport* is a hyperonym of *soccer*, etc. For this, you can usually define patterns that consider both the lexical and the syntactic information of the relationship to extract, which are usually called *lexical-syntactic patterns*.

Then a domain-independent method can try to discover relationships from texts that are even unknown until now. For this, we need to consider patterns that consider both lexical and syntactic information, usually called lexicon–syntactic patterns (Hearst, 1998). For example, consider that you want to update some knowledge base of cities and their characteristics and that you receive the sentence "In cities such as London, Rome and Tumbuntu, the pollution rates are medium". Surely, you had never heard of Tumbuntu, but the sentence is expressing a *hyperpermy* relationship between a city (i.e., represented as an NP) and Tumbuntu, so now you can *infer* that this is indeed the name of a city. Furthermore, generalizing with the other cities appearing in the word sequence, you can also infer that Tumbuntu's "pollution index" is medium.

To make this type of inference, a three-step procedure is usually applied:

1. *Define the patterns to instantiate*, for example, we can specify lexical-syntactic patterns such as: "NP_0 such as NP_1 (, NP_i)*", where NP_i is a noun phrase recognized in different positions of the sentence.

2. *Apply some kind of constituent parser* (i.e., PSG) to identify syntactic groups of interest such as NPs.

3. *Hypothesize new relationships to discover* in order to update some knowledge base or graph of relationships, using the previous patterns, being able to detect a new relationship, using the expression:

$$\text{For every } i, \text{hyperonym}(NP_0, NP_i)$$

For example, consider the following input text:

Older people and/or those with chronic diseases, such as respiratory problems, heart problems, or diabetes, are more likely to have a serious disease.

Then, applying the previous procedure, we can discover and infer the following relationships:

hyperonym ("chronic diseases", "respiratory problems")

hyperonym ("chronic diseases", "heart problems")

hyperonym ("chronic diseases", "diabetes")

An advantage of this approach is that human supervision usually offers high quality, which ensures that the relationships extracted are relevant, also explaining the negative examples. However, this method makes very expensive to label and/or annotate examples, and consequently, add new relationships, as it involves defining new patterns.

3. *Unsupervised learning methods* allows relationships to be extracted without the need to label training texts or write extraction rules. For this, a general set of restrictions and heuristics is defined, which must be triggered to generate and then filter the relationships of interest.

In general, in these types of approaches, the following steps are followed:

1. *Train a Classifier on a Small Corpus*:

   - For each sentence analyzed, you must find pairs of noun phrases (NP, NP2) with a sequence of terms that determines a relation r that connects them. Then you should label them as positive examples if they meet all restrictions or as negative otherwise.

   - Transform each triplet (NP1, r, NP2) into a characteristic's representation vector of (i.e. adding POS tags, NER tags, etc.).

   - Train a classifier to identify real candidate relationships.

2. *Extract Possible Relationships from the Corpus*:

   - Detect potential relationships from the corpus.

   - Maintain or discard candidate relationships depending on whether the classifier considers them real or not.

3. *Evaluate Relationships Based on a Redundancy Ranking of the Text*:

   - Normalize and combine identical relationships.

   - Count the number of different sentences where relationships are present and assign probabilities to each relationship, over the total.

This approach requires very few labeled training texts, not needing to manually specify any relationship of interest. However, the effectiveness of the method depends on the quality of the defined constraints and heuristics.

3.5 EVALUATION

Regardless of the nature of the type of information extracted (i.e., entities, relationships), performance can be seen as the ability of the IE task to predict such information, with which a template or something similar can be filled. To determine how well a method is learning to identify or categorize such information, the quality of the output produced by the task must be evaluated. For this, we need to answer the question, *how well is the information extracted from the documents?*

For this, we first need to separate the document corpus into two different datasets (i.e., 75% versus 25%): (1) The *training* corpus that contains texts annotated by humans who should correctly identify the specific information to extract for reference and which is used to prepare or train the IE task;

TABLE 3.1   Confusion Matrix

		Actual Class	
		Positive	Negative
Predicted Class	Positive	TP	FP
	Negative	FN	TN

and (2) the test corpus containing the annotation texts that will be used to *test* the IE task. Therefore, we can have predictions of feature classes, where some are correct and others are not with respect to these references.

Then we can use a **confusion matrix** or *error matrix* corresponding to a tabular display of a prediction model versus true information (see Table 3.1). Each row in the table represents the instances where some type of information was predicted (i.e., predicted class) while each column represents the instances of the actual information (i.e., actual class) that should be extracted (*target*).

Once an IE method has made the predictions, each cell in the matrix reports the following information:

- TP (*True Positives*): number of samples that were correctly classified as positive.

- FP (*False Positives*): number of samples that were incorrectly classified as positive.

- TN (*True Negatives*): number of samples that were correctly classified as negative.

- FN (*False Negatives*): number of samples that were incorrectly classified as positive.

Note that the diagonal elements denote the correct predictions for the different classes while the non-diagonal elements represent the samples that were misidentified or classified.

Then we can calculate three metrics that evaluate the performance of the IE task:

- **Accuracy**, answers the question *How well was the model classified?* and is calculated as a ratio of the number of correct classifications (or *predictions*) to the total number of classifications. That is to say:

$$\text{Accuracy} = (\text{TP} + \text{TN})/(\text{TP} + \text{TN} + \text{FP} + \text{FN})$$

In general, this metric is useful in the categorization of problems that have a good balance between classes.

- **Precision**, answers the question *What proportion of the positive classified samples were actually correct?* and is calculated as a proportion between the total number of correct positive classifications over the total number of positive classifications. That is to say,

$$Precision = TP/(TP+FP)$$

In general, this is a useful metric when you want to be sure about the predictions (i.e., prediction of fraud). Otherwise you might blame innocent customers.

- **Recall**, answers the question *What proportion of the actual positive samples were correctly classified?* and is calculated as a proportion of the total number of correct positive classifications over the total number of samples that actually belong to the positive class (i.e., samples weren't rated as positive, but that were actually positive). That is to say,

$$Recall = TP/(TP+FN)$$

In general, this is a useful metric when you want to capture as many positives as possible (i.e., in cancer prediction, we would like to classify the disease even if we aren't sure about its existence).

Note that *Precision* and *Recall* have an inverse relationship, and usually when *Precision* is increased, *Recall* is decreased and vice versa. Hence to find a balance between the two, there is a combined metric called F1, which corresponds to the harmonic mean of *Precision* and *Recall*. That is, F1 = 2*Precision*Recall/(Precision+Recall). This metric is also useful to compare the performance of different IE systems giving different priority levels to *Recall* or *Precision* (Büttcher et al., 2010).

For example, suppose that from several *Twitter* comments, an IE system should identify those having words expressing positive sentiments and others expressing negative sentiments. Consider that the test corpus possesses 1,100 opinions (100 positive opinions, and 1,000 negative opinions), producing the *confusion matrix* of Table 3.2.

Frequencies can be interpreted as follows:

- Of 100 positive reviews, the model correctly identified 90 of them (TP) and incorrectly identified 10 of them (FN).

TABLE 3.2   Example of a Confusion Matrix

		Actual Class	
		Positive	Negative
Predicted Class	Positive	90	60
	Negative	10	940

- Of 1,000 negative reviews, the model identified 940 of them correctly (TN) and incorrectly identified 60 of them (FP).

From this example, it appears that 1,030 opinions (940+90) are correctly classified out of the total of 1,100 (90+60+10+940), resulting in an Accuracy=1030/1100= 93.6%. On the other hand, 90 opinions were effectively identified as positive out of 100 that were classified as positive, producing Precision=90/100=90%, while for the negative class, Precision=940/950= 98.9% was obtained. This means that the extraction model is doing a better job identifying negative class opinions, because it has seen more negative examples during training. For both classes, the performance values are then Recall (positive)=90/100= 90% and Recall (negative)=940/1000= 94%. Finally, the harmonic mean or F1 of the positive class is 2*0.6*0.9/(0.6+0.9)= 72%.

3.6 SUMMARY

IE is the task of detecting and extracting specific preestablished information from textual information sources, ignoring irrelevant information. For this, there are multiple approaches such as those based on RE, supervised learning methods (i.e., classifiers that are trained to detect specific information from a training corpus), and unsupervised learning methods that can be used to detect information based on constraints and heuristics defined by the designer. IE systems can identify both entities named in documents and also relationships between these entities. The patterns used to extract this type of information can be manually defined or automatically learned from annotated corpuses with correct texts and relationships. These patterns can incorporate lexical-syntactic information to extract much more precise information in terms of semantic relationships that aren't evident in a text.

3.7 EXERCISES

This section shows some practical examples of methods to extract simple information from natural language texts. In particular, we review program examples for rule-based extraction (i.e., REs), simple relationship identification, and NER.

3.7.1 Regular Expressions

For the first example, you can download the program "regexp.py" from the book site. We need to import a language model from SpaCY and the regex library for RE[2]:

```
import regex
```

Then we define a function that searches for a simple REs (Simple Search(..)). Particularly, given a text, this function will search if there's any match or coincidence of an integer in this text to then extract it. Clearly, we cannot specify all number combinations as they're infinite, so we must define an RE. First, we define an RE that recognizes a digit in a range between 0 and 9, using the expression "[0–9]". However, we need to expand it for a sequence of 1 or more digits, so we iterate it with the repeat operator "+", defining the RE as "[0–9]+". In simple terms, this is instructing the RE recognizer to search and extract a character sequence that contains one or more digits. Then, we use the "findall(pattern, text)" method of the regex library to search for the strings matching the pattern, returning a list of matched strings:

```
def SimpleSearch(text):
    r = regex.findall('[0-9]+',text)
    return(r)
```

Now we need a function to do something a little more complex: take each of the lines of an input text, search and extract those words that only correspond to common or proper names (ExtractNounsFromDocument(..)). For this, we first need to perform POS tagging for each of the sentences in the text, and then extract those words whose POS tags correspond to a proper name (PROPN) or a common name (NOUN). We could extract compound names, but for now we'll only focus on simple names.

Our function POS_Tagger(..), defined in the exercises in Chapter 2, outputs POS-tagged texts in the following format:

Word1 / tag Word2 / tag … Word _ n / tag

---

[2] https://docs.python.org/3/library/re.html

Therefore, we must look for a pattern with the following format: word/tag, where the tag can be PROPN or NOUN. Note that you don't know what the word is, so we must define a general expression that describes it. A character inside a word is recognized as the "\w" expression, but a word is formed by one or more characters, so we can use the operator "+" to search for words with more than one character, "\w+" Then our expression should be defined as "\w+/PROPN|NOUN", where the special character "|" fits one expression or the other. However, if this pattern fits in any text, we don't have a way to indicate that it must extract a word or a label. To solve this, an RE allows to "group" expressions using the special characters "(..)", so that we can access it later through a position: group 1, group 2,.. group n. The RE that defines the search pattern thus stays as "(\w+)/(PROPN|NOUN)". Then, we must search for this expression in each line of the document and store the matches in a list, so we could use the previous findall(..) method to search a pattern which returns a list of all the matching strings. Our function creates a new list with each of the word list fitting each line.

```
def ExtractNounsFromDocument(Lines):
    noun_list = []
    pattern = r'(\w+)/(PROPN|NOUN)'
    for line in Lines:
        WordList = ExtractNounsFromLine(pattern,line)
        if WordList != []:
            noun_list.append(WordList)
    return(noun_list)

def ExtractNounsFromLine(pattern,line):
    text      = line.rstrip()
    tagged_text = POS_tagger(text)
    WordList    = [w for (w,t) in regex.findall(pattern,tagged_text)]
    return(WordList)
```

Now, let's extend the use of RE to identify relationships between names. For example, suppose we have this type of sentence: "Richard Sears, advisor to the Ministry", from which we want to know who's in which position in which institution. In this example, clearly the person corresponds to "Richard Sears", his position is "advisor", and he's working for the "Ministry". In simple terms, the expression should contain:

- A sequence of one or more words tagged as proper names or PROPN (person's name): "(\s*(\w+)/PROPN)+" (note that each word with its tag can be separated from zero or more spaces, so we repeat using the operator "+", the blank space "\s", defining "\s*").

- A punctuation (",") tagged PUNCT: "\s*\,/PUNCT" (since a character "," can be an RE operator; the operator \ indicates that it shouldn't
  be interpreted as an operator but as a simple character).

- A word tagged as NOUN (position): "\s*(\w+)/NOUN"

- A word tagged as proposition (ADP): "\s*\w+/ADP"

- A word tagged as determiner (DET): "\s*\w+/DET"

- A word tagged as PROPN (Simple Institution Name): "\s*(\w+)/PROPN".

Then our complete pattern is defined as:"(\s*(\w+)/PROPN)+\s*\,/PUNCT
\s*(\w+)/NOUN\s*\w+/ADP\s*\w+/DET\s*(\w+)/PROPN"

Remember that each expression or RE that we want to extract is grouped
with (..); so, in the defined expression we established five groups that interest us. On the other hand, although we define the pattern by observing an
example sentence, the expression depends on tags and not on words, so
it can match any string that has such an N-gram structure. For example,

John Basel, leader of the party

Charles, advisor to the president

Our last function (SearchRelation(..)) takes a text, tags it, and looks for
a match in the previously defined pattern:

```
def SearchRelation(text):
    tagged_text = POS_tagger(text)
    name         = '(\s*(\w+)/PROPN)+\s*'
    position     = '\,/PUNCT\s*(\w+)/NOUN'
    separator    = '\s*\w+/ADP\s*\w+/DET\s*'
    organization = '(\w+)/PROPN'
    pattern      = name + position + separator + organization
    match = regex.search(pattern, tagged_text)
    return(match)
```

In the main program, we can invoke our SimpleSearch(text) function.

```
text = "The number of infected people went from 1000 to 2000 in one week"
lista = SimpleSearch(text)
print(lista)
```

In this case, what's extracted is a list with all the numbers that fit the
expression ["1000", "2000"].

To use our ExtractNounsFromDocument(..) function, we first load the
language model, read it as a set of lines from a text file, and then we invoke
our function:

```
nlp = en_core_web_sm.load()
FILENAME = 'E:/JOHN/BOOK/ENGLISH/TextAnalytics-Examples/CORPUS/sports/d1.txt'

lines = open(FILENAME)
Nouns = ExtractNounsFromDocument(lines)
print(Nouns)
```

The result is a list with all the names that have been extracted from each line, so the following phrase appears on the screen:

```
□  Terminal 1/A
    ...:
    ...: lines = open(FILENAME)
    ...: Nouns = ExtractNounsFromDocument(lines)
    ...: print(Nouns)
[['Jack', 'Leslie', 'campaign', '000', 'statue', 'Leslie', 'striker',
'English', 'club', 'Plymouth', 'Argyle', '1920s', '1930s', 'England',
'Gary', 'Lineker', 'Leslie', 'story', 'extrordinary'], ['Leslie', 'England',
'National', 'Football', 'Museum', 'call', 'up'], ['sport', 'news', 'videos',
'features'], ['selection', 'committee', 'boy', 'Leslie', 'years',
'incident'], ['bit', 'uproar', 'papers', 'Folks', 'town', 'Plymouth', 'one',
'official', 'reason', 'mum', 'English', 'daddy', 'Ace', 'Spades'],
['reason', 'cap'], ['Leslie', 'parentage', 'England', 'footballer'], ['Viv',
'Anderson', 'title', 'century', 'Leslie', 'line', 'debut'], ['years',
'time', 'driver', 'motorsport', 'color', 'barrier'], ['READ', 'study',
'bias', 'TV', 'football', 'commentary'], ['Leslie', 'goals', 'appearances',
'Argyle', 'promotion', 'tier', 'football'], ['campaign', 'statue', '000',
'English', 'Football', 'Association', 'Luke', 'Pollard', 'Member',
'Parliament', 'Plymouth', 'Sutton', 'Devonport'], ['Jack', 'Leslie',
'player', 'England', 'shirt', 'colour', 'skin', 'Pollard', 'Twitter']]
```

Finally, we can use our SearchRelation(..) function based on a single input text:

```
rel = SearchRelation("Rogers Sanders, advisor to the Ministry")
if rel is not None:
    print(rel.captures(2))
    print(rel.captures(3))
    print(rel.captures(4))
```

In this case, if a relationship is found (i.e., it's not None), we're interested in capturing groups 2 to 4 according to the previously defined pattern. Note that group 1 isn't only of interest, but represents the entire group of name words, while we're only interested in individual words. Then, the result that's displayed on the screen is the following:

```
In [50]: rel = SearchRelation("Rogers Sanders, advisor to the Ministry")
    ...: if rel is not None:
    ...:     print(rel.captures(2))
    ...:     print(rel.captures(3))
    ...:     print(rel.captures(4))
['Rogers', 'Sanders']
['advisor']
['Ministry']
```

A limitation of the previous methods to extract information is that explicit rules or patterns must be defined to identify the information of interest. However, there're several situations where there's no clarity in the rules that govern expressions, depending on the contexts surrounding the words. In such cases, more powerful methods for entity recognition are required.

3.7.2 Named-Entity Recognition

For this exercise, we downloaded the example program "ner.py" available on the book site, which uses libraries for the language model and another library to display the SpaCY results called displacy:

```
import en_core_web_sm
from spacy import displacy
```

Then we define a function that allows to extract all the named entities (NE) in a text. For this, we use the SpaCY docker that allows us to extract each of the entities by accessing the doc.ents attribute of each recognized entity to form with them a list:

```
def ExtractEntities(text):
    doc = nlp(text)
    entities = [NE for NE in doc.ents]
    return(entities)
```

The types of entities to extract include people (PER), location (LOC), organization (ORG), and miscellaneous (MISC). Perhaps, for certain types of applications you would like to know only certain types of entities; so, given a list of extracted entities, we would like to filter them by type. For this, we define the function FilterEntities(..), which generates a list of entities of a certain type from the original list. Once a docker is created, the entity type can be accessed using the attribute label_, so the function must simply loop through the list of entities, creating a new list with each entity that corresponds to a specified type.

```
def FilterEntities(entities, entitiesType):
    filtered_entities = list()
    for Ent in entities:
        if (Ent.label_ == entitiesType):
            filtered_entities.append(Ent.text)
    return(filtered_entities)
```

Finally, the main call function program looks as follows:

```
FILENAME = 'E:/JOHN/BOOK/ENGLISH/TextAnalytics-Examples/CORPUS/sports/d1.txt'

nlp = en_core_web_sm.load()
text = open(FILENAME, 'r').read()
text.rstrip("\n")

entities = ExtractEntities(text)
print(entities)
entitiesType = FilterEntities(entities,'ORG')
print(entitiesType)
```

This loads the language model, reads a text from any text file, extracts the entities mentioned in that text, and then filters only those that correspond to organization names (ORG), producing the following output:

```
Terminal 1/A

In [53]: print(entities)
[Jack Leslie, 124,000, Leslie, English, the 1920s and, 1930s, England, Gary
Lineker, Leslie, Leslie, England, 1925, the National Football Museum,
Leslie, years, Plymouth, English, Leslie, Jamaican, England, first, Viv
Anderson, 1978, more than half, Leslie, 25 years ahead, Leslie, 1988, 137,
401, Argyle, third, English, between 1924 and 1931, 31,000, the English
Football Association, Luke Pollard, Parliament, Devonport, Jack Leslie,
first, England]

In [54]: print(entitiesType)
['Leslie', 'Leslie', 'the National Football Museum', 'Leslie', 'Leslie',
'Argyle', 'the English Football Association', 'Luke Pollard', 'Parliament',
'Devonport']
```

These lists of named extracted entities can be carried over for further analysis tasks (i.e., document clustering). However, there are moments in which the key task is to visually identify these entities in the text itself. For this, we can use the displacy library, allowing the automated visualization of the entities (ent) identified in the docker:

```
doc = nlp(text)
displacy.serve(doc, style="ent")
```

Once we run this display service, we can see some of the result in the address http://localhost:5000:

The Jack Leslie PERSON campaign hopes to raise Â£100,000 ($ 124,000 MONEY) for a statue to honor Leslie ORG , a striker for English NORP club Plymouth Argyle in the 1920s and DATE 1930s DATE . Former England GPE international Gary Lineker PERSON has described Leslie PERSON 's story as extrordinary.

Leslie ORG was picked to play for England GPE in 1925 DATE , according to the National Football Museum ORG , but the call-up was later rescinded.

CHAPTER 4

Document Representation

4.1 INTRODUCTION

Usually, sources of textual information consist of documents that may contain words, sentences, and/or paragraphs. However, the inherent unstructured and noisy nature of textual information makes it difficult to directly apply textual analysis methods. Because of this, efficient mechanisms are required to extract relevant *features* used to represent documents (Chapter 3). To understand this intuitively, consider the following excerpts adapted from news titles and suppose you want to determine the closeness between them to perform some further clustering task:

News 1:

>*Is K-Pop Behind Protests in Chile?: Koreans Reacted to Big Data Report*

News 2:

>*It's revealed that the government big data report on the protests was made by a Spanish company linked to the government*

News 3:

>*The Korean K-Pop group reports that has nothing to do with those groups.*

DOI: 10.1201/9781003280996-4

You can easily see that the news extracts are strongly related to each other, therefore, apparently it wouldn't be so difficult to group them. Ideally, to accomplish this we should be able to understand each of the excerpts, generate their respective mental representation, and then look for *similarities* between them. However, considering the large amount of news that we could be analyzing and their size, understanding everything in depth, could be out of reach for efficiency reasons, so we need intermediate solutions. An intermediate alternative may be to extract the main and determining characteristics of each of the documents. But this isn't enough since a computational method in general can only manipulate numerical representations. Then, once we managed to generate these numerical representations, we could try to measure some closeness or mathematical similarity between them.

Consider in principle each of the words contained in each of the sample news and that you've properly removed all punctuation symbols or separators. You'll realize that many of them don't contribute with anything, linguistically speaking, since they're really frequent in both news; so, they provide low amounts of information and, consequently, their discriminatory power is very low. In addition, there are *stopwords* in the examples in the form of lexical categories (i.e. articles, adverbs, prepositions), that occur too frequently, making them rather irrelevant. Therefore, these types of words, usually called *stopwords* could be removed while searching for characteristics, since their frequency in all documents is so high that it doesn't contribute as a document's discriminator. It's important to note that this is only applicable in text analytics tasks because when you want to build NLP applications all the linguistic elements have a role in language (Chapter 2).

On the other hand, there are two concepts that appear to be slightly different, in terms of the words contained in "big data report" of news item 1, and "government big data report" in news item 2, unless you have prior knowledge that leads one to think that both correspond to the same thing. If we now consider news item 3, we will notice that the word "reports" appears, which makes the similarity between all the news more evident. Although we could group concepts such as word or entity frequencies (Chapter 3), for simplicity, for now, we will only consider individual words to identify entities or more complex terms. To determine the features of each news item, we'll pre-process each one of them, removing all *stopwords*, performing POS tagging to only keep names and adjectives, and then lemmatizing to reduce the morphological variability and therefore the vocabulary size. This produces the following list of features for each news item:

For *news 1*: [K-Pop, protests, Chile, Koreans, report, big, data]

For *news 2*: [report, big, data, government, protest, company, spanish, government]

For *news 3*: [group, Korean, K-Pop, groups]

If you look at the list of features of each document, and try to determine the similarity, seen as the number of common words, you will notice that two of them have the words big and data in common. However, this approach is not always effective for the following reasons:

- If full texts are considered and not just titles, similarities will change, as their features will vary.

- If we add many more news to this analysis and they all contain the words big and data, their relevance becomes low.

- If the features of the documents occur more than once, and if there are some of them that are more important than others, a simple comparison isn't enough.

- If the number of features of each document is variable, a simple comparison of words or terms isn't practical since we'll be comparing documents with several different features.

Clearly, we need more efficient methods to select and represent the characteristics of texts, so that further analysis tasks are effective.

4.2 DOCUMENT INDEXING

The complete process of creating and selecting textual features can be seen in Figure 4.1.

Suppose that there's a corpus with the three previous news items:

Is K-Pop Behind Protests in Chile?: Koreans Reacted to Big Data Report

It's revealed that the government big data report on the protests was made by a Spanish company linked to the government

The Korean K-Pop group reports that has nothing to do with those groups.

From these, a set of unique words or terms must be identified, generating a *vocabulary* V:

Is, K-Pop, behind, protests, in, Chile, Koreans, reacted, to, big, data, report, it, revealed, that, the, government, report, on, protests, was, made,

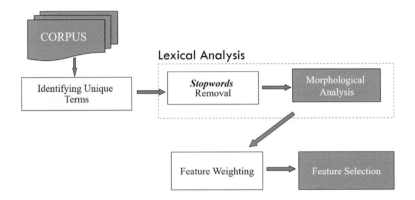

FIGURE 4.1 The indexing or characteristics generation task.

by, a, Spanish, company, linked, Korean, group, reports, has, nothing, do, with, those, groups

Depending on the language and the depth of linguistic analysis required, we should remove *stopwords* from the previously identified terms:

Is, K-Pop, behind, protests, Chile, Koreans, reacted, big, data, report, revealed, government, report, protests, made, Spanish, company, linked, Korean, group, reports, nothing, those, groups

In order to reduce the morphological variability of the terms and therefore the size of the vocabulary, the terms previously identified should be lemmatized, generating:

Is, K-Pop, behind, protest, Chile, Korean, react, big, data, report, reveal, government, report, protest, made, Spanish, company, link, Korean, group, report, nothing, that, group

Since the vocabulary terms will appear more frequently in some documents than in others, the importance or weight of each characteristic must be determined, i.e., in terms of its occurrence producing:

Is (1), K-Pop(2), behind(1), protest(2), Chile(1), Korean(2), react(1), report(3), big(2), data(2), reveal(1), government (2), made(1), company(1), Spanish(1), link(1), group(2), those(1)

Note that the terms could also be more complex entity names as discussed in Chapter 3. Finally, the weight assigned to each feature will determine those terms that are most relevant in the set of documents, using feature selection methods. For this purpose, different *weights* depending on the occurrence of each term in different documents could be assigned, and then select the best (i.e., {K-Pop, protest, Korean, report, big, data, group}).

4.3 VECTOR SPACE MODELS

The only way that our textual data can be computationally managed is to transform them to some numerical representation of the characteristics selected in the indexing step. A classic approach is encoding documents in the form of *Vector Space Models* (VSM), which allow documents with a high number of dimensions or features to be represented (Büttcher, et al., 2010). An advantage of representing information vectorially is that we can then perform traditional mathematical operations on them, such as comparing vectors, grouping vectors, etc., according to measures such as *Euclidean* distance, *Cosine*, etc., which constitutes a basic input for further tasks.

Thus, each document d can be represented as a set of words w, for now ignoring the order between them, producing a simple *Bag of Words* (BOW), just like the previous indexing task. Thus, considering the example of the three initial news items, their corresponding BOW lists are shown in Table 4.1.

By creating a list with the unique terms of the entire corpus, a vocabulary is obtained:

V=[Chile,big,korean,data,company,Spanish,gobern,group,report,K-pop, protest]

Then we have to determine how we represent each document using V. There are three basic approaches to this: Boolean representation models, term frequency representation models, and inverse frequency representation document models.

4.3.1 Boolean Representation Model

The simplest way to represent a document d is using a Boolean model, where each document is simply encoded as a vector indicating the *existence* (1) or non-existence (0) of each vocabulary word in the respective

TABLE 4.1   Sample Documents and Terms

News	BOW	Unique Terms
d1	K-Pop protest Chile Korean report big data	K-Pop protest Chile Korean report big data
d2	Report big data govern protest company Spanish govern	Report big data govern protest company Spanish
d3	Korean group k-Pop	Korean group k-Pop

	chile	big	korean	data	company	spanish	govern	group	report	k-pop	protest
d1	1	1	1	1	0	0	0	0	1	1	1
d2	0	1	0	1	1	1	2	0	1	0	1
d3	0	0	1	0	0	0	0	2	0	1	0

(a)

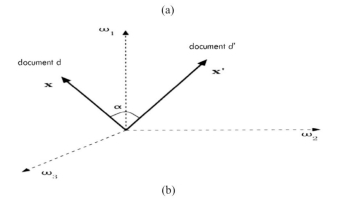

(b)

FIGURE 4.2　Vector representation of sample texts.

document. The length of each vector is fixed and is equal to the length of V or |V|, where |V| is much greater than |d|, due to data dispersion.

This model ensures that the features match the content of the documents. In this case, vectors with a length 5, for each document, are represented as shown in the matrix in Figure 4.2 (a). Note that this model can be used to represent both news documents (rows) and words (columns). Therefore, mathematically, we can apply vector operations that compare words or compare documents.

In order to geometrically understand this representation, let's only consider in the figure the first dimensions of the vectors, and take them into a 3-dimensional space, generating the vectors in Figure 4.2 (b). It can be seen that vector d1 is very close to vector d3, so the document represented by d1 may be talking about the same topics as the document represented by d3. Geometrically speaking, the angle between d1 and d2 is smaller compared to the other vectors, or equivalently, the value of *Cosine(d1,d2)* is closer to 1 than to the other vectors. However, in the example documents, the words occur more than once, which should affect their importance within the respective documents; however, this model doesn't account for this.

4.3.2 Term Frequency Model

If you look again at the documents in Table 4.1, you'll notice that there's a detail: There are more frequent words, so they should be more important than others in the same set of documents. However, the binary representation model doesn't account for this.

The *Term Frequency* (TF) seems to be a more natural way of weighing terms by their occurrence within a document. This is because in a corpus each document has a different length, so it's possible that a term appears more frequently in longer documents than in shorter ones. Then the *weighting* of a term *i* in a document *j* is simply:

$$W(i,j) = TF(i,j)$$

Where *TF(i,j)* is the number of times the term *i* appears in document *j*. If we take the sample documents in Table 3.1, now represented by the *TF*, the following weight vectors are produced:

	Chile	big	korean	data	company	spanish	Govern	group	Report	k-pop	protest	Total
d1	1	1	1	1	0	0	0	0	1	1	1	7
d2	0	1	0	1	1	1	2	0	1	0	1	8
d3	0	0	1	0	0	0	0	2	0	1	0	4

Note that each cell in the matrix can take values greater than or equal to 0, so further vector operations might not be as efficient when considering different ranges or scales. To avoid this, we can usually normalize the values, using different transformations, such as dividing the TF value by the total number of terms in each document. Table 4.2 shows the cells normalized TF values.

Whether in its canonical or standardized version, this representation can encapsulate characteristics with a good discriminating power. Thus, if several words or terms occur a lot in a document, but not in others, these characteristics can be good discriminators for that document in further analysis tasks. Note in the matrix shown in Table 4.2 that the word report (1st component of the vector representing documents) occurs in all documents, so its discriminating power should be significantly reduced, and something similar also occurs with the word *data* (2nd component).

TABLE 4.2   Normalized TF Vector Representation

	Chile	big	korean	data	company	spanish	govern	group	report	k-pop	protest
d1	0.14	0.14	0.14	0.14	0.00	0.00	0.00	0.00	0.14	0.14	0.14
d2	0.00	0.13	0.00	0.13	0.13	0.13	0.25	0.00	0.13	0.00	0.13
d3	0.00	0.00	0.25	0.00	0.00	0.00	0.00	0.50	0.00	0.25	0.00

4.3.3 Inverse Document Frequency Model

A disadvantage of the TF-based model is that it only weighs the importance of a term within a document, but it doesn't reflect that relevance in the document's body. An intuitive approach to address this is to *penalize* a term based on the number of documents where it appears: the greater the number of documents where a term appears, the greater its *penalization* should be, and therefore its initial relevance should be reduced.

So far, our focus has been on how frequent a term inside a document is. Now instead, we're considering the impact of each term on all documents. This representation model is called *Inverse Document Frequency* (IDF), which corresponds to a weight associated with the TF value of each term. In simple terms, IDF tries to *penalize* terms contained in many documents, since they reduce the discriminatory power of those terms.

Intuitively, when calculating the IDF factor, this should be really low for terms that occur in many documents (i.e., *stopwords* have this behavior). If the number of documents in the corpus is N, and DF (i) is the number of documents containing the i-th term, the IDF factor for the i-th term should be calculated as $IDF(i) = N/DF(i)$.

However, there are some considerations with this way to determine the IDF:

- In the case of large corpuses (i.e., millions of documents), the IDF value will clearly be very large for some words (i.e., thousands of times) compared to others, so, to distinguish a document, so the scaling factor would be very big. Because of this, these values should usually be normalized by calculating the *logarithm* of the previous factor, so that it provides a factor that's easier to compare.

- When trying to compare document vectors that contain words that weren't in the original corpus used to create the model, words that weren't in the vocabulary may appear, so their DF value will be 0. Since we cannot divide by 0, the value must be smoothed by adding a 1 to the denominator.

Thus, the IDF factor for a term i is normalized as:

$$IDF(i) = \log\big(N/(DF(i)+1)\big)$$

Then, the weighting of the term i in a document j, is expressed as the model called TF×IDF as follows:

$$W(i,j) = TF(i,j) * IDF(i)$$

Finally, if we consider the TF vectors in the example in Table 4.2, the new weighted vectors according to the TF×IDF model would be:

	chile	big	korean	data	Company	spanish	govern	group	report	k-pop	protest
d1	0.08	0.00	0.00	0.00	0.00	0.00	0.00	0.00	0.00	0.00	0.00
d2	0.00	0.00	0.00	0.00	0.07	0.07	0.15	0.00	0.00	0.00	0.00
d3	0.00	0.00	0.00	0.00	0.00	0.00	0.00	0.29	0.00	0.00	0.00

DF	1	2	2	2	1	1	1	1	2	2	2
IDF	0.58	0.00	0.00	0.00	0.58	0.58	0.58	0.58	0.00	0.00	0.00

Based on this model, we could think of some task that compares document vectors to give us some indication of their proximity. Suppose that the comparison is made according to some correlation between vectors such as *Pearson* (Baron, 2019). The result of the *Pearson* measure among all document vectors for both the TF and the TFxIDF model, can be seen in Table 4.3.

The associations begin to reveal some interesting data for the news d1, d2 and d3 that are being analyzed from the initial example:

- There's an important negative association (-0.67) between the news item d2 and d3 when the TF model is used. However, we implicitly know that they're referring to closely related news about the same event. This is improved while associating these news items (-0.18), which increases in the TFxIDF model.

- There's little association (-0.16) between the news item d1 and d3 when using the TF model. However, we know that both speak of the same group. This association is slightly improved (-0.10) when using the TFxIDF model.

TABLE 4.3 Correlation between Document Vectors: (a) TF Model (b) TFxIDF Model

	(a)				(b)		
	d1	**d2**	**d3**		**d1**	**d2**	**d3**
d1	1,00	-0,33	-0,16	d1	1,00	-0,18	-0,10
d2	-0,33	1,00	-0,67	d2	-0,18	1,00	-0,18
d3	-0,16	-0,67	1,00	d3	-0,10	-0,18	1,00

4.4 SUMMARY

A text by itself cannot be computationally managed, so we need mathematical-computational models to efficiently represent the most important *features* of text documents. For this, we must first index or select the best set of characteristics or *indexes* of a corpus. Then, we must create vector models based on documents to represent those weighted sets of characteristics. Common representation models include binary, frequency-based models (TF) and document inverse frequency models (TFxIDF).

4.5 EXERCISES

In this section you'll see a practical exercise to generate a Vector-Space Model (VSM) to represent documents in a corpus, for a document retrieval task.

4.5.1 TFxIDF Representation Model

For this example, you must download the "TFxIDF.py" program from the book site. To start, we must import a few libraries that we've previously used, and others for handling files and directories (joblib,os). In order we must import NumPy,[1] to handle vectors and matrices, and to handle models and machine learning tasks like SkLearn[2], and some utilitarian functions like *Cosine*. All of these are included in our "utils.py" function library, so we can load them as:

```python
from past.builtins import execfile
execfile('E:/JOHN/BOOK/ENGLISH/TextAnalytics-Examples/utils.py')

from sklearn.feature_extraction.text import TfidfVectorizer
from scipy.spatial.distance import cosine
```

First, we're going to define a function to create a document corpus (CreateCorpus(..)). For this, it's possible to use some sample document's directory provided on the book site. This function takes each of the file names of the selected directory in a path (os.listdir(path)), reads them and generates two lists, one storing the text results of each file (corpus), and another storing the name of those files (doc_id):

---

[1] https://numpy.org/
[2] https://scikit-learn.org/stable/

```
▾ def CreateCorpus(path):
    directory = os.listdir(path)
    corpus = []
    doc_id = []
▾   for filename  in directory:
        text = open(path+filename,'r').read()
        corpus.append(text)
        doc_id.append(filename)
    return(corpus,doc_id)
```

From the created corpus, we need a function (CreateVSM(..)) to create a vector space representation model (VSM). Since we can produce several model types (i.e., TF, TFxIDF, binary), we'll define a function that's flexible enough to be reused in other exercises. Because of this, the function receives four parameters:

1. The set of input texts to represent (texts).

2. The file name where the model will be stored (ModelName).

3. A boolean flag indicating if we want to generate an IDF model (by default, model_idf=True).

4. A boolean flag indicating if we want to generate a binary model (By default, binary_model=False).

Then, we initialize the vector generation method (TfidfVectorizer(..)) with the model types to transform the pre-processed texts into a document matrix by *features* (model.fit_transform(texts)). With the generated array, we can access its vocabulary (model.vocabulary_), the array converted to an "array" format (.toarray()), and a list of IDF factors that were created for a TFxIDF model (otherwise empty) in case it was another selected model. Once we create the model, we store its different components into a file (SaveModel(..)). Keep in mind that this model is only created once and later only its vectors will be used in the respective applications, unless the document corpus grows dramatically every so often, which would justify to re-generate the TF-IDF model:

```
▾ def CreateVSM(texts,ModelName,model_idf=True,binary_model=False):
▾   model   = TfidfVectorizer(use_idf=model_idf,
                              norm=None, binary=binary_model)
    features_matrix  = model.fit_transform(texts)
    vocabulary       = model.vocabulary_
    dtm              = features_matrix.toarray()
▾   if (model_idf):
            idf = model.idf_
▾   else:
            idf = []
    SaveModel(ModelName,dtm,idf,vocabulary)
```

Then we need functions to pre-process the corpus and save the model. To pre-process the corpus, we use basically the same function from Chapter 2, but this time we add the lemmatization to each input text:

```
def PreProcessing(texts):
    cleanText = []
    for text in texts:
        text = RemoveStopwords(text.lower())
        text = Lematize(text)
        text = RemoveNumbers_Puntuactions(text)
        if len(text)!=0:
            text = regex.sub(' +', ' ', text)
            cleanText.append(text)
    return(cleanText)
```

On the other hand, saving the model so it can be used later (SaveModel(..)), we simply take a directory name where we want to store the model (ModelName) and create three files using the Joblib library, representing the following components: the model itself (TFxIDF), the IDF factors and the vocabulary:

```
def SaveModel(ModelName,model,idf,vocab):
    exists = os.path.isdir(ModelName)
    if not exists:
        os.mkdir(ModelName)
    joblib.dump(model, ModelName +"/"+'tfidf.pkl')
    joblib.dump(idf,   ModelName +"/"+'idf.pkl')
    joblib.dump(vocab, ModelName +"/"+'vocab.pkl')
```

Furthermore, we also need a function to load a previously generated model (TFxIDF matrix, IDF factors, vocabulary) from ModelName (i.e., a folder name).

```
def LoadModel(ModelName):
    model = joblib.load(ModelName+"/"+'tfidf.pkl')
    idf   = joblib.load(ModelName+"/"+'idf.pkl')
    vocab = joblib.load(ModelName+"/"+'vocab.pkl')
    return(model,idf,vocab)
```

Then, we will use the model built for a task to retrieve documents relevant to a query provided by a user. For this, the procedure will follow the following steps:

1. Load the TFxIDF vector model.

2. Input a user query.

3. Convert the query into a vector.

4. For each vector of documents:

   1. Compute the cosine similarity between each vector and the query vector.

5. Order the similarity values from highest to lowest.

6. Display the documents related with each similarity.

First, a function is required that's able to create the query vector from the input terms (CreateQuery(..)). It takes a string of terms (terms), the IDF vector and the vocabulary. The function performs three fundamental steps: (1) Create a vector of the same length as the vocabulary; (2) assign the value 1 in the vocabulary position of each of the (lemmatized) terms of the input query; and (3) weight the previous vector by the IDF factor. This looks as follows:

```python
def CreateQuery(terms,idf,vocabulary):
    query = np.zeros(len(vocabulary))
    termsList = Tokenize(Lematizar(terms))
    for t in termsList:
        try:
            ind = vocabulary[t]
            query[ind] = 1
        except KeyError:
            ind = -1
    if (np.count_nonzero(query) != 0):
            query = query * idf
            return(query)
    return([])
```

Note that vocabulary has a dictionary structure, so given a word or term (t), you can retrieve its position (*ind*) and then complete the binary vector in the position of the corresponding query vector. The final weighting is achieved by simply multiplying the query's binary vector by the IDF vector. Then we require a function that retrieves the relevant documents from a corpus (RetrieveRelevantDocuments(..)) from the query vector (query), the document representation model (model), and the identification of each document (doc_id).

```python
def RetrieveRelevantDocuments(query,model,doc_id):
    RelDocs = []
    for ind_doc in range(len(doc_id)):
        filename = doc_id[ind_doc]
        sim = 1 - cosine(query,model[ind_doc,:])
        RelDocs.append((sim,filename))
    return(sorted(RelDocs,reverse=True))
```

For each of the documents (ind_doc), we calculate the cosine similarity between the query vector and the current document vector (model[ind_doc,:]), and then this is added to a list together with the name of this document (filename), obtained from the list of names (doc_id) generated by the CreateCorpus(..) function. The list is then ordered from highest to lowest *cosine* values.

Finally, we've a function that simply takes the list of relevant documents previously generated and displays them along with their similarity value:

```
def DisplayDocuments(Docs):
    print("List of documents relevant to the query:\n")
    for (sim,d) in Docs:
        print("Doc: "+d+" ("+str(sim)+")\n")
```

The main program invoking the previous functions initializes our language model and creates the corpus from a path where the documents to be analyzed (PATH) are located. From the corpus, a vector model is created and saved in the "my_model" directory.

```
PATH = "E:/JOHN/BOOK/ENGLISH/TextAnalytics-Examples/CORPUS/sports/"
nlp             = en_core_web_sm.load()
corpus,docsID = CreateCorpus(PATH)
texts  = PreProcessing(corpus)
CreateVSM(texts,"my_model")

(tfidf, idf, vocabulary) = LoadModel("my_model")
```

For this example, model creation and model loading happen at the same time. However, in a real application, model loading is something that occurs much later or by another program, so there it would make sense to load it to work with those data. Finally, the core of the program requests the term strings to be searched in the documents, becoming a query vector, and then retrieves and displays the relevant documents ordered by similarity.

```
print("*********************************************")
print("welcome to the document search!")
print("*********************************************")

terms = input("Enter query: ")
query_vector = CreateQuery(terms,idf,vocabulary)

if len(query_vector)==0:
    print("ERROR in query vector, documents cant be retrieved!..")
else:
    RelDocs = RetrieveRelevantDocuments(query_vector,tfidf,docsID)
    DisplayDocuments(RelDocs)
```

Once we run the program, we can see a sample of some of the variables, such as the corpus with the content of the 10 sample documents:

```
In [63]: len(corpus)
Out[63]: 10

In [64]: corpus
Out[64]:
['The Jack Leslie campaign hopes to raise Â£100,000 ($124,000) for a statue
to honor Leslie, a striker for English club Plymouth Argyle in the 1920s and
1930s. Former England international Gary Lineker has described Leslie\'s
story as extrordinary.\nLeslie was picked to play for England in 1925,
according to the National Football Museum, but the call-up was later
rescinded.\nVisit CNN.com/sport for more news, videos and features\n"They
[the selection committee] must have forgotten I was a colored boy," Leslie
said years after the incident.\n"There was a bit of an uproar in the papers.
Folks in the town [Plymouth] were very upset. No one ever told me official
like but that had to be the reason; me mum was English but me daddy was
black as the \'Ace of Spades.\'\n"There wasn\'t any other reason for taking
my cap away."\nWere he to have played internationally, Leslie, who had
Jamaican parentage, would have been England\'s first black footballer.
\nInstead, it is Viv Anderson who gained that title in 1978 -- more than
half a century after Leslie was in line to make his debut.\nREAD: \'I was 25
years ahead of my time,\' says driver who shattered motorsport\'s color
barrier\nREAD: New study reveals \'evident\' racial bias in TV football
commentary\nLeslie passed away in 1988 having scored 137 goals in 401
appearances for Argyle, which has just earned promotion to the third tier of
English football, between 1924 and 1931.\nThe campaign to build the statue
has so far raised more than Â£25,000 ($31,000) and is being supported by the
English Football Association and Luke Pollard, Member of Parliament for
Plymouth Sutton and Devonport.\n"Jack Leslie should have been the first
black player to appear in an England shirt but was dropped once selected
```

Then comes a summary of the generated TFxIDF matrix for the documents in the corpus and a vocabulary of 643 words, as follows:

```
 Terminal 1/A

In [72]: tfidf.shape
Out[72]: (10, 643)

In [73]: tfidf
Out[73]:
array([[0.        , 0.        , 0.        , ..., 2.29928298, 0.        ,
         2.90397025],
       [0.        , 0.        , 0.        , ..., 0.        , 0.        ,
         0.        ],
       [0.        , 0.        , 0.        , ..., 0.        , 0.        ,
         1.45198512],
       ...,
       [0.        , 0.        , 0.        , ..., 0.        , 0.        ,
         0.        ],
       [0.        , 0.        , 0.        , ..., 0.        , 0.        ,
         4.35595537],
       [0.        , 0.        , 0.        , ..., 0.        , 0.        ,
         1.45198512]])
```

And a sample of the vocabulary as (words, index) pairs is as follows:

```
In [75]: len(vocabulary)
Out[75]: 643

In [76]: vocabulary.items()
Out[76]: dict_items([('jack', 289), ('leslie', 318), ('campaign', 82),
('hope', 262), ('raise', 451), ('statue', 545), ('honor', 261), ('striker',
554), ('english', 185), ('club', 107), ('plymouth', 424), ('argyle', 36),
('england', 184), ('international', 282), ('gary', 225), ('lineker', 327),
('describe', 155), ('story', 550), ('extrordinary', 195), ('pick', 419),
('play', 422), ('accord', 3), ('national', 379), ('football', 215),
('museum', 377), ('later', 310), ('rescind', 464), ('visit', 611),
('cnncomsport', 109), ('news', 385), ('video', 609), ('feature', 200),
('selection', 496), ('committee', 117), ('forget', 218), ('color', 112),
('boy', 71), ('say', 490), ('year', 642), ('incident', 272), ('bit', 65),
```

```
☐  Terminal 1/A ✕                                            ■ ✎ ⋮
*****************************************
welcome to the document search!
*****************************************

Enter query: football open
List of documents relevant to the query:

Doc: d1.txt (0.1377110283726578)

Doc: d8.txt (0.1064125543746105)

Doc: d4.txt (0.03812889922281848)

Doc: d9.txt (0.0)

Doc: d7.txt (0.0)

Doc: d6.txt (0.0)

Doc: d5.txt (0.0)

Doc: d3.txt (0.0)

Doc: d2.txt (0.0)

Doc: d10.txt (0.0)
```

Finally, we run our search engine, with the query "national football":

Where apparently the most relevant documents are "d1.txt" and "d8.txt", among others.

CHAPTER 5

Association Rules Mining

5.1 INTRODUCTION

Suppose you have a large set of customer feedback on products they've purchased from an e-commerce site. You have the suspicion that the occurrence of certain products in the comments are associated with the occurrence of certain others; that is, there should be a link that *associates* them in many of those comments. Checking this suspicion could be extremely beneficial for your business as it would improve your marketing campaigns, allowing to create special offers, have changes in the virtual *layout* of your products, etc.

Consider the following news headlines featured in international media:

News 1:

> *"Is K-Pop behind Chilean protests? Korean media reacted to the questioned Big Data report"*

News 2:

> *"They reveal that the Government Big Data report as a result of the protests was made by a Spanish company"*

Then, we represent each news by the terms or characteristics important to each one, removing *stopwords* and lemmatizing when necessary, obtaining:

- For news 1: k-pop, protests, chilean, media, Korean, questioned, report, big, data

- For news 2: company, protests, Spanish, government, report, big, data

DOI: 10.1201/9781003280996-5

You can notice some common patterns in both news items: The occurrence of the word big is associated with the occurrence of data; however, this doesn't represent anything interesting since both words collocate very frequently. On the other hand, the occurrence of the words big and data is associated with the occurrence of the word protest. Furthermore, the word protest could be associated with the occurrence of k-pop. Although we need more evidence for these last associations, we're being provided with knowledge that could be very interesting to produce *insights* for decision-making.

To perform this type of association analysis, robust methods are required that are capable of not only finding these associations but also selecting the most relevant and reliable patterns.

Association analysis or *shopping basket analysis* attempts to find common patterns of association between items in data transactions, commonly seen as the analogy of "products" that a customer would place in a supermarket *shopping basket*. These transactions may take the form of products purchased by customers, documents containing certain terms, etc. The working assumption is that these transactions could contain nonobvious associations between items, which would be worth detecting. The analysis applications are varied and include online recommendation systems, analyses of purchase *reviews* on e-commerce sites, monitoring of user clicks, etc.

5.2 ASSOCIATION PATTERNS

Usually, a *pattern* which can be detected is in the form of *association rules*, so the objective of the analysis is to find an interesting set of *rules*, made up of combinations of *frequent itemsets*. For example, the following are some *rules* involving frequent *itemsets*, resulting from analyzing different data types and application domains:

- *In a customer complaint, the terms "problem" and "delivery" are associated with "quality".*

- *Shopping at Amazon.com, over 80% of customers who bought books on climate change also bought books on industrial revolutions.*

The extraction of this type of rules is possible, thanks to the assumption that customers have certain habits when purchasing *items* (products), so there are certain *regularities* which can be discovered. Hence, the *shopping basket analysis* can be seen as the process of analyzing a *customer's* buying habits in order to discover *associations* between the items that customers place in their *shopping baskets* (Tan et al., 2018). This is equivalent to the fact that certain documents are characterized by containing certain implicit associations between terms or entities mentioned in the documents.

In general, a *shopping basket* can be viewed as a transaction or "purchase" of various items or "products" performed by a supermarket customer. In the case of a set of documents, each one represents a transaction, and each word contained in them represents an item (i.e., Product), as shown in Figure 5.1.

Intuitively, transactions can show associations or patterns of interest. For example, between transactions 1–3 it can be seen that the occurrence of the item Chile is associated with the item big while between transactions 1 and 5 the occurrence of Korean is associated with the item company, which could show a potentially interesting and novel association. On the other hand, between transactions 5 and 6, the occurrence of govern is associated with the occurrence of Korean, which perhaps doesn't represent a very interesting relationship.

Formally, an **association rule** is a pattern form of the form:

$$A \rightarrow C$$

where A and C are the antecedents and consequents of the rule, respectively. Each of them can contain a certain set of items or *itemsets*, so it's usually interpreted as the occurrence of an itemset in A that is associated with the occurrence of an itemset in C; that is, "IF A THEN C". Alternatively, this can be seen as *The purchase of the items in A is strongly related to the purchase of the items in C in the same transaction*. For example, if an itemset that could eventually be frequent is {Bread, Eggs, Milk}, a

t1	chile	big	korean	company
t2	chile	big	korean	
t3	chile	big		
t4	chile	data		
t5	govern	big	korean	company
t6	govern	big	korean	
t7	govern	big		
t8	govern	data		

FIGURE 5.1   Documents transactions as shopping baskets.

potential association rule could be "IF {Bread, Eggs} THEN {Milk}" or "IF {Milk, Bread} THEN {Eggs}". It's necessary to highlight that, unlike other methods that generate rules, such as decision trees, association rules indicate co-occurrence and not decision rules for predictive purposes.

5.3 EVALUATION

The example above assumes that some method was able to determine that there were frequent itemsets (i.e., {Bread, Eggs, Milk}) from many transactions. On the other hand, it's also assumed that good association rules (i.e., IF {Milk, Bread} THEN {Eggs}) can be produced from *frequent itemsets*, so there must be a way to evaluate the quality of this association.

There are three specific metrics for evaluating both the quality of an itemset and the association strength of a produced rule: *Support, Confidence, and Lift.*

5.3.1 Support

Support measures the relative frequency (i.e., importance) of an itemset L in all transactions or the probability of occurrence of L in other words, P(L). In general, an itemset is frequent (i.e., *Frequent itemset*) if its *support* value exceeds a minimum support threshold defined by a user (*MinSup*); in other words, it must support the rest of the transactions.

In many instances, we need high support to ensure that this is a useful association between items. However, there may be instances where low *support* is useful if we're trying to find irregular associations.

For example, consider *itemset1*={bread} and *itemset2*={shampoo}. There will be many more transactions containing bread than those containing shampoo. Hence, *itemset1* will generally have a higher *support* than *itemset2*. Now, consider *itemset1*={bread, butter} and *itemset2*={bread, shampoo}. Many transactions will have both bread and butter in the basket, but not so many will have bread and shampoo. Then, *itemset1* will have a higher *support* than *itemset2*. Formally, the support of an itemset X containing several items is defined as:

$$\text{Support}(X) = \frac{\text{Number of Transactions containing itemset X}}{\text{Total Number of Transactions}}$$

The *support* value helps identify relevant *itemsets* that can be used later to generate possible association rules. For example, consider an itemset that occurs at least 50 times in 10,000 transactions; that is, it has a support=0.005, in other words, it's not a very relevant itemset, and thus we don't have enough information to generate an interesting pattern.

5.3.2 Confidence

Unlike *Support*, this metric is associated with a rule, so the probability for the occurrence of an *itemset* (in consequent **C**) is measured since another itemset (in antecedent **A**) occurred in the same "basket". The objective of *confidence* is to determine, of all the transactions that contain a certain consequent, how many would also have a certain antecedent in them. For example, for the rule {bread} → {shampoo, diapers}, a confidence of 0.5 would mean that in 50% of the cases where {bread} was purchased, the basket also included {shampoo, diapers}. For product recommendations, a confidence of 50% might be acceptable, but in a medical situation, this threshold would clearly not be adequate. The confidence value is maximum (1) for a rule when the items in the consequent and antecedent always occur together. Note that the metric isn't symmetric, so the A → C confidence is different from the C → A confidence. Formally, the confidence of an A → C rule is defined as:

$$\text{Confidence}(A \rightarrow C) = \frac{\text{Support}(A \rightarrow C)}{\text{Support}(A)}$$

However, consider the following situation: What would be the confidence of {butter} → {bread}? That is, what proportion of transactions that have butter also had bread? Surely, its value will be very high (close to 1). What would happen with {Yogurt} → {milk}? The value would also be high since {milk} is a very frequent itemset, so it would exist in all other transactions. Then, regardless of what's in the antecedent for such a frequent consequence, the *confidence* value will always be high.

Let's now take the rule {Toothbrush} → {Milk}, where the number of transactions containing {Toothbrush, Milk} and Toothbrush, is 10 and 14 respectively, which gives a *Confidence* of 0.7, which can be seen as a high value. However, we intuitively know both products have a weak association, so there is something misleading about this high confidence value. Consequently, only taking *confidence* values into account limits our ability to make inferences about this association.

5.3.3 Lift

Unlike *confidence*, this metric determines how often the antecedent and consequent of a rule occur together more than what one would expect if they were statistically independent. In other words, this can be seen as the rise that an antecedent A gives to our *confidence* for having the consequent C in the basket. Then the lift metric indicates the ratio of reported support to expected support, if both rules were independent. Formally, the lift of a rule A → C is defined as:

$$\text{Lift}(A \rightarrow C) \frac{\text{Confidence}(A \rightarrow C)}{\text{Support}(C)}$$

In cases where A is actually associated with C in the basket, the *lift* value will be greater than 1 (i.e., there's a dependency between A and C); so, it would indicate a useful association pattern while values close to 1 would mean that items in the rule are completely independent. For example, consider the rule {Toothbrush} → {Milk}. The probability of having milk in the basket with the knowledge that a toothbrush is present would be: $10/(10+4)=0.7$. Now, putting this in perspective, consider the probability of having milk in the basket; without knowing if there is a toothbrush, it would be: $80/100=0.8$, so clearly the rule is expressing a relationship between items that are independent.

5.4 ASSOCIATION RULES GENERATION

As mentioned, customer purchase transactions can exhibit certain association patterns, in the form of co-occurring *itemsets*, some of which may be more interesting than others. From them, we should try to generate the "best" association rules which allow to produce good *insights*.

This is not a simple task: databases (i.e., purchase transactions, document corpus, etc.) could have thousands of different items to choose from. For example, having itemsets of length 15, evaluating and generating all the possible rules made up of pairs of antecedent and consequent would involve exploring a space of approximately 2^{15} possible rules! This increases exponentially as the number of items increases, not to mention the high computational cost involved in evaluating each of the candidate rules in order to select the best ones.

There are several computational methods to efficiently generate frequent itemsets and association rules. One of the most popular is the APRIORI method which tries to discover all the *interesting* patterns in the data that satisfy certain conditions. Since this is a complex search task, the challenge of a method of generating rules from itemsets is to find a good balance between three aspects:

1. *Complexity of Patterns*: Simple patterns should be generated as the more complex ones may not be of interest.

2. *Understandability of Patterns*: A pattern must be understandable to be able to interpret it and generate knowledge.

3. *Computational Complexity*: Finding all possible patterns is a very expensive task, so efficient ways must be found to reduce the search space for solutions.

To address these challenges, the APRIORI method views rule generation as a two-step process: (1) find all frequent itemsets and (2) generate rules from identified itemsets:

1. *Generation of Frequent Itemsets*: This step finds all combinations of frequent itemsets; that is, those that exceed a certain minimum *support* (MinSup) threshold. For example, if there are six items {Bread, Butter, Eggs, Milk, Notebook, Toothbrush} in all transactions combined, possible itemsets could include {bread}, {butter}, {bread, Notebook}, {milk, Toothbrush}, {milk, eggs, vegetables}, etc. Then, we must select those items that are frequent.

Thus, the itemset {bread, Notebook} might not be a frequent itemset if it occurs only 2 out of 100 (0.02) times. To efficiently find all frequent itemsets, by checking their support, the APRIORI method establishes the following principle:

An itemset can be frequent only if all subsets of items are frequent.

Formally, for two itemsets A and B, it must be fulfilled that: $P(A, B) <= P(A)$ and $P(A, B) <= P(B)$, where $P(X)$ represents the *support* of the itemset X. In simple words, this means that the generation of an itemset that joins a subitem A with a subitem B is only possible if both itemsets separately are frequent and so on. This is equivalent to saying that the number of transactions containing the items {bread, eggs} is greater than or equal to the number of transactions that contain {bread, eggs, Vegetables}. If the latter occurs in 30 transactions, the former will occur in all of them and possibly in even more transactions. Then, if the support value of {bread, eggs, Vegetables}, that is, $30/100 = 0.3$, exceeds the MinSup, we can be sure that the *support* of {bread, eggs} ($> 30/100$) will also be greater than the MinSup threshold. This feature is called the **anti-monotony property** of support: if we remove an item from an itemset, the support value of the newly generated itemset *will* either be the same or an increment.

This principle brings two important consequences from the point of view of efficiency:

1. *Itemsets Pruning*: All supersets of an itemset that don't exceed the MinSup are *pruned* or cut. This cut significantly reduces computational power as the number of items increases.

2. *Incrementality*: The task of incrementally finding frequent itemsets is reduced, finding the individual frequent itemsets first (1 item), then the itemsets of length 2 (2 items), and so on.

Given a *MinSup* threshold, the APRIORI algorithm tries to extract frequent itemsets and generate association rules as follows:

1. Initially generate all frequent itemsets (support ≥ MinSup) with a length of 1 (a single item).

2. Repeat from $k=1$ until there are no more itemsets to generate:

   a. Generate itemsets with a length of $k+1$ from all combinations of previous itemsets with a length of k.

   b. Prune those itemsets whose support doesn't exceed *MinSup*.

An example of the algorithm operation is shown in Figure 5.2 on a corpus of four documents. Once there's an initial corpus and an item vocabulary, it's possible to generate size 1 itemsets (candidates of length

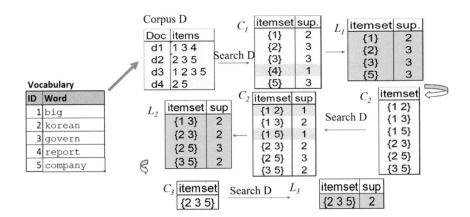

FIGURE 5.2   Generating frequent itemsets using the APRIORI method.

1 or C_1); then the support of each one is calculated and those that don't exceed the MinSup are removed (long 1 candidates that exceed the *MinSup* or L_1). The created itemsets are then combined to produce length 2 itemsets to generate the C_2 candidates and subsequently filter those relevant ones producing L_2, and so on until we reach the itemsets that cannot be combined with any other subset, that is, *frequent itemsets*.

Despite the simplicity and power of the method, there are some efficiency considerations that should be addressed. For example, the itemsets generation step (2.a) requires calculating the *support* value. This involves accessing the matrix that represents the documents and occurrences of items and performing the count, which can be very computationally expensive. Hence there are multiple variations of the method that consider hash tables to store temporary values, nonlinear structures to store the itemsets that are generated, more compact itemsets, nonuniform *MinSup* values depending on the sizes of the itemsets, etc.

2. *Rule Generation*: This step generates all the best rules from frequent itemset combinations obtained from step (1). The rules are made up of binary partitions (i.e., antecedent consequent) of each frequent itemset. Thus, if a frequent itemset L has the length k (k items in L), there are 2^k-2 candidate association rules, ignoring empty lists in L → ∅ and ∅ → L. For example, if a frequent itemset is {bread, eggs, milk, butter}, there would be 14 candidate rules, including: (eggs, milk, Butter → bread), (bread, milk, butter → eggs), (bread, eggs → milk, butter), (eggs, milk → bread, butter), and (butter → bread, eggs, milk).

However, perhaps not all rules represent good quality associations, so there should be efficient combinations. These are then weighed depending on whether they exceed any minimum *confidence* threshold, better known as *MinConf*.

As the *support* of all the rules produced from the same itemset is the same, only the *confidence* denominator needs to be calculated. As the number of items in an itsemset decreases, their *support* increases (i.e., anti-monotony property), and therefore the value of *confidence* decreases. Considering this property, we create a search space with all the possible combinations of rules (Figure 5.3). In order to avoid an exhaustive search for rules, a search subspace is cut with those combinations of rules that don't exceed the *MinConf*.

Low-confidence rules

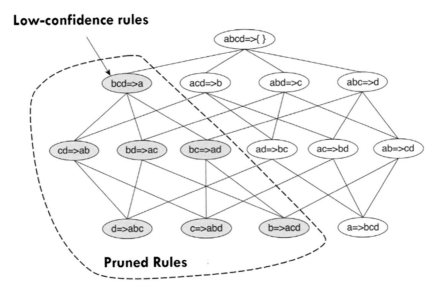

FIGURE 5.3 Association rules search space.

Given a user-defined *MinConf* threshold, rule generation proceeds as follows:

1. For each of the frequent itemsets:
   a. Build rules with only one consequent.
   b. Prune those rules that don't exceed the *MinConf*.
   c. Repeat until only one item remains in the antecedent:
      1. Build rules using a combination of consequents of the rest.

Clearly, the number of rules generated can vary depending on the threshold value. In order to filter the subset of candidate rules, it's also possible to select those that meet certain dependency conditions given by high *lift* values.

In the case of applying APRIORI to generate association rules from documents, the following steps should be considered:

1. Create the document corpus.

2. Preprocess and clean the corpus (i.e., remove punctuations, stopwords).

3. Extract basic features (i.e., nouns, proper nouns).

4. Generate a *binary* matrix of documents versus terms (each cell will be 1 if the term is contained in the document or 0 otherwise).

5. Extract frequent itemsets with *APRIORI* with a *MinSupport* threshold.

6. Generate rules with a *MinConf* threshold.

5.5 SUMMARY

One approach to discovering *insights* in a corpus is on mining hidden patterns between items contained in documents. For this, it's necessary first to find what combinations of items can be interesting to then discover what patterns can be detected from them. A usual pattern has the form of an association rule that allows the co-occurrence of items contained in the same transaction to be represented. One of the popular methods to extract such a pattern is the APRIORI algorithm. This can create frequent itemsets that exceed a certain threshold of support. The method can then explore a wide range of candidate rules by combining these itemsets and filtering them according to a certain confidence threshold. The ultimate goal is to obtain association rules that are potentially interesting and novel for decision-making. The rule extraction method can be used both on traditional transaction databases and on document corpuses.

5.6 EXERCISES

This section shows a practical example for generating association rules from a corpus of documents, using the APRIORI algorithm.

5.6.1 Extraction of Association Rules

For this example, you can download the program "apriori.py" from the book site. Before starting, you must install the following packages that allow you to use the functionalities to analyze association rules:

```
pip install mlxtend
```

We'll need to import a few libraries that we've previously used, so we'll load our function library "utils.py":

```
from past.builtins import execfile
execfile('utils.py')
```

In addition, we'll add new libraries, such as panda[1] to create and handle *dataframes* (panda) and Mlxtend,[2] which is an extended library for machine learning tasks:

```
import pandas as pd
from mlxtend.frequent_patterns import apriori, association_rules
```

We extend the preprocessing function defined in Chapter 2. In our new version (PreProcessingWithNouns(..)), we only add the function called ExtractNounsFromLine(pattern, text) to extract and work only with the common or proper names of each sentence of each text from a corpus:

```
def PreProcessingWithNouns(texts):
    clean_text = []
    pattern = r'(\w+)/(PROPN|NOUN)'
    for text in texts:
        text = List_to_Sentence(ExtractNounsFromLine(pattern,text))
        text = RemoveStopwords(text)
        text = Lematize(text)
        text = RemoveNumbers_Puntuactions(text)
        if len(text)!=0:
            text = regex.sub(' +', ' ', text)
            clean_text.append(text)
    return(clean_text)

def ExtractNounsFromLine(pattern,line):
    text      = line.rstrip()
    taggedText = POS_tagger(text)
    WordList   = [w for (w,t) in regex.findall(pattern,taggedText)]
    return(WordList)
```

This function uses the POS tagger to identify and extract names, which is trained on the entire original corpus written in natural language. Because of this, this is the first task that must be performed for each text before continuing with the cleaning and normalization tasks. On the other hand, the rest of the functions that we'll use will be based on those already defined and included in "utils.py".

The main program invokes the functions, loads the language model, and creates the corpus from a document directory indicated by PATH. To generate the association rules, we need a set of binary item transactions, so we must create a vector space model with binary values (i.e., binary_model=True) so that all calculated frequency greater that 0 is considered as 1. This is performed using the same function CreateVSM(..), used in other chapters but indicating that we don't want a TFxIDF model (i.e.,

---

[1] https://pandas.pydata.org/.
[2] http://rasbt.github.io/mlxtend/.

model_idf=False), only needing binary value arrays. The model output is then written to the transaction's directory. The previously generated model is then loaded with the binary document vectors and the vocabulary. In this case, there's no interest in using IDF weights, so anything is assumed ("_"):

```
PATH = "E:/JOHN/BOOK/ENGLISH/TextAnalytics-Examples/CORPUS/sports/"

nlp = en_core_web_sm.load()
corpus,_ = CreateCorpus(PATH)
texts = PreProcessingWithNouns(corpus)
CreateVSM(texts,"transactions",False,True)

(binary_docs,_,vocabulary) = LoadModel("transactions")
```

Since the transaction matrix (documents×vocabulary) may be too large and our algorithm therefore may take a while, we adjust a VocabLength variable with the maximum length of the vocabulary we want to use. If we want to run our algorithm with all the vocabulary words, we can simply adjust the variable as VocabLength=len(vocabulary). We must then create a table that represents our transactions; so, unlike a normal matrix, we must indicate each of the vocabulary words as column names so that the algorithm can identify them. For this, we can build a panda *dataframe*[3] from document representation, where the column names correspond to the list with the first VocabLength words:

```
VocabLength  = 30

basket = binary_docs[:,0:VocabLength]
ColumnNames = [ list(vocabulary)[x]  for x in range(0,VocabLength)]
df = pd.DataFrame(basket, columns = ColumnNames)
```

Now we can run our algorithm *a priori* from that dataframe (df) to generate the frequent itemsets, setting a MinSupport of 0.005 and indicating that it uses the column names (True) as the item names. Once the itemsets are obtained, we can generate the association rules, specifying the desired evaluation metric, in this case lift, with a minimum threshold of 1. Once the rules are obtained, they are sorted in descending order according to their confidence and then their lift.

---

[3] https://pandas.pydata.org/pandas-docs/stable/reference/api/pandas.DataFrame.html.

```
itemsets = apriori(df, min_support = 0.05, use_colnames = True)
rules = association_rules(itemsets, metric ="lift", min_threshold = 1)
sorted_rules = rules.sort_values(['confidence', 'lift'],
                                        ascending =[False, False])

print(sorted_rules[['antecedents','consequents','confidence','lift']])
```

When executing the program, we can show a sample of the generated itemsets:

```
In [98]: itemsets
Out[98]:
        support                                       itemsets
0         0.1                                          (jack)
1         0.1                                        (leslie)
2         0.1                                      (campaign)
3         0.1                                        (statue)
4         0.1                                       (striker)
..        ...                                           ...
129       0.1              (museum, video, story, committee)
130       0.1             (national, selection, sport, news)
131       0.1             (jack, museum, leslie, boy, lineker)
132       0.1       (committee, museum, story, video, campaign)
133       0.1       (national, striker, selection, sport, news)

[134 rows x 2 columns]
```

This extracts 134 frequent itemsets, starting with length 1 until reaching length 5 itemsets (i.e., "national, striker, selection, sport, news"). We can then show some of the 648 generated rules and their characteristics (i.e., antecedent, consequent, confidence, lift):

```
In [101]:
print(sorted_rules[['antecedents','consequents','confidence','lift']])
        antecedents                     consequents  confidence  lift
0         (leslie)                          (jack)         1.0   10.0
1           (jack)                        (leslie)         1.0   10.0
2        (lineker)                          (jack)         1.0   10.0
3           (jack)                       (lineker)         1.0   10.0
6            (boy)                          (jack)         1.0   10.0
..           ...                             ...          ...    ...
584       (museum)       (lineker, boy, leslie, jack)    0.5    5.0
613    (committee)     (museum, video, story, campaign)  0.5    5.0
614       (museum)   (committee, story, video, campaign)  0.5    5.0
72        (museum)                      (committee)       0.5    2.5
73     (committee)                         (museum)       0.5    2.5

[648 rows x 4 columns]
```

CHAPTER 6

Corpus-Based Semantic Analysis

6.1 INTRODUCTION

Many text analytics applications require determining some kind of closeness or similarity between documents or words to make decisions about hidden patterns. This could include grouping news items that talk about similar topics, categorizing a document according to its meaning, detecting the emotion behind an opinion, recommending *reviews* of similar products, calculating the similarity between a user's *query* and potential documents that can be retrieved by a search engine (i.e., Google, Bing), etc.

Consider the following snippet from a text taken from a pet site:

Going for a walk with our furry friend should be a pleasant experience for both of US, but sometimes it's only for him because it can be really annoying when he barks when seeing other animals.

Understanding its meaning can be the fundamental input for various textual analysis tasks, including:

- How similar is this fragment with another text that talks about animals or dogs (i.e., document clustering)?

- What's the emotion expressed when talking about the furry friend (i.e., sentiment classification)?

DOI: 10.1201/9781003280996-6

- If I wanted to search for texts on the term dogs, would the previous fragment be retrieved (i.e., information retrieval)?

- etc.

In the first instance, answering these questions involves using Natural-Language Processing (NLP) techniques (Chapter 2) to automatically reason about previously constructed representations or meanings for sentences, etc. However, due to computational efficiency considerations, this is out of scope when trying to analyze a lot of textual information. On the other hand, not all the knowledge delivered by some semantic representation is always required.

Intuitively, all the questions associated with the previously described tasks have a common element: they all involve determining some *closeness* of meaning or *similarity* between the representation of one text and that of another. Then we should be able to answer two questions:

1. *How to efficiently represent the meaning of the words or sentences of a document?*

2. *How to determine the closeness between these representations?*

If you had some kind of specialized electronic dictionary, you could search for the terms contained in a text and then associate them with their properties, thus producing their representation. Furthermore, you could do the same with other documents and then determine their common properties as a way to establish their *semantic closeness*. Soon after walking, you would realize that if you carry out the above process on texts that have different terms, clearly their closeness would be very low. However, one of the texts talks about animals and the other one about dogs, so in reality both texts are somehow related. The problem arises because the *dictionary* isn't capable of providing knowledge of the specific relationships connecting the terms; in this case, animal is a general case of dog, or linguistically speaking, both are connected by a semantic relation of *hypernym* (Bermúdez, 2020; Eisenstein, 2019; Gillon, 2019). One way to have this type of relationship is by using a knowledge base or taxonomy. The proximity between those terms can then be seen as a path that must be traveled between the terms of these texts; in other words, the conceptual distance between animal and dog is much less than between animal and truck (Kendall & McGuinness, 2019).

One problem with this type of knowledge-based approach is that building and updating dictionaries or taxonomies is a very demanding task. On the other hand, there are no knowledge bases such as dictionaries or taxonomies for all domains, so the methods couldn't represent closeness or similarities between terms and documents.

A more reliable alternative that doesn't require knowledge bases is to generate representations based on the *context* where the words occur in the documents. The context can be seen simply as the environment or window that surrounds a word and that somehow determines its meaning. A common way to encode such *contexts* is by using vector representations for either words and/or documents (Chapter 4). Then, determining the proximity is relatively simple as it results in computing distance between vectors. However, given that the number of contexts or features can grow significantly and that not all of them are relevant in the representation, some dimensional reduction method is usually required that allows the representations to be encoded efficiently in a reduced number of dimensions (Bishop, 2006).

Since words can have more than one possible meaning (i.e., several possible semantic relationships), semantic ambiguity problems must be solved efficiently (Chapter 2). Some approaches use an unsupervised machine learning technique to generate the best semantic representations of words and/or documents from certain similarity measures. On the other Hand, in a supervised machine learning approach (Aggarwal, 2018), representations are generated by *training* a classifier from a set of documents (i.e., corpus). These are annotated with the meaning of the words in a context to then generate a classification model that determines the best sense or context that corresponds to the words.

6.2 CORPUS-BASED SEMANTIC ANALYSIS

Remember that we're trying to generate efficient representations to encode the meaning of the words (*semantic* representation) in order to carry out a similarity analysis. Eventually, vector representations based on TF- or TFxIDF-type models (Chapter 4) could be used to assess the semantic similarity. However, there are two fundamental problems with this kind of representation:

1. The actual linguistic relationships between words aren't encoded. In fact, if we notice the way both models are generated (TF or TFxIDF), it's easy to notice that there's no way to directly encode the association

of one word with others, and the relationship only accounts for the weight of each word associated with each document of a corpus.

2. They can express too many *features* or dimensions of the words or documents. This can cause major computational efficiency problems when processing such vectors due to the dimensionality curse (Bishop, 2006). More importantly, many dimensions can cause "text" noise, hindering the actual relationship between words in a context.

Then, computational techniques are required to transform this type of highly dimensional representation into a low-dimensional representation model, which also allows to capture the hidden or latent relationships between words and/or documents. This process of transformation to generate low-dimensional vectors of words is known as *Word Embedding* (Bokka et al., 2019; Goldberg, 2017). Figure 6.1 shows the process of transformation or *embedding* of words represented in many dimensions, to their *embeddings* in two dimensions. It can be seen that the transformation allows to capture close relationships that were *hidden*, and that, when grouped together, they seem to reflect some real linguistic relationship.

Any method that allows generating word *embeddings* should be able to *learn* the best vector representation of each word, considering the multiple or *distributed* context affecting its meaning. In other words, generating those vectors should faithfully represent the closeness that exist between words in a similar context of use.

There are several techniques to generate this type of embedding. However, due to their results in document analysis, the following stand out:

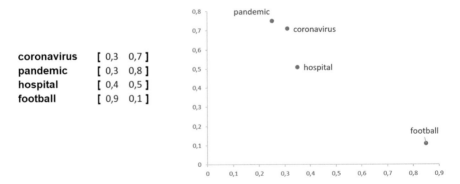

FIGURE 6.1   Word embeddings representation.

- *Latent Semantic Analysis (LSA)*: This is an unsupervised learning technique (Aggarwal, 2018) that, using dimensional reduction techniques, reconstructs an initial vector space in less dimensions.

- *Word2Vec*: This is a group of supervised learning models that, using artificial neural networks (Goldberg, 2017), are able to predict the context of words and their vector representations based on context examples.

6.3 LATENT SEMANTIC ANALYSIS

In general, there are computational efficiency limitations when generating good semantic representations based on words from texts, using traditional vector space models (Landauer et al., 2014).

Let's assume the task of retrieving documents relevant to a user-specified *query* (i.e., term list). Linguistically speaking, two fundamental problems arise:

1. *Polysemy*: A language phenomenon that occurs when the same word has several possible meanings. The effect in the previous task is that the word analysis could retrieve *irrelevant* documents, that is, documents that contain the same words as the query but with different meanings.

2. *Synonymy*: An identity or similarity semantic relationship that occurs when different words have a similar (or identical) meaning. The effect on document retrieval is that the word analysis would fail when trying to retrieve *relevant* documents, since synonym relationships wouldn't be detected.

Intuitively we know that if two documents talk about the same topics, their representation vectors should be close. However, this can be easily obstructed due to the high number of dimensions or characteristics, so we could try to reduce these dimensions in order to capture the hidden characteristics of the words. Interestingly, in this process, unknown or *latent* relationships could appear between the words of the documents.

A corpus-based *unsupervised learning* technique that allows to generate previous semantic spaces is called *LSA*. The main assumption is that there's a latent structure in the use of words—hampered by variability in word selection. LSA is a theory and method that allows to extract and represent meaning based on the contextual use of words through certain statistical transformations applied to a large corpus (Landauer et al., 2014).

Unlike other analysis methods, the *associations* between the input items, from which the LSA infers the representations, are between the unitary expressions of meaning (i.e., meaningful words and complete sentences where they occur) rather than between successive words. That is, the LSA uses as initial data not only contiguous pairs of word co-occurrences but specific patterns of occurrences of many words over a large number of contexts with local meaning (i.e., sentences or paragraphs). On the other hand, the LSA doesn't consider the influence of word order while determining the meaning of a sentence when capturing how differences in word selection are related (Chapter 2).

On the other hand, LSA doesn't use human-built dictionaries, knowledge bases, or grammars, so the technique can be seen as an unsupervised way of discovering hidden or *latent* synonym relationships in a corpus. To extract and understand patterns from texts, the LSA makes three fundamental assumptions:

1. *The meaning of a sentence is the sum of the meaning of all the words that make it up.* On the other hand, the meaning of a word is the average representation of all the documents where it occurs.

2. *Semantic associations between words are present* but not explicitly, being *latent* in the language sample.

3. *Words with close meanings* will occur in similar parts of a text (*distributional hypothesis*).

LSA assumes that dimensionality reduction from initial contexts in a much smaller number of dimensions will produce much better approximations of human cognitive semantic relationships. Unlike other methods, LSA uses a preprocessing step in which the distribution of words over their usage context is taken into account, independent of their correlations with other words. This also represents a considerable improvement compared to other dimensional reduction techniques, such as *Principal Component Analysis* (Bishop, 2006), which could also be used on textual information once it has been encoded in vectors.

6.3.1 Creating Vectors with LSA

The general idea behind LSA is quite simple: from a corpus of documents, a simple vector space model (TF or TFxIDF) is constructed, which represents the initial contexts on a large number of dimensions (initially equivalent to the number of documents). Then, a matrix decomposition method is used to finally reconstruct the vector space in a smaller number of dimensions. This reduction has an important effect since it *collapses* the influence of the dimensions and contexts, in the importance or *weight* that each word could have in the documents.

Given a C corpus, a new representation of reduced dimensions can be created from the original documents, called *semantic vectors*, by performing the following steps:

1. Create a frequency matrix X from C: This matrix should contain the frequency in which terms or words (t) appear in documents and other contexts (d). Note that the set of m unique terms extracted correspond to the corpus vocabulary and that the set of n documents corresponds to the initial vector dimensions. In addition, some cleaning and preprocessing might be required at this stage (Chapter 2)

    Consider a corpus of four documents with a vocabulary of six terms or words, whose frequencies are represented in the 6×4 matrix of dimensions in Table 6.1.

2. Decompose the original matrix X using the linear algebra technique known as *Singular Value Decomposition* (SVD) (Klein, 2015). This factorizes X as the product of three separate matrices $X = U*S*V^T$, as shown in Figure 6.2, where:

   - U is the left singular component matrix that describes the relationship between terms or words (rows) with their orthogonal factor vectors or *features*. Remember that a matrix is singular if its determinant is 0 or is squared if it doesn't have an inverse.

   - S is the diagonal matrix of the singular values of X, with nonnegative descendant values, formally known as the *singular values*.

TABLE 6.1   Initial Matrix of Terms by Documents

	d1	d2	d3	d4
Covid	2	2	0	0
hospital	2	2	0	0
Virus	3	3	0	0
infections	0	0	2	2
City	0	0	1	1
Transport	0	0	2	2

		X			=			U			x		S			x			Vt	

	d1	d2	d3	d4
covid	2	2	0	0
hospital	2	2	0	0
virus	3	3	0	0
infections	0	0	2	2
city	0	0	1	1
transport	0	0	2	2

	f1	f2	f3	f4
covid	0,48	0	0	0
hospital	0,48	0	0	0
virus	0,72	0	0	0
infections	0	-0,66	0	0
city	0	-0,33	0	0
transport	0	-0,66	0	0

	f1	f2	f3	f4
f1	5,8	0	0	0
f2	0	4,24	0	0
f3	0	0	0	0
f4	0	0	0	0

	d1	d2	d3	d4
f1	0,7	0,38	0	0
f2	0	0	-0,7	-0,7
f3	0	0	0	0
f4	0	0	0	0

FIGURE 6.2 Matrix decomposition using Singular Value Decomposition (SVD).

Each nonzero value represents a *feature* and the main diagonal has a value of zero. The magnitude of the values describes how much dispersion each *feature* describes in the data.

- V^T is the transposed right singular matrix that describes the relationship between *features* (rows) and documents (columns).

3. Reconstruct the original matrix, X', with a smaller number of dimensions: This reconstruction involves multiplying the decomposed matrices but with a smaller specified number of dimensions t. Usually, t can be selected as the largest t singular values of S, only keeping the first t columns of U and V. Another way to reduce it is by doing a reconstruction, removing the coefficients from the diagonal matrix S starting with the smaller.

As a general rule, for large corpus sizes, t can vary between 100 and 500 dimensions. For small corpus, it's recommended to construct an *importance* histogram (i.e., square of singular values) versus *singular values* (or dimensions) as shown in the graph in Figure 6.3. Then, the number of singular values that have the greatest *importance* can be chosen, discarding the first dimension, as for document vectors the first dimension correlates with the length of the document while for terms or words this correlates with the frequency of words in all documents.

4. The vector model or matrix finally constructed corresponds to the semantic vector space X', which can be used to obtain the term's and document's vectors as shown in Figure 6.2. In the case of the term vector space, it's reconstructed as U*S with the reduced number of t dimensions. Similarly, the document vector space is reconstructed with t dimensions like V^T*S. Both reconstructions can be interpreted as follows, assuming t=2:

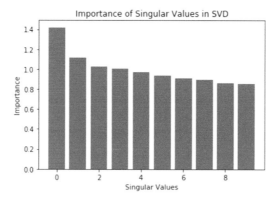

FIGURE 6.3   Selecting the best number of dimensions.

- *U * S*: This describes the relationship between the terms or words (rows) and the features (columns); in other words, it corresponds to the vectors that represent the terms:

	f1	f2	f3	f4
Covid	2,82	0	0	0
hospital	2,82	0	0	0
virus	4,24	0	0	0
infections	0	−2,82	0	0
city	0	−1,41	0	0
transport	0	−2,82	0	0

Again, we can see that the terms covid, hospital, and virus are associated with the **f1** feature, while the terms infections, city, and transport are associated with the **f2** feature. Furthermore, we can see that virus has a stronger association with **f1** than covid or hospital, showing that virus occurs more frequently. In the same way, city has a weaker association with **f2** than infections, showing that city occurs less frequently.

- *V^T *S*: Describes the relationship between documents (rows) and *features* (columns); in other words, it corresponds to the vectors that represent the documents:

	f1	f2	f3	f4
d1	4,1	0	0	0
d2	4,1	0	0	0
d3	0	−3	0	0
d4	0	−3	0	0

If we take into account only two dimensions to reduce ($t=2$), we can notice that if we use any distance metric, there will be a greater distance between documents **d1** and **d2** with respect to documents **d3** and **d4**.

With these term and document vectors, we can easily apply usual measures to compare vectors (i.e., *Cosine, Euclidean*) to evaluate:

- The similarity between vectors of different documents for a clustering task.

- The similarity between vectors of different terms or words for an association detection task.

- The similarity between term vectors and documents for a document retrieval task.

For example, if we take the document space with the first two dimensions ($t=2$), we can calculate the *Euclidean* distance between all the documents, obtaining the following distance matrix:

	d1	d2	d3	d4
d1	0,00	0,00	5,09	5,09
d2	0,00	0,00	5,09	5,09
d3	5,09	5,09	0,00	0,00
d4	5,09	5,09	0,00	0,00

This shows that documents **d1** and **d2** are close in terms of their subjects (distance=0) while documents **d2** and **d3** appear to speak of more distant subjects (distance=5.09). Although this represents data with very few dimensions, it can give us an indication of which documents we could group and which ones should be separated.

In general, the LSA is a simple method for distributed generation of low-dimensional vectors, which is easy to understand and implement. In addition, the technique offers better results than traditional vector space models for managing synonymy. However, the computational cost of performing SVD increases significantly as the corpus size increases. On the other hand, it's difficult to incorporate new terms into the model since it needs to be regenerated with the new corpus.

6.4 WORD2VEC

Word2Vec is a group of machine learning models that's used to produce low-dimensional word vectors or *word embeddings*. This type of model uses *Artificial Neural Networks* (ANN) that are trained to predict and reconstruct word contexts (Bokka et al., 2019; Goldberg, 2017). To achieve this, a corpus of texts is taken as input, which is divided then into sentences where words are found in context. Then, we proceed to learn to predict the correct context for the words, while the network simultaneously adjusts the best feature vectors that allow that prediction. Finally, each word will have a vector in low dimensions obtained from the *hidden layers* of the network.

Unlike the LSA, this kind of method has three fundamental differences:

1. This is a *supervised learning method* (Aggarwal, 2018) to generate word vectors, so those vectors are learned and positioned in a low-dimensional space. This allows that vectors which share common contexts in the corpus to learn to locate themselves close in that space, adjusting their vectors accordingly.

2. The initial input representation is based on a simple coding which uses a vector to express the existence of a word in a vocabulary (one-shot encoding) and not a weighting proportional to its frequency as in TF models.

3. They can incorporate new words or sentences into the vocabulary, only re-training the words in the corresponding contexts.

The main objective of *Word2Vec* is to generate *word embeddings* that allow *predicting the context of each input word*. For training efficiency purposes, a three-layer artificial neural network model is used:

- *Input layer:* Contains the windows encoding of words in a corpus, where the size of the window determines the number of words in the context.

- *Hidden layer:* Contains the input embedding as different dimensions or characteristics vectors.

- *Software layer:* Contains the coding of the possible prediction results (i.e., words, labels, etc.).

In general, *Word2Vec* allows you to *learn word embeddings* using two specific methods: *Continuous Bag of Words* (CBOW) and *Skip Gram*.

CBOW takes the context of a word as input (i.e., words that surround it in a certain window) and tries to predict the word that's missing in that context (Figure 6.4 on the left), while *Skip Gram* takes the word of interest and attempts to predict its context (Figure 6.4 on the right). *Skip Gram* is similar to *CBOW* but inverted and with multiple contexts. Given its more frequent use in data analysis applications, the *CBOW* model has been more popular.

Given the context of a word, the *CBOW* model must learn to determine the probability that a *vocabulary* word (or label) is a neighbor of the word that was initially delivered. Once the neural network is trained, we can extract the weight vectors from the hidden layer of a certain number of dimensions (or neurons), which represent the embeddings of each vocabulary word.

The initial encoding of the word context is done in a certain size window. However, the larger the size, the more difficult it is to predict the context of a word as the search space grows, and, at the same time, it imposes more

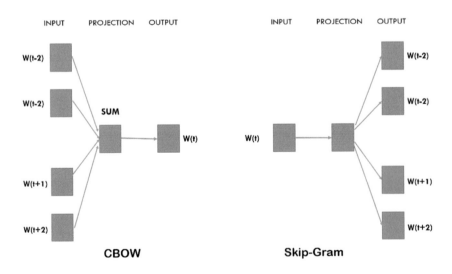

FIGURE 6.4   Types of Word2Vec models.

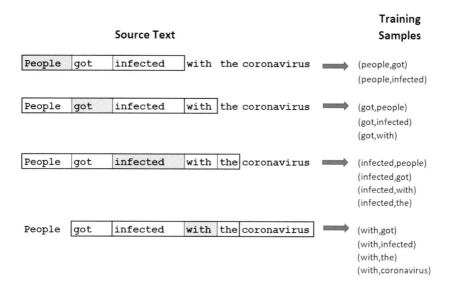

FIGURE 6.5   Examples of context windows for training.

restrictions on the training corpus. Therefore, they're usually considered windows with a maximum size of 2 or 3. Figure 6.5 shows an example of training samples for the model, which uses size 2 windows (i.e., word pairs).

Each word in the input context is encoded as a binary value vector or **one-hot vector**, that is, a vector whose length has the size of the vocabulary, where each word occupies a position in that vector. Each cell is simply a bit representing the existence of the word: A bit with a value of 1 indicates that it corresponds to the word that's encoded, and all the rest of the vectors have a value of 0. For example, consider the sentence: "People got infected with the coronavirus", so the vocabulary would be V={people, got, infected, with, the, coronavirus}; hence, the one-hot vector encoding for each of the six vocabulary words is as follows:

people	[1,0,0,0,0,0]
got	[0,1,0,0,0,0]
infected	[0,0,1,0,0,0]
with	[0,0,0,1,0,0]
the	[0,0,0,0,1,0]
coronavirus	[0,0,0,0,0,1]

To visualize these encodings, we can imagine a space in five dimensions, where each word occupies one of the dimensions and has no relation to the rest (i.e., there are no projections in the other dimensions). This means that *coronavirus* and *infected* are as different as *people* and *with*, which isn't true. The objective of the model is to generate vector representations of words with a similar context so they should occupy close spatial positions (i.e., the angle between these vectors should be close to 0).

6.4.1 Embedding Learning

To generate a *word embedding model*, a training corpus is initially taken from which all the sentences are extracted separately. For each sentence, word sequences of L length (i.e., context window size) are extracted, as shown in Figure 6.9, with training word sequences with a length of 2. Each word in a sequence is represented with the *one-hot vector* encoding previously described.

The general form of the architecture model that allows to transform the input into the output can be seen in Figure 6.6.

Neural network training with CBOW then proceeds as follows:

1. *Create two random weight matrices*: one that connects the input layer (i.e., *one-hot* encodings of vocabulary **V**) with the hidden layer of **N** neurons **Wvn** (matrix V*N) and the context matrix, which corresponds to the connections between the **N** neurons of the hidden layer and the output layer **W`nv** (matrix N*V) that contains the possible predictions of words in context. The hidden layer contains **N** neurons (or dimensions) and the output is again a vector with a length of **V** with the elements to be predicted in the output layer or *Softmax* layer (Sherstinsky, 2020). Both weight matrices have an *embedding* for each vocabulary word when training ends.

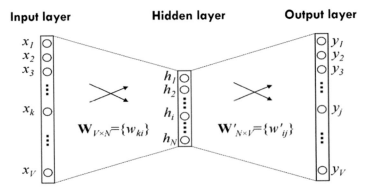

FIGURE 6.6   Architecture of a Continuous Bag of Words (CBOW) model.

2. For each training sample:

1. *Generate the Output Values of the Hidden Layer*: The result of the neuron processing of the hidden layer is done by performing the weighted sum of the product of the input values by the weight matrix **Wvn**. The effect of this product is only to select the matrix row corresponding to bit 1, as shown in Figure 6.7, for a one-hot encoding vector of the fourth word of a vocabulary.

   Because of this, the hidden layer is working like a lookup table, so the output of that layer is a vector of words that's associated with the input word.

   The neurons in the hidden layer then simply copy a weighted sum of the inputs to the next layer, without going through any intermediate firing functions.

2. *Generate the Output Layer values*: The model output layer contains another vector the same length as V and represents the probability that each target word is a *neighbor* (context) of the encoded words in the input (Figure 6.8). To predict each of the values of the output layer (y), each weight vector of each *neuron* of this layer (Vw0) is multiplied by the vector created by the hidden layer (Vwi), creating the output values.

$$[0 \quad 0 \quad 0 \quad 1 \quad 0] \times \begin{bmatrix} 17 & 24 & 1 \\ 23 & 5 & 7 \\ 4 & 6 & 13 \\ 10 & 12 & 19 \\ 11 & 18 & 25 \end{bmatrix} = [10 \quad 12 \quad 19]$$

FIGURE 6.7   Updating hidden layer values.

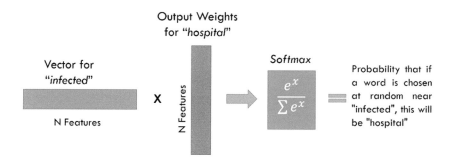

FIGURE 6.8   Computing values for output neurons.

Since this will generate real values, we must transform them into probability values so that we can decide the best output word. For this, a *SoftMax* type function is applied to the previously calculated value (Figure 6.9). This corresponds to a generalization of a logistic (*exponential*) function that's used to represent a categorical function, that is, a probability distribution over a certain number of possible outputs, thereby ensuring that all values are between 0 and 1.

Unlike other ANN models, this represents the only nonlinearity of the CBOW model. Therefore, *SoftMax* estimates the probability of an output word (w_o), given an input word (w_o), as a ratio between the exponential of the result of each output neuron and the sum of the exponential of all values of output, i.e.:

$$P(w_o \mid w_i) = \frac{e^{V_{wo}V_{wi}^T}}{\sum_{w=1}^{W} e^{V_w V_{wi}^T}}$$

3. *Update the Embedding Weights*: Once the best output word (w_i) is predicted from the previous stage, each is compared with the one-hot vector of the input encoding (Figure 6.10). Then the error is calculated as the difference between the probability of output and the one-hot vector of the input. With this error, the network weights are updated using *gradient back propagation methods* (Bokka et al., 2019).

Figure 6.11 shows a training with a hidden layer of **N = 300** neurons (dimensions of the final vectors or *embeddings*). Then the final embedding

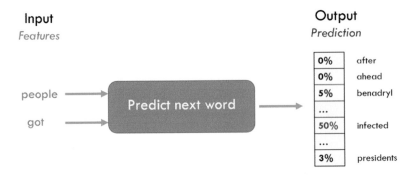

FIGURE 6.9   Output words prediction using the SoftMax classifier.

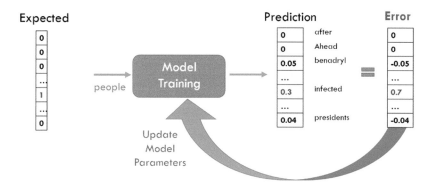

FIGURE 6.10   Continuous Bag of Words (CBOW) training process to generate predictions.

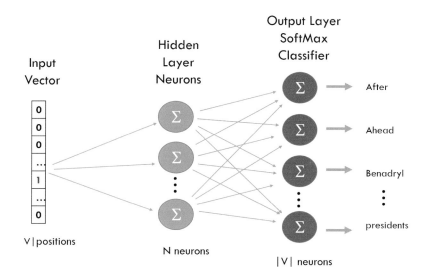

FIGURE 6.11   General network structure for context prediction.

vector matrix will have 10,000 rows (one per word in **V**) and **N** columns (one for each feature or neuron).

6.4.2 Prediction and Embeddings Interpretation

Once the model is trained and the word vectors (*embeddings*) are created, the prediction of a word, given a context, is calculated in three steps: (1) search for the embedding of a word, (2) calculate the prediction, and (3) project the word in the output vocabulary. Note that the number of dimensions or characteristics of the embedding vector is equivalent to N, the number of neurons in the hidden layer.

As mentioned in previous sections, the generated embeddings can be used to perform word similarity calculations in documents for various text analytic tasks. The generated vectors interpretation, even with few dimensions, is not very evident. However, intuitively, we could understand how the features are distributed in these embeddings. For example, consider a vector of 51 *features* or dimensions for the word nurse that has been learned by CBOW for some corpus:

0.47	0.56	−1.54	0.001	0.68	0.82	0.005	0.76	...	0.43	0.68
0	1	2	3	4	5	6	7	...	49	50

Clearly, we can't say much by just looking at the values. However, we could generate a visualization so that we can compare them with other vectors. For this, let's color-code the vector cells based on their values: being red if the value is close to 2, white if the value is close to 0, and blue if the value is close to −2. This produces the following color distribution for the vector:

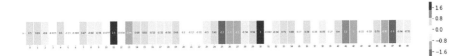

Next, let's ignore the numbers and look only at the colors to indicate the cell's features and contrast the nurse vector with the man and woman vectors:

It can be seen that men and women are more similar to each other than to each other than men and nurse. This shows that these embeddings can effectively capture a lot of information about the meaning of the words, depending on the learning achieved from the words in the context.

In general, *Word2Vec* type models such as CBOW produce efficient distributed word representations (*embedding*), and you can easily incorporate new words into vocabulary. However, this approach doesn't address problems such as polysemy, so the meaning of a given word type varies depending on its context.

Unlike LSA, the method is a bit vulnerable and not robust, so its results aren't uniform. Furthermore, the training time required for large vocabularies is an important limitation, which is why other methods to generate embeddings are required although several current solutions consider the use of pretrained models of this type (Yang et al., 2020).

6.5 SUMMARY

There are many textual analysis applications where determining semantic similarity is essential. For these cases, we need to create efficient word or document representations which are able to capture the meaning in their context. These are several corpus-based semantic analysis techniques that allow the creation of this type of representation in the form of low-dimensional vector models (i.e., word embedding). One of the popular models is called LSA, which is an unsupervised model that allows to create semantic vectors for words or documents in low dimensions, using decomposition matrix methods. While performing the dimensional reduction, latent relationships that were implicit between the words and whose dimension variability didn't allow to detect them can be captured. On the other hand, other models such as Word2Vec are supervised learning methods to predict word contexts while simultaneously learning the vectors that best represent the words in a context.

6.6 EXERCISES

This section will show some examples to generate and use Word embedding models, such as LSA and Word2Vec, from a corpus of documents. For this, the "lsa.py" and "word2vec.py" programs can be downloaded from the book site. Before starting, it's necessary to install the following GenSim package[1] for machine learning functionalities:

pip install -U gensim

6.6.1 Latent Semantic Analysis

For the LSA management example ("lsa.py") we will need to re-use several previously defined functions, so we load our "utils.py" library:

```
from past.builtins import execfile
execfile('utils.py')
```

We'll also add the matplotlib[2] library for data visualization:

```
import matplotlib.pyplot as plt
```

We must define a new function to create an LSA model (i.e., the semantic space) from a corpus (CreateLSASpace(..)) based on the following steps.

1. Preprocess a corpus to generate a text list.

2. Create an initial TFxIDF matrix from the previous texts.

3. Generate the previous matrix transpose (.T), so that the rows can represent word vectors.

4. Decompose the initial matrix using SVD, so it creates three matrices: U, Sigma and V^t.

5. Reconstruct the matrix in terms of U*diagonal(Sigma) with a reduced number of dimensions NumDim.

6. Reconstruct the document matrix in terms of diagonal(Sigma)*V^t with a reduced number of dimensions NumDim.

7. Get the vocabulary from the list of *features* in the original matrix (.get_features_names()).

8. Save the model for further use.

---

[1] https://pypi.org/project/gensim/.
[2] https://matplotlib.org/.

Thus, the function receiving a previously built corpus and the name of the file to store the model is as follows:

```
def CreateLSAspace(corpus,numDim,ModelName):
    texts  = PreProcessing(corpus)
    transf = TfidfVectorizer()
    tf = transf.fit_transform(texts).T
    U, Sigma, VT = np.linalg.svd(tf.toarray())
    terms = np.dot(U[:,:numDim], np.diag(Sigma[:numDim]))
    docs = np.dot(np.diag(Sigma[:numDim]), VT[:numDim, :]).T
    vocab = transf.get_feature_names()
    SaveLSAmodel(ModelName, Sigma, terms, docs, vocab)
```

Note that we use various methods corresponding to the NumPy (np) library, such as the diagonal of a matrix (np.diag(..)) and the dot product between two matrices (np.dot(..)). The functions to save the model to a file (SaveLSAmodel(..)) and to load it later (LoadLSAmodel(..)) are similar to those described in the exercises in other chapters. The first takes the arrays and vocabulary and writes them to the specified directory while the second loads an already created model from a model (i.e., directory name) into the corresponding matrices:

```
def SaveLSAmodel(ModelName,Sigma,terms,docs, vocab):
    exists = os.path.isdir(ModelName)
    if not exists:
        os.mkdir(ModelName)
    joblib.dump(Sigma,   ModelName +"/"+'sigma.pkl')
    joblib.dump(terms,   ModelName +"/"+'terms.pkl')
    joblib.dump(docs,    ModelName +"/"+'docs.pkl')
    joblib.dump(vocab,   ModelName +"/"+'vocab.pkl')


def LoadLSAmodel(ModelName):
    sigma = joblib.load(ModelName+"/"+'sigma.pkl')
    terms = joblib.load(ModelName+"/"+'terms.pkl')
    docs  = joblib.load(ModelName+"/"+'docs.pkl')
    vocab = joblib.load(ModelName+"/"+'vocab.pkl')
    return(sigma, terms, docs, vocab)
```

With these functions, we can use either term vectors or document vectors for various tasks. For example, we could visualize the dispersion of the terms or documents, so we must define a function which allows us to graph the provided vectors (VisualizeVectors(..)). For this, we need to perform two basic steps:

1. From the input vectors, create two data lists: one for the x coordinate (position 0) and the other for the y coordinate (position 1), as a single vector can have multiple dimensions.

2. Graph each of the pairs (x, y) by adding a name tag (annotate(..)) that corresponds to the vocabulary (words or names of documents). In order to differentiate each of the points, they are assigned with different colors.

Then the function that receives the list representing the vocabulary (vocab) and the vectors is as follows:

```python
def VisualizeVectors(vocab,vectors):
    x = []
    y = []
    for value in vectors:
        x.append(value[0])
        y.append(value[1])
    plt.figure(figsize=(7, 7))
    plt.title("Vector Representation")
    for i in range(len(x)):
        plt.scatter(x[i],y[i])
        plt.annotate(vocab[i],
                    xy=(x[i], y[i]),
                    xytext=(5, 2),
                    textcoords='offset points',
                    ha='right',
                    va='bottom')
    plt.show()
```

One of the aspects that we have assumed so far is that, when constructing the LSA vector space, we should have an idea of the appropriate number of dimensions to use for the reconstruction of the original vector space. For this, we should choose that number of dimensions (i.e., number of singular values of the Sigma matrix) that maximizes the *importance*, where it corresponds to the square of each singular value. The function that allows displaying these values is the following:

```python
def ShowImportance(Sigma):
    NumVaNumValues = np.arange(len(Sigma))
    Importance = [x**2 for x in Sigma]
    plt.bar(NumVaNumValues,Importance)
    plt.ylabel('Importance')
    plt.xlabel('Singular Values')
    plt.title('Importance of Singular Values in SVD')
    plt.show()
```

Another relevant technical aspect is that matrices generated at this stage are vectors whose rows are numerically indexed, so they're accessible only by position. However, many applications require to manipulate key-indexed vectors (i.e., words or file names) in a specific way (i.e., you want to compare the vector of the word "coronavirus" with another vector, but you don't know its position.). To solve this, usually the original matrix must be converted to another structure, so that there are keys instead of indexes, either through a *dataframe* or a dictionary. We chose the last alternative to define a function (CreateDictionary(..)) that, given the vectors and a vocabulary, creates a dictionary in which the indices will correspond to each of the identifiers of the vocabulary and the content will correspond to the vector itself:

```
def CreateDictionary(Vectors,vocabulary):
    word_dict = {}
    for  v in range(0,len(vocabulary)):
        word_dict[vocabulary[v]] = Vectors[v]
    return(word_dict)
```

Then our main function call program loads our usual language model, adjusts a number of dimensions to be reduced, creates the corpus from a document directory specified in PATH (CreateCorpus(..)), and creates the LSA model, saving it in a directory called "my_lsa", with a number of (reduced) dimensions of six (NumDim=6):

```
nlp = en_core_web_sm.load()
NumDim =  6
corpus, docsList = CreateCorpus(PATH)
CreateLSAspace(corpus,NumDim,"my_Lsa")
```

The LSA space is created once to then asynchronously load the model and use it in other applications. In our case, for the purpose of the example, the load is in the same program, in order to obtain singular values (Sigma), vectors of terms and documents, and the list of words (vocabulary):

```
(Sigma, vect_terms, vect_docs, wordList) = LoadLSAmodel("my_Lsa")
```

An analysis that we would like to carry out is to determine the best number of dimensions to reduce, so we invoke our previously defined function:

```
ShowImportance(Sigma)
```

When executing it, the following graph is shown, where the maximum number of singular values corresponds to the number of documents in the corpus, and, after discarding the first dimensions, for reasons previously explained in this chapter, it's reasonable that this begins to converge approximately in the fourth dimension so it seems like a proper number:

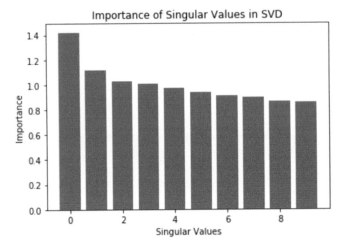

However, in practice we must consider other factors by analyzing, for example, how the method can retrieve synonyms between words, given a certain dimension of the vectors used.

The program then uses the generated vectors to create scatter plots for both words and documents. In order to make the visualization understandable, the graphing function will only consider vectors of the first 20 words and the vectors of the first five documents:

```
VisualizeVectors(wordList, vect_terms[0:20])
VisualizeVectors(docsList, vect_docs[0:5])
```

Which generates the following scatter chart of words:

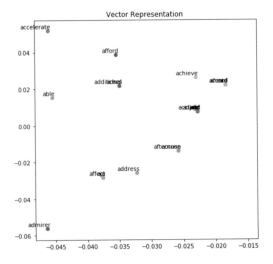

And the document scatter visualization:

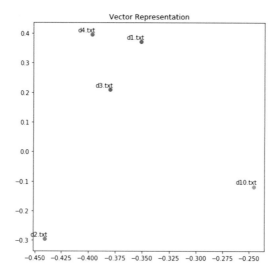

Note that due to the proximity of their vectors, although the graphics are only using two dimensions, they already show a proximity between some documents, such as "d1.txt" and "d4.txt". These findings are key to grouping documents into tasks such as clustering as it would indicate that both documents in the example should be in the same clusters.

Finally, we can convert word and document vectors into dictionaries that can be accessed later (i.e., word or document name):

```
terms = CreateDictionary(vect_terms, wordList)
docs  = CreateDictionary(vect_docs , docsList)
```

An interesting exercise is to compare the closeness of document vectors that were apparently close in the previous graph (two dimensions) with the closeness using all reduced dimensions (NumDim=6). The first thing we'll do then is obtain document vectors that were apparently very close in the previous graph and calculate their real closeness in terms of the cosine similarity:

```
Terminal 1/A ✕                                          ■ ▰ ≣

In [114]: v1 = docs['d1.txt']

In [115]: v2 = docs['d4.txt']

In [116]: v1
Out[116]:
array([-0.35124706,  0.37231276, -0.41361377,  0.43301844, -0.03714862,
        0.07015526])

In [117]: v2
Out[117]:
array([-0.39662126,  0.39513006, -0.1014932 ,  0.3472915 ,  0.14131775,
       -0.08035729])

In [118]: 1-cosine(v1,v2)
Out[118]: 0.861300781212611
```

Now, if we take only the first two dimensions for each vector, the following similarity is obtained:

```
Terminal 1/A ✕                                          ■ ▰ ≣

In [119]: v1 = v1[0:2]

In [120]: v2 = v2[0:2]

In [121]: v1
Out[121]: array([-0.35124706,  0.37231276])

In [122]: v2
Out[122]: array([-0.39662126,  0.39513006])

In [123]: 1-cosine(v1,v2)
Out[123]: 0.9995198739109804
```

You may notice that indeed, documents appear more similar in two dimensions than using the original six dimensions given in the reduction. In fact, just looking at the value ranges of each vector component, you can already see that there's a certain closeness without using additional functions.

6.6.2 Word Embedding with Word2Vec

In order to generate word embeddings using *Word2Vec*, we'll use the program "word2vec.py". For this, we load our previously defined functions in "utils.py":

```
from past.builtins import execfile
execfile('utils.py')
```

We must add two libraries: gensim for document management and retrieval and a *cosine* function extension, which allows to calculate distances between multiple vectors:

```
from gensim.models import Word2Vec
from sklearn.metrics.pairwise import cosine_similarity
```

To train a word embedding model of the Word2Vec type, we need to preprocess the input corpus and separate each text from a read file into a token list; so we need to slightly adapt the preprocessing function defined in other chapters:

```
def PreProcessingSentences(texts):
    cleanText = []
    for text in texts:
        text  = RemoveStopwords(text)
        text  = Lemmatize(text)
        text  = RemoveNumbers_Puntuactions(text)
        if len(text)!=0:
            text = regex.sub(' +', ' ', text)
            tokens = Tokenize(text)
            cleanText.append(tokens)
    return(cleanText)
```

The difference is that each corpus text that we're preprocessing and adding to a list is divided into a token list, so the function returns a token list. So, we need to train our Word2Vec model with these preprocessed texts using a function called "TrainModel(..)", which trains and produces the word embeddings model and saves it in a certain location (.save(ModelName)):

```
def TrainModel(sentences,ModelName):
    model = Word2Vec(sentences, size=4, window=2, min_count=1)
    model.save(ModelName)
```

This training phase requires several parameters, but we've included only the fundamental ones: The input token list (sentences), the number of dimensions of the embedding vectors (size=4) that's equivalent to the number of neurons in the hidden layer from the model's neuronal network, and the size of the training window (window=2) in each sentence. Then the function loading the training model (LoadW2Vmodel(..)) is defined as:

```
def LoadW2Vmodel(ModelName):
    model = Word2Vec.load(ModelName)
    vocabulary = [term for term in model.wv.vocab]
    return(model,vocabulary)
```

This function loads the model from a location (ModelName), creates a list of all the vocabulary terms (model.wv.vocab), and returns the model and its vocabulary.

The main program loads the language model, creates the corpus based on the directory location (PATH), and trains the model by saving it in the location "my_word2vec":

```
nlp = en_core_web_sm.load()
corpus,_doc_id = CreateCorpus(PATH)
sentences = PreProcessingSentences(corpus)
TrainModel(sentences,'my_word2vec')
```

Since the model was already trained, we can download it:

```
model, vocabulary = LoadW2Vmodel('my_word2vec')
```

Then, we can use the vectors created by the model in the task we want. However, the Word2Vec model library[3] provides facilities for several basic tasks such as the following:

- Find the word that has the vector most similar for a given word (.most_similar(..)).

- Calculate the similarity between words in a list (.similarity(..)).

- Perform vector operations.

- etc.

An example of the above is in the main program:

```
print(model.wv.most_similar('celebrate'))
print(model.wv.similarity("celebrate","give"))

v1 = model.wv['great']
v2 = model.wv['coach']
v3 = model.wv['cheerleader']

model.wv.similar_by_vector(v1-v2+v3)
```

When running in parts, the following is displayed:

---

[3] https://code.google.com/archive/p/word2vec/.

```
In [126]: print(model.wv.most_similar('celebrate'))
    ...: print(model.wv.similarity("celebrate","give"))
[('place', 0.9826940298080444), ('good', 0.9807543158531189), ('additional',
0.977787435054779), ('opener', 0.9712570309638977), ('Travelers',
0.963854193687439), ('kidnap', 0.9514890313148499), ('Stenmark',
0.9495529532432556), ('matter', 0.9480329751968384), ('lose',
0.9475122690200806), ('mind', 0.9441789388656616)]
0.46081167
```

First, a list of words is shown whose vectors are similar to the word celebrate. Furthermore, the similarity (*cosine*) between the vectors for the words celebrate and give from the input texts is shown.

While running the third part, the words that are most similar to the resulting vector generated by the operation $v1-v2+v3$ are shown, where $v1$, $v2$ and $v3$ are the great, coach, and cheerleader, respectively:

```
In [128]: v1 = model.wv['great']
    ...: v2 = model.wv['coach']
    ...: v3 = model.wv['cheerleader']
    ...:
    ...: model.wv.similar_by_vector(v1-v2+v3)
Out[128]:
[('evident', 0.9842102527618408),
 ('available', 0.9707431793212891),
 ('Premier', 0.9678003787994385),
 ('worshipful', 0.9537631869316101),
 ('glitter', 0.9533646702766418),
 ('consecutive', 0.9490921497344971),
 ('issue', 0.9403780102729797),
 ('Organisers', 0.931625485420227),
 ('obviously', 0.9221462607383728),
 ('leave', 0.9190470576286316)]
```

The above becomes even more relevant when, from the semantic point of view, we can add the vector of a related or opposite feature of the word, which will assign another semantic space for the resulting word, since it changes its meaning.

Another interesting task that we can perform is to visualize the generated vector dispersion, as we did with the LSA through the VisualizeVectors(..) function which was already defined. However, only the first two dimensions will be used, and for visual comprehension purposes, the first 20 words.

```
VisualizeVectors(vocabulary,model.wv.vectors[:20,0:2])
```

When running, the following scatter plot is obtained:

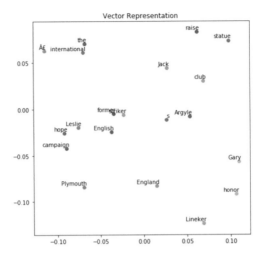

Note that several of the news talk about international soccer championships and/or players; so, at least in two dimensions, it makes perfect sense that terms such as England, Lineker, and Plymouth are close. On the other hand, improvements are observed that could be made in the preprocessing stage, as Gary and Lineker appear separated, even when they correspond to the same person, because the preprocessing task didn't include an NER task.

Finally, an interesting exercise that could be useful for other analysis tasks is to generate a similarities (or distances) matrix between all vectors, in order to allow the further analysis such as clustering and classification. The program does this by calculating the cosine similarity between all vectors (cosine_similarity(..)), generating a square similarity matrix and displaying it on a heat map, using the functions of the graphic library (plt):

```
sim = 1 - cosine_similarity(model.wv.vectors)
plt.matshow(sim[0:20,0:20])
plt.show()
```

To simplify the view when executing this code, only the graph with the first 20 words is shown.

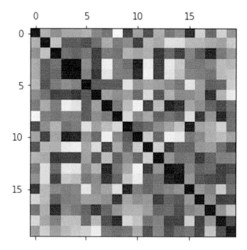

Where the matrix is symmetric and the darker colors represent areas of greater similarity, you can visually determine which documents are more distant or similar to each other (i.e., documents in positions 7 and 13) for other textual analysis and document retrieval tasks.

CHAPTER 7

Document Clustering

7.1 INTRODUCTION

There are many industrial and business applications that focus on discover hidden patterns of interest in the form of textual information clusters or segments, which can provide us with key knowledge for decision-making. Some of the current applications include:

- *Customer Segmentation*: Customer subdivision into groups or segments with similar market characteristics or related complaint behaviors.

- *Fraud detection*: Determine individual behavior patterns that allow groups of valid activity to be divided from those that deviate from the norm and are therefore abnormal, as in incident declarations.

- *Newsfeeds Generation*: Group news articles depending on their similarity so that they can be filtered, viewed, and browsed by different user profiles.

- *Customer Call Logs Analysis*: Understand customer segments and their needs in relation to the use of calls, SMS and Internet activity.

For example, suppose that you receive daily news headings that you want to group, such as the following:

1. *Amazon's virtual assistant could witness a homicide in Florida*

2. *Auto sales in Mexico hit low records due to pandemic*

3. *High-speed trains are close to doubling their speed*

4. *Coronavirus could last three more years in the United States*

You'll easily notice that there are two newsgroups that are related to each other: A g1 group made up of news (1) and (3) since they're talking about "technology", and another g2 group made up of news (2) and (4) since they're talking about "coronavirus", as shown in Figure 7.1.

This grouping is possible, thanks to your experience that makes you think that there are certain common patterns among them that couldn't only explain each news item but also connect them to make recommendations, segment them, etc. We could hypothesize the associations by looking for common words or phrases between them. However, soon after we start, some difficulties would begin to arise:

- As the size of the document collections increases, simply searching for such common patterns wouldn't be efficient.

- Documents contain many implicit relationships between words, so if you try to compare individual news, you probably won't be able to find many direct associations.

- As the dimensionality of the texts increases, it becomes more difficult to establish their corresponding groups (i.e., some documents could potentially belong to more than one group).

To address these problems, statistical distance metrics or semantic similarity analysis (Chapter 6) can provide a good start to then group nearby documents or words together. Intuitively, the grouping task looks simple because depending on the number of groups you want, the problem

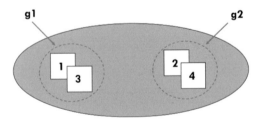

FIGURE 7.1   Simple news grouping.

Group 1	Group 2
d1	d2,d3,d4
d2	d1,d3,d4
d3	d1,d2,d4
d4	d1,d2,d3
d1,d2	d3,d4
d1,d3	d2,d4
d1,d4	d2,d3
d2,d3	d1,d4
d2,d4	d1,d3
d3,d4	d1,d2

FIGURE 7.2 Generating document groups.

becomes creating combinations of possible groups, subject to several restrictions: Texts remaining in each group should be very similar to each other and texts that belong to different groups shouldn't be similar between them.

Suppose we're looking to create two possible groups of related information from four documents (**d1, d2, d3,** and **d4**). The document similarity analysis should be performed among ten possible group combinations, such as those shown in Figure 7.2. For each group, we should evaluate, for example, those where the closest proximity between the documents is the least. It's easy to see that, as the number of documents grows, even with the same number of groups, the number of combinations will grow exponentially.

As a consequence of the above, evaluating and creating the best groups using *brute force*[1] algorithms will become clearly computationally impossible to handle. Because of this, efficient and robust methods are required to find the best groupings, which allow us to get relevant patterns. In other words, how do we efficiently choose related groups to help us understand more about documents?

7.2 DOCUMENT CLUSTERING

Clustering is the task of building groups or clusters of similar objects (i.e., documents) (Ignatow & Mihalcea, 2017; Srivastava & Sahami, 2009). In order to discover interest patterns from such data, we grouped data objects as the

---

[1] Combinatorial search that allows you to systematically list all the possible candidates for solving a problem.

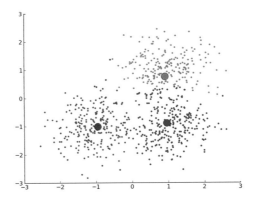

FIGURE 7.3   Example of three clusters represented by 2-dimensional vectors.

first step to understand a topic in a text analysis system that uses machine learning. For example, Figure 7.3 represents the results of clustering 16 sample documents into three clusters. To simplify its visualization, the results are only displayed using two components of the document vectors.

In general, a *clustering* method performs an unsupervised learning task, which groups data objects without prior information to characterize each cluster. In the case of textual information, there are many applications where document clustering is vital, including improved document rankings, clustering complains from users using a service, customer segmentation, topic identification, text summarization, and exploring or browsing similar documents.

In a typical document clustering system, as shown in Figure 7.4, an input corpus, a similarity, or distance measure are taken and an attempt is made to find the best document clusters, so that two conditions are met:

1. *Documents within a cluster should be very similar.*

2. *Documents from different clusters should be very distant.*

To accomplish this, it's necessary to address two aspects: *document representation* and *similarity measures*, and then to understand document clustering techniques.

a. *Document Representation* can usually use simple vector space models (Chapter 4) or *word embeddings* (Chapter 6). However, a cluster that was created might have more than a single document; therefore, the representation of a group of documents extends to its *center of mass* or *centroid*. The *centroid* r_c of a cluster c can be defined as the average of each one of the document vectors of the cluster d_c., that is:

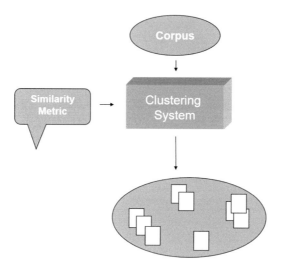

FIGURE 7.4   A document clustering system.

$$r_c = \frac{1}{|c|} \sum_{d_c \in c} d_c$$

where $|c|$ is the cluster size (i.e., number of documents). In general, the clusters generated should not overlap, as it would violate the second condition, which would be easily reflected by observing the distance between its centroids. For example, suppose we have the following four 3-dimensional document vectors, where each cell represents the normalized frequency of each of the three vocabulary words:

d_1	[0,33 0,17 0,50]
d_2	[0,25 0,50 0,25]
d_3	[0,17 0,33 0,50]
d_4	[0,00 0,56 0,44]

Also, consider that we have two candidate clusters: $G_1 = \{d_1, d_2\}$ and $G_2 = \{d_3, d_4\}$, then the centroids of both clusters are as follows:

$$r_1 = (d_1 + d_2)/2 = ([0,33\,0,17\,0,50] + [0,25\,0,50\,0,25])/2$$
$$= [0,29\,0,33\,0,38]$$

$$r_2 = (d_3 + d_4)/2 = ([0,17\,0,33\,0,50] + [0,00\,0,56\,0,44])/2$$
$$= [0,08\,0,44\,0,47]$$

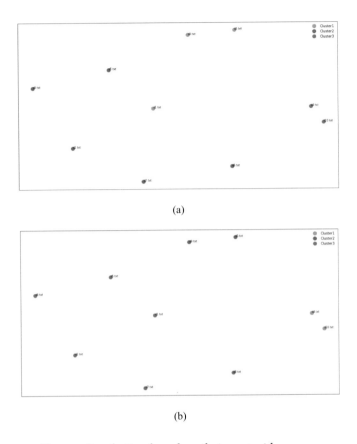

(a)

(b)

FIGURE 7.5   Clusters distribution based on their centroids.

On the other hand, Figure 7.5 shows an example of three clusters (i.e., green, blue, red) created by a method for ten documents, represented only in two dimensions (features), in order to facilitate their visualization.

Visually, it can be seen that the clusters generated for the configuration of (a) are worse than those created for the configuration (b), since not only documents are more distant but the cluster centroids are very close to the cluster centroids (green dots and red dots in clustering (b)). On the other hand, the quality of these clusters can be directly affected by the documents assigned to a cluster and these, in turn, by the measure of similarity used to assign a document to one cluster or another.

b. *Similarity Measures* reflect the conceptual closeness between different documents, so within a cluster, the value of this measure should be maximum for your documents, indicating a strong closeness between them and therefore a pattern of interest. In general, if you take a document and try to assign it to a cluster, it's necessary to measure the similarity between the vector of that document and that of each cluster, and then choose the one with the greatest similarity (or least distance). The similarity between a document vector d and a cluster c can be calculated as the average similarity between d and each of the documents in that cluster (d_c):

$$\text{sim}(d,c) = \frac{1}{|c|} \sum_{d_c \in c} \text{sim}(d,d_c)$$

Since documents and words can already be represented as vectors, it's possible to use similarity or distance measures between these vectors as a way of expressing the closeness of common themes between documents. This includes metrics such as the following:

a. *Euclidean Distance:* For two *n*-dimensional vectors of d_1 and d_2 documents, the Euclidean distance (norm L_2) is simply:

$$L_2(d_1,d_2) = \sqrt{\sum_{i=1}^{n}(d_{1i} - d_{2i})^2}$$

However, due to the *curse of dimensionality,* if *n* is very large, the distance between the two won't be very realistic to establish vector comparisons. A better alternative would be to calculate similarities based on the angle formed between both vectors: The smaller the angle between these vectors, the greater the similarity between them (i.e., both could be talking about the same topics).

b. *Cosine Similarity:* Measures the similarity between two non-null vectors as the cosine of their angle. The similarity value is 1 when the angle between the vectors is 0 and is lower than 1 for any other angle. Thus, the *cosine* similarity of two d_1 and d_2 documents with a length of *n* can be calculated as:

$$\frac{\sum_{j}^{n} d_{1j} \sum_{j}^{n} d_{2j}}{\sqrt{\sum_{j}^{n} d_{1j}^2} \sqrt{\sum_{i}^{n} d_{2j}^2}}$$

Note that the cosine distance can be simply determined as the complement of the previous measurement, that is, 1-cosine(d_1,d_2).

Suppose we have two document vectors (doc1 and doc2) and a vector that represents a user's *query*, all on a vocabulary formed by the terms [*term 1, term 2, and term 3*], therefore we have 3-dimensional vectors. The spatial distribution of the three vectors is shown in Figure 7.6. Surely, we would like to determine which documents could be more relevant to that *query*. For this, we would only need to determine the similarity between each document and the *query* vector. Then, we should sort the documents according to their similarity to the *query*. It can be noticed in the figure that the similarity between doc2 and the *query* is greater (i.e., greater cosine value or less angle) than the similarity between doc1 and the *query*; therefore, the order of the similarity of documents to be delivered is doc2 and doc1.

In the case of a clustering task, we don't have a reference point such as the *previous query*, so our clustering will depend on our chosen centroid, the metric used to measure the distance/proximity, and the number of dimensions of the documents. Because of this, clustering techniques must efficiently search for clusters in a very large scan space, depending on the above factors. In general, clustering techniques can be divided into two main types (Srivastava & Sahami, 2009; Aggarwal, 2013): (1) *hard clustering*, where each data point belongs to only one cluster, and (2) *soft clustering*, where each data point is assigned a certain probability of belonging

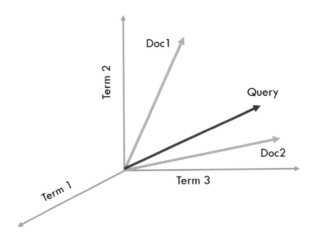

FIGURE 7.6 Spatial distribution of document vectors.

to each cluster (i.e., a data point can belong to more than one cluster). Imagine, for example, that you should assign a document that talks about topics like *The millionaire transfer of a soccer player from team X to team Y*. Clearly, this is associated with documents that contain terms related to *finance* as well as those that contain terms related to *sports*; therefore *soft clustering* should capture the fact that the document could belong to more than one cluster.

In general, there are many *clustering methods*, with different effectiveness depending on the nature of the data, the topology of the clusters, and the search strategies used. However, we'll focus on two clustering-oriented approaches for documents: (1) centroid-based algorithms (i.e., K-means) and (2) model-based algorithms (i.e., self-organizational maps).

7.3 K-MEANS CLUSTERING

The *K-means* clustering method seeks to efficiently search for non-overlapping clusters based on the distances to their centroids (or means) from the clusters. For a certain C clustering configuration on a set of x documents, this means:

- *Compact Clusters:* All documents ($x(i)$) inside each cluster (k) must be at a *minimum* distance from its centroid (r_k). This distance is usually called *within-cluster distance* or *wc* and is calculated as the sum of all the *wc* of each cluster:

$$wc(C) = \sum_{k=1}^{K} wc(C_k) = \sum_{k=1}^{K} \sum_{x(i) \in C_k} d\big(x(i), r_k\big)$$

where K represents the number of clusters previously identified, C_k identifies the k-th cluster, and $d(x(i), r_k)$ represents the distance between each document $x(i)$ in a cluster and its r_k centroid. The centroid of a cluster k is calculated as:

$$r_k = \frac{1}{n_k} \sum_{x(i) \in C_k} x(i)$$

where n_k corresponds to the number of documents in the cluster k.

- *Separate Clusters:* The distance between clusters must be maximum. This distance is usually called *between-cluster distance* or *bc* and is calculated as the sum of all distances between the centroid of the clusters.

$$bc(C) = \sum_{1 \le j \le k \le K} d(r_j, r_k)$$

The method iteratively assigns each data point *exclusively* to one of the K clusters based on a distance measure. The centroids of each cluster will be the coordinates that are further used to assign new data points to *nearby* clusters. Figure 7.7 shows the result dimensions of the clustering process in only two for $K=3$ for a certain data set, where the cross symbols represent the coordinates of the respective clusters. Note that the axis values are normalized to zero mean (Baron, 2019).

In each iteration, clusters adjust their centroid depending on the assigned documents: Adding data points to a cluster will possibly cause its centroid to be modified and therefore would make other documents closer or more distant. Consequently, the algorithm ends when a certain number of iterations has been reached or when the centroids (means) of the clusters stabilize, using a *Hill Climbing* search strategy (Russell & Norvig, 2016).

Based on a previously specified number of K clusters and a corpus of n documents, the *K-means* method groups as follows:

1. Select K random document vectors as initial centroids (seeds).

2. Repeat.

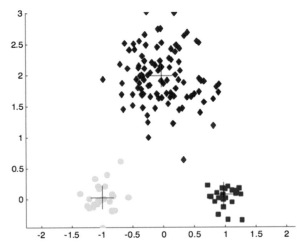

FIGURE 7.7   Generating three clusters from a corpus of documents.

1. Assign each document to the closest cluster according to the centroid.

2. Recalculate the centroid of each cluster.

3. Until there are no changes in the centroids or until reaching a certain number of iterations.

While the algorithm is quite simple, you'll notice at a glance that it doesn't generate uniform results, as the method depends on several factors:

- *Selection of Initial Centroids*: The selection of seeds representing the initial centroids of each cluster can affect the quality of the final clustering. For example, Figure 7.8 shows two results of the clustering task depending on the initial seeds chosen. One way to determine the best set is to simply generate multiple random seeds and then stick to the result with the lowest error value (*wc*).

- *Choosing the Right Number of Clusters*: Documents are highly dimensional data, which makes it difficult to view them and can greatly affect the quality of the final cluster configuration. In order to determine the optimal number of clusters, the relationship between various numbers of clusters and the *Sum of Squared Errors* (SSE) can be graphed for each configuration under evaluation. Note that SSE is similar to the *wc* metric for positive values of the sum of intra-cluster distances and for a C clustering configuration being calculated as

$$\text{SSE}(C) = \sum_{k=1}^{K} \sum_{x(i) \in C_k} d^2\left(x(i), r_k\right)$$

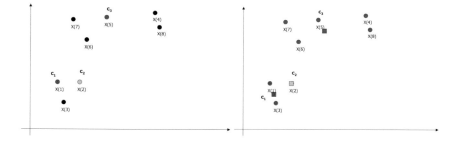

FIGURE 7.8   Different clusters based on their initial centroids.

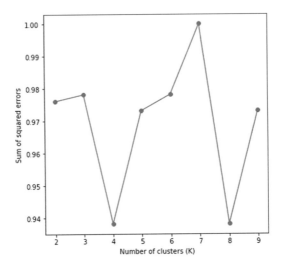

FIGURE 7.9   Selecting the best number of clusters.

You can then select the number of clusters where the change in SSE
begins to level off. In the example in Figure 7.9, it can be seen that the
best SSE is for $K = 4$, so this value is chosen as the optimal number of
clusters (i.e., there is also a low SSE for $K = 8$; however, the clustering
algorithm can take longer).

In the case of document clustering, there are two variants that can be
incorporated into K-means so that the final clusters are more informative:

- Consider vectors that represent each document as word embeddings vectors, either using LSA or Word2Vec models. (Chapter 6).
  This allows the measures of distance between documents to be based
  on the learned linguistic context and not only on the frequency of
  appearance of the words.

- Preprocess documents basically performing *stemming* and removing *stopwords*. This significantly reduces the dimensions of the
  vectors.

One of the biggest advantages of K-means clustering is that it's a relatively
efficient method and generates spherical clusters that are easy to interpret.
However, this method can fall into local optima and is only applicable
when defining the way to calculate the mean. On the other hand, the focus

is very sensitive to outliers and noise. As a whole, its algorithmic complexity depends on the number of clusters (K), the size of the corpus (*n*), and the number of iterations, which doesn't really make it competitive because small variations in these parameters can produce high computational complexity.

7.4 SELF-ORGANIZING MAPS

A *SOM* is a type of *Artificial Neural Network* (ANN) that uses unsupervised learning to produce document clusters represented in a discrete space of low-dimensional features called a *map* (Schmidt, 2019). Unlike other ANN models that generally use gradient descent error-based learning, SOMs apply competitive learning, so they use a *neighborhood* function to preserve the topological properties of the input space you want to learn to map in clusters.

The SOM method automatically discovers how to associate each input data to a cluster, where the clusters are represented as points on a mesh or geometric map. Since the method learns through processing layers (input layer and output layer), the underlying network adjusts the "weights" of the connections, which represent the strength with which each data object is associated with one or the other cluster. For this, the method tries to learn the best cluster *topology* or *mesh* from the input data, that is, geometric relationships between these clusters and the assignment of the input data to points in the mesh. Each point on the mesh or map is associated with a cluster. SOM-based clustering is considered an extension to K-means but with the following differences:

1. In K-means, the desired number of clusters (K) must be specified, while in SOM the method learns the best transformation of input data in a certain cluster topology. The number of neurons in the output layer has a very close relationship with the final number of clusters.

2. In K-means, clusters are independent of each other while in SOM clusters are connected to each other geometrically, so local optima are avoided.

3. K-means is very sensitive to noise present in the dataset and in the allocation of the clusters, while SOM can learn to treat noise as elements outside the clusters.

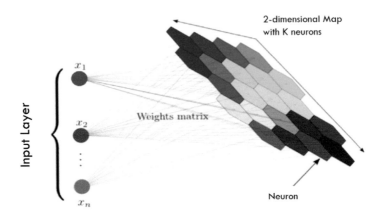

FIGURE 7.10   SOM general architecture.

SOM's basic architecture is based on a simple two-layer ANN, or process-ing layers, as shown in Figure 7.10:

1. *Input Layer*: represents the input data (i.e., document vectors).

2. *Output or Competitive Layer*: represents the interconnection topol-ogy between the different clusters and inputs (i.e., generally a 2-dimensional mesh).

The input layer is interconnected with the output layer (aka. *Kohonen layer*) through weight vectors. The vector's objective is to learn the best transformation of each input unit to its corresponding cluster, so that each input "competes" for its cluster representation.

To learn this transformation, we begin by initializing the weight vectors with random values. Then, we try to iteratively find the weights that best represent and connect the input data with the clusters in the mesh. For this, each weight vector takes into account its neighborhood, being able to learn who's closest to the clusters.

The selected weight is *rewarded* for being better than the one randomly selected while the neighbors of that weight are *rewarded* for being able to become the chosen vector. This allows the topological map (mesh) that's gen-erated to grow and have different shapes. In most of the cases, they're linear, rectangular, or octahedron in a 2-dimensional feature space (Figure 7.11).

7.4.1 Topological Maps Learning
The first step in the process of learning a SOM is to initialize all the con-nection weights that the input associates (i.e., vector representing each

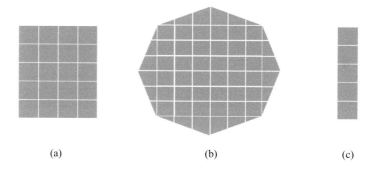

(a)   (b)   (c)

FIGURE 7.11   Some shapes of SOM topologies: (a) rectangle (2D), (b) octahedron (2D), and (c) linear (1D).

document) with a cluster. A random sample of training documents is used as a network input. With these, the distance of each cell of an input (*input*) vector of length n is calculated, with the weight that connects it to each of the n neurons (*weight*) of the output layer:

$$\text{Distance}^2 = \sum_{i=0}^{n} \left(\text{input}_i - \text{weight}_i\right)^2$$

Then the neuron is selected from the *map* with the shortest distance, called a BMU (*Best Matching Unit*). This means that the input vector can be represented with this transformation neuron on the cluster map. As a SOM is trained, the idea is that this distance is the closest it can to the received input data, that is, the connection weights are updated in a way that the distance is shorter every time. Simultaneously, BMU neighbors' weights are also modified so they're close to the input vector in a certain initial *radius*, which decreases while training a SOM. The next step while training a SOM is to calculate the radius value:

$$\sigma(t) = \sigma_0 e^{-\frac{t}{\lambda}}$$

where t is the current iteration, σ_0 is the initial radius of the map and λ is defined as $\lambda = k/\sigma_0$, and k is the number of iterations. The formula uses an exponential decay, causing the *radius* to decrease, thus indicating the stability of the elements of a cluster. In simple terms, this means that in each training iteration, the relevant points of the mesh will be brought close to the input data.

When the radius is calculated in the current iteration, the weights for all neurons within that radius are updated. The closer the neuron is to the BMU, the greater the change in its weights. This change is made by means of the following weight update rule at each time t:

$$\text{weight}(t+1) = \text{weight}(t) + O(t)L(t)\big(\text{input}(t) - \text{weight}(t)\big)$$

Here $L(t)$ represents the learning rate and $L(t) = L_0 e^{-\frac{t}{\lambda}}$ uses exponential decay to reduce the learning rate in each iteration. As there will be neurons that have a higher weight since they are closer to a BMU, $O(t)$ is calculated as:

$$O(t) = e^{-\text{BMU}\big/2\sigma(t)^2}$$

Thus, learning a SOM proceeds as follows:

1. Initialize weights

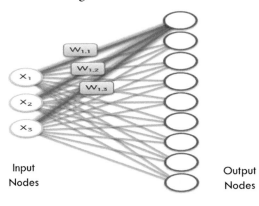

2. For every input vector:

   1. Select an input vector (words from each document) from the corpus and use it as a network input.

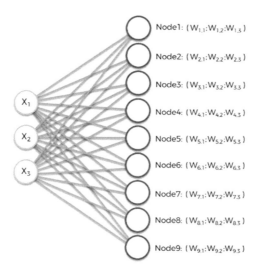

   2. Calculate the BMU

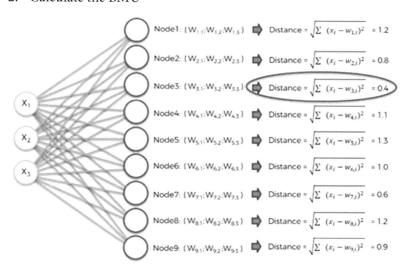

3. Calculate the radius of the neighbors that will be updated

4. Adjust the weight of the neurons within the radius to bring them closer to the vicinity of the input vector. Then update the radius so that the neighborhood gets smaller and smaller.

Intuitively, the geometric interpretation of how SOM clusters documents is simple and can be seen in Figure 7.12. Suppose you want to generate a mesh (blue grid) of $r \times s$, where each of its points is associated with a weight or mean of a cluster $\mu_{1,1}, \ldots \mu_{r,s}$ (i.e., centroid in K-means).

In each iteration, the method *moves* the mean of the cluster, maintaining the topology specified by the mesh. Then a data vector should be

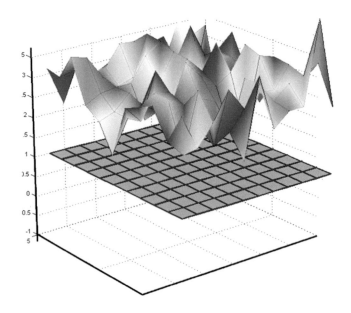

FIGURE 7.12 Geometric representation of clusters in Self-Organizational Map (SOM).

assigned to the cluster with the closest mean. As a consequence, nearby data objects will tend to map to nearby clusters.

In general, it should be noted that a SOM doesn't build a generative data model; that is, the method doesn't understand how the data was created. However, its adaptive nature allows it to adjust input data assignments to clusters efficiently, considering its neighbors. Remember that this feature is nonexistent in K-means, since searches there are local, and when the data is assigned to the clusters it cannot be undone.

7.5 SUMMARY

Similarity-based clustering documents to find patterns that characterize the data is one of the most important tasks in textual analytics applications. In the case of documents, clustering requires efficient approaches to represent and measure distances/closeness's between documents. From this, different cluster generation strategies can be used. One of the most popular strategies is the K-means clustering method, which fundamentally creates clusters based on the distance of the input data to the centers of the clusters, which is why groups are characterized by having concentric topologies. On the other hand, extensions of the technique, such as the SOM, allow not only to create clusters with different types of topology but to learn the best input data assignments to such clusters, considering the relationship with neighboring data points, which makes it attractive as a global optimum technique.

7.6 EXERCISES

This section shows some examples of document clustering using *K-means* and *SOM* methods from a corpus of documents. For this, you can download the "kmeans.py" and "som.py" from the book site.

7.6.1 K-means Clustering

For the K-means clustering task ("kmeans.py"), we need to import some already defined libraries and functions, found in "utils.py".

```
from past.builtins import execfile
execfile('./utils.py')
```

Now we import some new libraries to calculate the cosine similarity between multiple vectors, facilities for K-means, calculation of clustering metrics (Silhouette), and multidimensional scaling methods:

```
from sklearn.metrics.pairwise import cosine_similarity
from sklearn.cluster import KMeans
from sklearn.metrics import silhouette_score
from sklearn.manifold import MDS
```

We define a first function to initialize (Kmeans(..)) and perform K-means clustering (clustering(..)) from a data matrix (DataMatrix) and a specified number of clusters (K):

```
def clustering(DataMatrix,K):
    model = KMeans(n_clusters=K)
    model.fit(DataMatrix)
    return(model)
```

In order to visualize the results of the clustering task, we define a function (VisualizeClusters(..)) from the previously generated clusters (clusters), document names (titles), and the matrix representing those documents (DataMatrix). For this, the function performs the following steps:

1. Transform (Scale) the data vectors to a two-dimensional scale, giving new coordinates (x, y) for each instance of the data.

2. Define the colors of each cluster (maximum of five colors), and the cluster names or identifiers.

3. Create a *dataframe* with the following attributes of each document: coordinate (x,y), cluster names (labels), and the names of each of the documents (title).

4. Group each of the previous records by cluster name (label).

5. For each of the groups of previous records, place the legends in a position (x, y) with their name (label) and corresponding color (color).

6. For each of the dataframe records, graph the document name (title) in the coordinate (x, y).

```
def VisualizeClusters(clusters,titles,DataMatrix):
    (x_new,y_new) = Scale(DataMatrix)
    color_cluster = {0: '#1b9e77', 1: '#d95f02',
                     2: '#7570b3', 3: '#e7298a', 4: '#66a61e'}
    name_cluster = {0: 'Cluster1',
                    1: 'Cluster2',
                    2: 'Cluster3',
                    3: 'Cluster4',
                    4: 'Cluster5'}
    df = pd.DataFrame(dict(x=x_new,y=y_new,label=clusters,title=titles))
    groups = df.groupby('Label')
    fig, ax = plt.subplots(figsize=(17, 9))
    for name, group in groups:
        ax.plot(group.x, group.y, marker='o', linestyle='',
                label=name_cluster[name], color=color_cluster[name])
    ax.legend()
    for i in range(len(df)):
        ax.text(df.loc[i]['x'], df.loc[i]['y'], df.loc[i]['title'], size=8)
    plt.show()
```

The function that performs the scaling (Scale(..)) takes the data matrix to perform the following steps:

1. Calculate the distance matrix between all the vectors in the data matrix.

2. Initialize the multidimensional scaling method[2] (MDS) with only two components (n_components=2).

3. Transform the distance matrix from (1) with MDS into a new (scaled) position matrix.

4. Obtain the new coordinates (x,y) from the first two components of the previous matrix.

```
def Scale(data_matrix):
    dist = 1 - cosine_similarity(data_matrix)
    mds = MDS(n_components=2, dissimilarity="precomputed")
    pos = mds.fit_transform(dist)
    x, y = pos[:, 0], pos[:, 1]
    return(x,y)
```

Finally, we define a function (ShowMetricEvolution(..)) that allows us to visually inspect the best number of clusters from the data vectors (Data). The maximum number of clusters to evaluate corresponds to the maximum number of documents or MaxDoc). The function allows an evaluation considering two possible metrics:

1. SSE (sum of the squared errors with respect to the centroid of each cluster): The lower the value, the better the quality of the clustering performed.

---

[2] http://www.analytictech.com/networks/mds.htm.

2. *Silhouette*[3] Coefficient (how similar is a data to its own centroid compared to other centroids): The higher the value, the better the quality of the clustering performed (range [−1,1]).

The basic idea is that the function iterates for all K values between 2 and MaxDoc, performing the clustering task with the initial data and the K value, and stores the calculated metric values in a list: clusters.inertia_ or SSE or, silhouette_score(Data, Clusters.labels_) for the Silhouette metric, where Clusters.labels_ corresponds to a list containing the cluster identifiers for each piece of data. The function then generates the graph with each of the K values and its corresponding metric value (list of values):

```
def ShowMetricEvolution(Data,MaxDoc,metric="sse"):
    MetricDescription = {"sse":"Sum of squared errors",
                         "sil":"Silhouette Coefficient"}
    score = []
    list_k = list(range(2, MaxDoc))
    for k in list_k:
        Clusters = clustering(Data,K)
        if metric =="sse":
            value = Clusters.inertia_
        else:
            value = silhouette_score(Data, Clusters.labels_)
        score.append(value)
    score = NormalizeMetric(score)
    plt.figure(figsize=(6, 6))
    plt.plot(list_k, score, '-o')
    plt.xticks(list_k)
    plt.xlabel(r'Number of clusters (K)')
    plt.ylabel(MetricDescription[metric])
```

In case you want to compare a metric for different models that have different scales in the data vectors, ShowMetricEvolution(..) invokes a function that simply normalizes the values dividing them by the maximum score in the list, so that all are in the range from 0 to 1:

```
def NormalizeMetric(scores):
    max_value = np.max(scores)
    new_values = [x/max_value for x in scores]
    return(new_values)
```

If you want to work with the original values, without normalization, simply eliminate the call to that function.

The main program loads the language model and then uses functions already defined in other chapters and available in "utils.py" to create the

---

[3] https://scikit-learn.org/stable/auto_examples/cluster/plot_kmeans_silhouette_analysis.html.

corpus from the documents in the path specified by PATH, preprocesses the corpus, and creates the a TFxIDF model:

```
nlp = en_core_web_sm.load()

(corpus,docID) = CreateCorpus(PATH)
texts   = PreProcessing(corpus)

CreateVSM(texts,"my_tfidf")
```

Next, we can download our model and perform K-means clustering from the document vectors, assuming for now that we want only four clusters ($k=4$). We then display the list of clusters identifiers for each document vector:

```
(vectors, _idf, vocabulary) = LoadModel("my_tfidf")

K = 4
model = clustering(vectors,K)
print(model.labels_)
```

By executing this part of the code, we can see that the following list is displayed for the documents in the corpus:

```
In [168]: print(model.labels_)
[1 3 0 0 1 2 2 3 2 3]
```

Each data point was assigned to clusters ranging from 0 to 3, so the first element belongs to cluster 0, the tenth element belongs to cluster 3, etc. If we want to display the distribution of the clusters and documents in two dimensions, we simply execute our display function from the list of clusters generated (model.labels_), the list of document identifiers (docID), and the their vectors:

```
VisualizeClusters(model.labels_,docID,vectors)
```

This is displayed in the following graph, where you can not only see which documents are in which clusters but also how distant they are from each other:

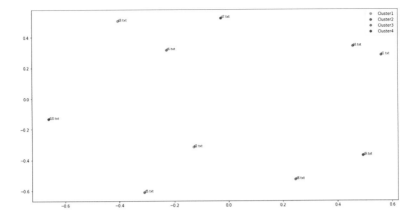

However, this K-means execution used a defined number of clusters (K=4), and we're not really sure if it's the most appropriate to use. To find the best K value, we could use our previously defined function to visualize the possible K values and their SSE ("sse") and Silhouette ("sil") metric values in two separate graphs:

```
MaxDoc = 10

ShowMetricEvolution(vectors,MaxDoc,"sse")
ShowMetricEvolution(vectors,MaxDoc,"sil")
```

When running them, you can see the following visualizations:

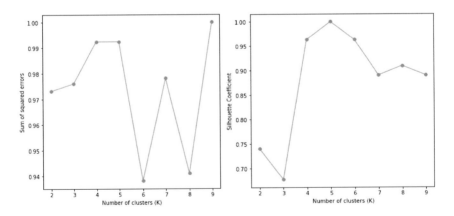

From the SSE point of view, the smallest value is approximately reached with K=6, therefore our initial assumption was not that good. On the other hand, observing the Silhouette coefficient, we can notice that the highest value is reached approximately for k=5, so the decision will depend on what we want to measure, whether it is only the intra-cluster error (SSE) or the proportion between data of a centroid compared to the others.

On the other hand, observing the SSE error, we can see that in general they are high values along the different values of k. One of several possible causes of this may be related to the vectors we're using that are represented as TFxIDF models. To address this, we could try to perform the same clustering task above but using vectors generated from an LSA model. For this, we can reuse the LSA vectors generated for the same corpus in the LSA exercises, using our the LoadModelLSA(..) function defined in "utils.py" with the name of the preexisting model called "my_lsa" (with 4-dimensional vectors). It's necessary that the "my_lsa" directory is accessible from our working directory, otherwise it won't be possible to add the full path where that directory is located. Next, we take just one of the arrays returned by the function, the document vectors (vectors), and then we invoke the same clustering and visualization functions above:

```
dirLSA = "E:/JOHN/BOOK/ENGLISH/TextAnalytics-Examples/Ch6-SemanticAnalysis/"
(_Sigma, _term, vectors, _vocab) = LoadLSAmodel(dirLSA + "my_lsa")

model = clustering(vectors,K)
print(model.labels_)

VisualizeClusters(model.labels_,docID,vectors)

ShowMetricEvolution(vectors,MaxDoc,"sse")
ShowMetricEvolution(vectors,MaxDoc,"sil")
```

When executing this part, the following cluster identifiers are displayed, where it can already be seen that the assignments are quite different from the previous case of K-means:

```
In [172]: print(model.labels_)
[1 3 0 0 1 2 2 3 2 3]
```

The display of the new clusters is shown as follows:

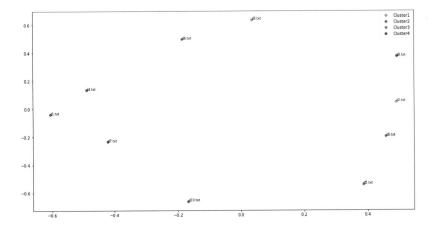

It's possible to notice some differences between the distances of these clusters compared to those previously generated. However, we cannot conclude much about it, so we need to analyze both the new SSE and Silhouette in the generated graphics:

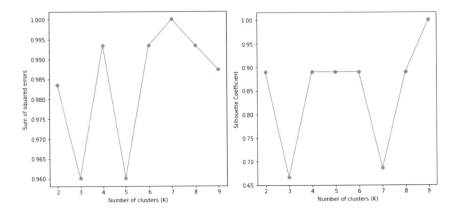

The results show that in average, the LSA vector representation is effectively capturing closer documents (by synonym) in the corresponding clusters. The SSE metric shows smaller values than in the previous case, reaching the smallest value for K=3. On the other hand, the values of the Silhouette metric are also higher than for the previous case, reaching approximately its maximum value for K=9.

7.6.2 Self-organizing Maps

For the other SOM-based clustering technique, we use the example program "som.py". Also, we need to install the SimpSOM library to train SOM:

pip install simpsom

Then we import some libraries and functions already defined, which are found in "utils.py":

```
from past.builtins import execfile
execfile('utils.py')
```

And we add the one that corresponds to the SimpSOM[4] package:

```
import SimpSOM as sps
```

For this example, we need to define only one function that performs the SOM training (TrainSOM(..)) from the input data (data) and some default values, such as the number of epocs and the rate initial learning (learningRate):

```
def TrainSOM(data,epocs=500,learningRate=0.01):
    my_map = sps.somNet(10, 10, data)
    my_map.train(learningRate, epocs)
    my_map.save("my_som")
    return(my_map)
```

Using the sps module, the network is initialized with a 2-dimensional 10×10 map over the input data to train the neural network (my_map.train(..)), record the weights learned in the file "my_som", and return the learned map. The main program loads the language model and reuses the functions already defined in "utils.py" to create and preprocess the corpus and to create the TFxIDF model:

```
nlp = en_core_web_sm.load()

(corpus,docID) = CreateCorpus(PATH)
texts    = PreProcessing(corpus)
CreateVSM(texts,"my_tf")

(tfidf, _idf, vocabulary) = LoadModel("my_tf")
```

The generated document vector model has several dimensions, so we'll use only the first six to speed up the training task (TrainSOM(..)) of the neural network:

```
data = tfidf[:,0:6]
som = TrainSOM(data)
```

---

[4] https://simpsom.readthedocs.io/en/latest/.

Once we carry out the training and generate the map, we can perform two tasks:

- Project the document vectors and their names (docID) in that 2-dimensional map.

- Generate the corresponding clusters.

```
projected = som.project(data,labels=docID,show=True, colnum=0)
clusters  = som.cluster(data,show=True)
print(clusters)
```

A color map (from 1 to 3) is assigned according to the value of the cell of the network weight vector, given its position, in this case colnum=0:

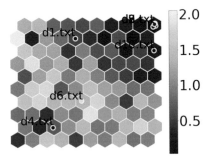

When creating the clusters, the following list is displayed on screen:

```
Terminal 1/A
In [181]: print(clusters)
[[1, 2, 3, 5, 7, 8, 9], [0, 4, 6]]
```

There each sub-list represents one of the two clusters generated, such as cluster [0,4,6] that contains the document vectors of positions 0, 4, and 6, respectively, and so on with the other clusters.

Finally, note that there are important differences between the clusters generated by K-means and those generated by SOM. Since SOM's global search for clusters is much more effective than K-means, it requires considerable training time to generate the maps. Because of this, it's convenient that for the clustering of many documents, you not only consider metrics such as errors but also the creation time of the clusters.

CHAPTER 8

Topic Modeling

8.1 INTRODUCTION

Document clustering methods (Chapter 7) allow you to partition data (i.e., documents) into *coherent* groups that ideally can exhibit interesting patterns. The meaning of coherence and the way partitioning is performed varies between different clustering methods. Despite their benefits, they are unable to discover any hidden structure in these groups.

For example, consider the following news headlines in international media and that no additional source of knowledge is available:

1. *Amazon's virtual assistant could witness a homicide in Florida*

2. *Auto sales in Mexico hit low records due to pandemic*

3. *High-speed trains are close to doubling their speed*

4. *Flower market in Mexico closed due to covid-19*

5. *Coronavirus could last 3 more years in the United States*

With some ease, you might notice that there are two related newsgroups: A g1 group made up of news (1) and (3) about technology, and another g2 group made up of news (2), (4), and (5) about covid-19. Surely, a *clustering* method should also come to the same conclusion. Let's assume that there's a "hidden" structure that connects the words of group g1 and another that connects those of group g2 (i.e., Which terms are more important to characterize each group?). If you were to "discover" these structures, not only could you incorporate new documents into a group since you

DOI: 10.1201/9781003280996-8

would know the model that governs the group but also these structures would give information about what topics each group "speaks" about. As the number of news items in the analysis begins to grow, determining that structure becomes much more complex. On the other hand, you surely noticed that group g1 talks about *technology*-related issues while group g2 talks about coronavirus-related issues. However, to make such an inference, you had to use your experience of similar situations seen in the past. Unfortunately, a traditional clustering method has no way of determining such a structure or knowing what it refers to, unless we provide it with additional knowledge sources.

To discover such a *hidden* structure, we should undertake a *generative* process to describe the way in which documents are generated from words that occur in similar contexts. Given this assumption, we could then infer the hidden structure of the model, usually in the form of *themes* or *topics* associated with the documents. One of the most common types of generative models for carrying out this task are called *topic models*, and they can help us organize and provide ideas that allow us to understand relationships in a corpus of documents.

Topic modeling is an unsupervised machine learning technique that allows you to discover hidden semantic structures in a body of documents. These structures usually take the form of patterns in the occurrence of similar words and phrases within these documents and they are automatically grouped to characterize topics or topics of interest.

Intuitively, since a document deals with a particular *topic*, one would expect particular words to appear in the document more frequently. For example, the words match and *court* will appear more frequently in documents that talk about *soccer*, the words *table* and *ball* will appear in documents about *table tennis*, and *player* will appear equally in both. Usually, a document contains multiple topics in different proportions; thus, in a document that is 10% about *table tennis* and 90% about *soccer*, there would probably be nine times as many *soccer* words as *table tennis* words.

Thus, a topic model formally captures the intuition that allows examining a corpus of documents and *discovering* what topics could be and what the balance of topics for each document is, based on some statistical distribution of words.

8.2 TOPIC MODELING

In its simplest form, topic modeling is a text analytics technique that enables topics to be discovered in a collection of documents. A topic contains a frequently co-occurring group of words, and topic models can connect words that have similar meanings and can distinguish different uses with multiple meanings. As documents are made up of words, a topic can be covered in more than one document and can therefore be expressed as a combination of strongly connected words. Furthermore, any document could be associated with more than one topic (Atkinson et al., 2016; Aggarwal, 2018).

Thus, topic modeling refers to the process of dividing a collection of documents (i.e., corpus) based on two assumptions, as shown in Figure 8.1:

1. *Each document is seen as a mixture of topics.* There is a distribution of topics that can be obtained by "combining" all the distributions of the topics covered. Imagine that each document can contain words from multiple topics in different proportions. For example, in a model of two topics A and B, it could be said that document 1 is 90% about topic A and 10% about topic B while document 2 is 30% about topic A and 70% about topic B.

2. *Each topic is seen as a mixture of words.* Imagine a model of two topics A and B can be discovered from news articles but their meaning is unknown. The most frequent words associated with topic A could be president, congress, and government, while for topic B, these could be movies, television, and actor. No one has informed you what topic A or topic B refers to nor is there any historical information to infer; but you may have already realized that topic A probably refers to *policy* issues while topic B speaks of *entertainment* themes. Also note that there are words that can be shared between topics. For example, the word budget could appear in both topics.

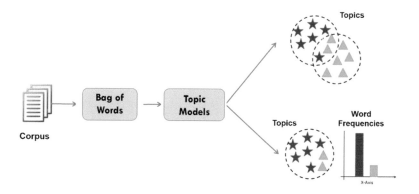

FIGURE 8.1 Topic distribution, words and documents.

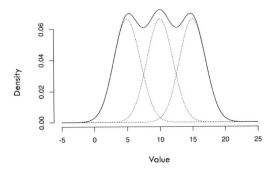

FIGURE 8.2   A mixture of three distributions.

In simple terms, a mixture or *mixture* distribution is a combination of two or more probability distributions. Random variables are sampled from more than one original population to create a new distribution. Distributions can be constructed from different types of distributions (i.e., normal, multinomial, etc.) or the same type of distribution with different parameters. For example, Figure 8.2 shows a mixture of three normal distributions (aka. Gaussian mixture model), each with a different mean.

A topic modeling technique should understand what topics are present in the documents, and how strong such a presence is based on a mixture distribution. There are several methods of modeling topics, the most popular being a variant of the LSA called *Probabilistic LSA* (pLSA) and *Latent Dirichlet Allocation* (LDA) (Aggarwal, 2013; Atkinson et al., 2016; Beaujean, 2014; Aggarwal, 2018).

LSA is an unsupervised learning method that allows to generate semantic spaces for words or documents from a corpus in low dimensions (Chapter 6). Based on the generated vector representation, one could consider that the vectors of the words can be expressed in terms of *topics*, which corresponds to the reduced dimensions of the original data. In general, LSA is fast and efficient to use, but it has three difficulties as a topic model:

1. Vectors are not interpretable, so it wouldn't be possible to determine what the topics are about.

2. A very large corpus and vocabulary is required to obtain accurate results, which impacts computational efficiency and vocabulary management.

3. The generated representation isn't as efficient, so a lot of noise can be produced in the representation of the meaning of words when the number of dimensions grows.

To address these problems, pLSA uses a probabilistic method instead of SVD (Klein, 2015). The main idea is to find a probabilistic model of *topics* or latent structures that can *generate* the data that we observe in the initial document-by-word matrix ($D \times W$). In particular, we're looking to model $P(D, W)$, so that, for any d document and w word, $P(d, w)$ corresponds to that entry in the matrix. Although pLSA approaches the problem in a different way from LSA (Landauer et al., 2014), it only adds a probabilistic treatment of topics and words on the original model; so it has two disadvantages in relation to other techniques:

- There are no parameters to model **P(D)**, so the methods for assigning probabilities to new documents are unknown.

- The number of parameters linearly grows with the number of documents, so the probabilistic method is subject to *overfitting*.

Due to this, pLSA isn't so used by itself, so when looking for a topic model, it quickly turns to methods such as the LDA, as it somehow extends pLSA to address the above aspects.

8.3 LATENT DIRICHLET ALLOCATION

The topic modeling technique called *LDA* is a generative model that allows you to transform each document in a corpus into a set of topics that cover an important part of the document's words. This is possible thanks to the assumption that the documents are written with a certain distribution of words and that this distribution determines the topics, ignoring the order of the words (i.e., without considering the syntax).

LDA is based on two fundamental assumptions:

1. *The distributional hypothesis*: Establishes that similar topics use similar words.

2. *The mixing hypothesis*: Establishes that documents talk about various topics, so a statistical distribution of *mixing* of topics can be determined.

In general, LDA assigns a topic model that contains two outputs: (1) a list of topics containing frequently co-occurring word groups and (2) a list of documents that are strongly associated with each topic. Ideally, each topic should be distinguishable from other topics. For this, the method assumes that all the words of a document can receive a *probability* of belonging to a *topic* and that *topics* or latent variables are independent. For this, we use *Dirichlet* distributions (Beaujean, 2014) that allow us to model the document-*topic* and word-*topic* distributions. We can see a *Dirichlet* as a distribution over distributions, which answers the question: "Given this *type* of word distribution, what are some of the current probability distributions that I'll see?" Technically, *Dirichlet* is a multivariate generalization of the Beta distribution (Baron, 2019).

To intuitively understand how topic assignment works, suppose we must compare probability distributions of topic mixes over a corpus that contains documents that speak of three very different topics (A, B, and C) that we don't know. The distribution that models this will be one that strongly weights a specific topic and that doesn't give much weight to the rest. Thus, if we have three topics, probability distributions that we would like to see could be expressed as *mixtures* of topics:

- Mixture X: 90% topic A, 5% topic B, 5% topic C

- Mixture Y: 5% topic A, 90% topic B, 5% topic C

- Mixture Z: 5% topic A, 5% topic B, 90% topic C

If we choose a random probability distribution from this *Dirichlet* distribution, parameterized by large weights in each topic, we'll probably obtain a distribution that strongly resembles either mixture X, mixture Y, or mixture Z.

As a consequence, it would be highly unlikely to generate samples from a distribution that is 33% of topic A, 33% of topic B, and 33% of topic C. This is what a *Dirichlet* distribution basically provides: A way to sample probability distributions of a specific type. Formally, a *Dirichlet* distribution samples on a probability simplex; that is, on a set of numbers that add up to 1, for example, **(0.6,0.4)**, **(0.1,0.1,0.8)**, which represent probabilities on **K** different categories or topics. In the case of the example, **K=3**, a model can be generated that represents a k-dimensional vector of α values.

When categorical distributions are handled and we're uncertain about the distribution, the simplest way to represent that uncertainty as a probability distribution is a *Dirichlet*. A *K*-dimensional Dirichlet has *K* positive number parameters (i.e., Can be normalized to represent probabilities) that become the mean value of the *Dirichlet*. Thus, all samples will be centered around that *simplex*. The farther you are from a point in the simplex, it usually represents one of the corners of the K dimensions, such as (**0,0,1,0**). A simple way to understand this is geometrically, as shown in Figure 8.3. Here is a corpus of eight documents represented by the blue data points, and we assume that the vocabulary consists of three words (i.e., each document is a 3-dimensional vector) whose axes represent the multinomial probability distributions (**θ**) of each of the words. Furthermore, we've chosen to represent **K = 2** topics.

Remember that a multinomial distribution is a type of probabilistic distribution that's used to calculate the results of experiments involving two or more random variables (i.e., occurrence of words in a document). Each experiment is the result of a finite number K of the probabilities $p_1, \ldots p_k$ of the independent variables $x_1, \ldots x_k$ (aka vector), where $\sum_{i=1}^{k} p_i = 1$. Then the probability of the multinomial distribution in n experiments (tests) is given by:

$$P\left(X_1 = x_1 \; y \ldots \; X_k x_k\right) = \begin{cases} \dfrac{n!}{x_1! \ldots x_k!} p_1^{x1} \ldots p_k^{xk}, \text{ when } \sum_{i=1}^{K} x_i = n \\[2mm] 0, \text{ otherwise} \end{cases}$$

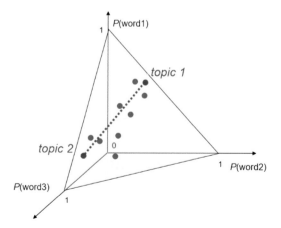

FIGURE 8.3 Geometric interpretation of topics.

Each document may contain one or more vocabulary words but with a different output occurrence probability, where the *multinomial* distribution θ requires that the values sums to 1; that is, $P(\text{word1}) + P(\text{word2}) + P(\text{word}) = 1$. In addition, each document can cover $K=2$ possible topics, so the resulting model is a *mixture of 2 topics*. In turn, there's a certain probability distribution of each word associated with each of these topics. As a result, topics can be viewed as probability distributions over the vocabulary of a corpus. If we observe the triangle formed by the three axes, then we would like to know the *probability density* at each of its points.

Formally, a *Dirichlet* distribution defines a *probability density* for an entry of k categorical (topical) values in a vector α that has the same number of characteristics as the multinomial parameter θ. A *Dirichlet* of parameter α or Dir(α) for a certain number of topics k is defined as:

$$\text{Dir}(\alpha) \rightarrow p(\theta|\alpha) = \frac{\Gamma\left(\sum_{i=1}^{k} \alpha_i\right)}{\prod_{i=1}^{k} \tau(\alpha_i)} \prod_{i=1}^{k} \theta^{\alpha_i - 1}$$

where Γ is the *Gamma* distribution (Baron, 2019) and $p(\theta|\alpha)$ tries to answer the question *What is the probability density associated with the θ distribution, given that our Dirichlet distribution has the parameter α?*

Formally, these dependency relationships between documents and topics and between words and topics can be modeled with a simple *Bayesian* approach, as shown in Figure 8.4:

- Given a document d, topic z is present in that document with a probability of $P(z|d)$.

- Given a topic Z, a word w is generated from z with a probability of $P(w|z)$.

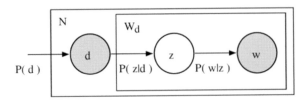

FIGURE 8.4   Dependency modeling between documents, topics and words.

Formally, the joint probability of observing a document D and a word W is:

$$P(D,W)=P(D)\sum_Z P(Z|D)P(W|Z)$$

Intuitively, the right side of the equation tells us how likely it is to observe some document D, and then, based on the distribution of topics Z in that document, how likely it is to find a certain word W within that document.

In this case, $P(D)$, $P(Z|D)$, and $P(W|Z)$ are the model parameters, where $P(D)$ can be directly estimated from the corpus, $P(Z|D)$ and $P(W|Z)$ are modeled as multinomial distributions (θ) which can be trained using algorithms of *Expectation-Maximization* (Baron, 2019). If you look at this formulation as a generative process, $P(D,W)$ is equivalent to the following expression using three different parameters:

$$P(D,W)=\sum_Z P(Z)P(D|Z)P(W|Z)$$

There we start with the topic $P(z)$, and then the document is generated independently with $P(d|z)$ and the word with $P(w|z)$, assuming that the topics are independent of each other. A *Dirichlet* distribution provides a way to sample this probability distribution.

From the sampling of documents, topics and words, the approach is extended to model the topics according to the *Dirichlet* distribution, generating a random sample representing the distribution of topics (or mix of topics) of a document. From the distribution of topics (θ), a topic Z is selected based on this distribution. Then, from another *Dirichlet* distribution Dir(β), a random sample is selected that represents the word distribution of topic Z. Finally, from the word distribution (φ), a word w is selected (Figure 8.5).

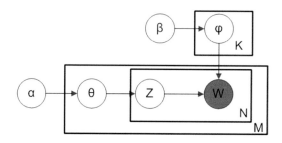

FIGURE 8.5   Modeling topics with Dirichlet distribution.

The method that performs the topic assignment using LDA is summarized as follows:

1. Given a number of documents M, a number of topics K and a vocabulary length of N.

2. Estimate the hyperparameters α and β.

3. For each document $d \in \{1...M\}$:

    I.   Choose θ (topic distribution) from a $Dir(\alpha)$.

       – Θ_{dk} is the probability that a document $d \in \{1...M\}$ has a topic $k \in \{1...K\}$.

    II. Choose φ (word distribution) from a $Dir(\beta)$.

       – φ_{kv} is the probability that a word $v \in \{1...N\}$ is in a topic $k \in \{1...K\}$.

    III. For each W_i word in the document d:

       i.   Choose a topic Z_i from a multinomial distribution(θ_d).

       ii. Choose a word (W_i) from a multinomial distribution (φZ_i).

If a number of topics K is chosen that's less than the number of documents, the effect produced is a reduction in the dimensionality of the original corpus. Once these latent variables or hidden topics in fewer dimensions are obtained, other unsupervised learning techniques can be applied.

Since the parameters $\boldsymbol{\varphi}, \boldsymbol{\theta}$ that maximize p (**w**; **α,β**) must be estimated, we need to obtain the hyperparameters **α** and **β**, which control the similarity of documents and topics, respectively:

- *The α parameter represents the density between documents and topics.* A lower value of α (under 1.0) will assign few topics to each document. For example, this can be seen with many topic distribution samples that are in the corners of the 3-dimensional space—near the topics, in Figure 8.5. If the value is too low, it will probably end up showing α vectors in which only one element is 1.0 and all the rest are 0 (i.e., (**1.0,0.0,0.0**)), which indicates that a document only has one topic. If the value of α is 1.0, it means that any space on the surface of the triangle in the figure is evenly distributed.

On the other hand, a high value of α (greater than 1.0) will assign many topics, producing documents that are more similar in terms of the topics they contain. This would mean that the samples would begin to congregate in the center of the triangle of the figure. That is, as the value of α increases, it's highly probable that the samples are uniform, that is, they represent a mixture of all topics.

- The *β parameter* represents the density between topics and words: a low value of *β* will use few words to model a topic. On the other hand, a high value of *β* will use more words, producing topics that are more similar in terms of the words they contain.

With these parameters, the LDA tries to find *the* best model for each topic; that is, the one with the highest concentration in the distribution.

For example, Figure 8.6 shows how the 3-dimensional parameter α governs the shape of the distribution. In particular, note that the sum of the values of α controls the *strength* of that distribution (e.g., how large its peak is). As the value of α increases, the distribution becomes more focused in the center of the *simplex*, as shown in the figure with the data points in red (words). On the other hand, if this sum approaches 0, the distribution will tend to be focused in points with few large proportions.

To estimate these hyperparameters that generate the best concentration, we usually need parameter estimation and inference methods. Although

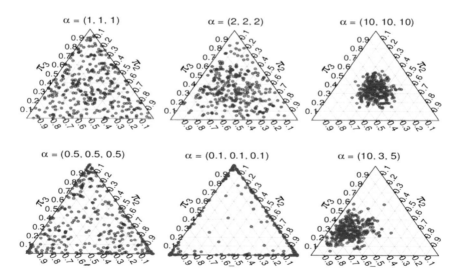

FIGURE 8.6   Dirichlet distribution on a 2-simplex for different values of α.

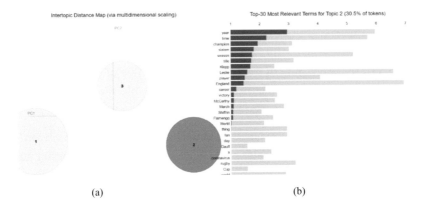

FIGURE 8.7 Topic visualization for a sample corpus.

this problem is generally impossible to work with, there are some approximation methods such as Gibbs sampling, Expectation-Maximization (*EM*), and Variational Inference (Baron, 2019; Bishop, 2006).

As an example of a topic model for $K=3$, a certain body of documents with the adjusted parameters of the LDA is shown in Figure 8.7. The result is visualized using multidimensional scaling (Baron, 2019) of the distance between the topics (Figure 8.7a).

For a chosen topic such as topic 3 (red color), Figure 8.7b shows the result of the distribution of words associated with that topic. Words can be shared between topics but with different *strength*; so, for the total frequency of each word, one part corresponds to that of the current topic (red) while the rest corresponds to the other two topics (light blue).

8.4 EVALUATION

There is an assumption that the latent structure discovered by LDA is generally significant and useful. However, evaluating this is very challenging in unsupervised learning. Ideally, we would like to capture information to determine if the right thing has been learned, in a simple metric that can be maximized and compared.

To address the above, there are two evaluation approaches (Beaujean, 2014):

- *Intrinsic Assessment Metrics*: They measure the ability of the method to capture the semantics of the model or coherence and to interpret the topics, so as to reduce uncertainty in decision-making.

- *Extrinsic Evaluation Metrics*: Measure how good the model is at performing specific pre-defined tasks, such as grading or supervised learning.

The most popular measures of interest include *perplexity* and *topic coherence*. Perplexity is a statistical measure of uncertainty, so a good model is one with low perplexity. The perplexity for a probability distribution p on a variable x can be calculated as: $2^{-\sum_x p(x)\log_2 p(x)}$. An intuitive way to understand this metric is how well a probability model predicts an unknown sample. In the case of LDA, the topic model can be estimated for a given value of K. Then, given the word distributions represented by the topics, we can compare them to the current topic mixes or the word distribution in the corpus documents.

The graph in Figure 8.8 shows the perplexity value for a different number of topics K, reaching the lowest value when $K=6$ (topics). However, optimizing a model based on this measure won't produce interpretable results; hence we need other metrics.

The quality of the latent structure generated by LDA can also be assessed for *topic coherence.* In general, a set of expressions or facts is said to be coherent if they support each other. In this way, *topic coherence* measures an individual topic by calculating the degree of semantic similarity between high-weight words on the topic. This helps to distinguish between

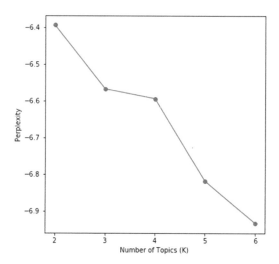

FIGURE 8.8   Evaluating a topic model according to perplexity.

topics that are semantically interpretable and topics that are objects of statistical inference.

Topic coherence is applied to the best words in each topic and is defined as the average of the similarity scores between the words in each topic. This similarity can be measured using various approaches, including:

- *C_v:* Measures the co-occurrence of words in a moving window within a topic. These values are then used to calculate the *Normalized Pairwise Mutual Information* (NPMI) of the N best words with other best words.

- *U_mass:* This measures co-occurrence by comparing a word only with its preceding word and its subsequent word, respectively. This uses a pairwise evaluation function that corresponds to a logarithmic conditional probability.

A good model will generate coherent topics, that is, topics with a high *coherence score*.

The graph in Figure 8.9 shows the relationship between coherence (calculated as *u_mass*) and different numbers of topics. Since the coherence score seems to increase with the number of topics, it makes sense to select the model that gives the highest coherence value, before a decrease, so in this case we select *K=6*.

In general, the LDA usually works better than the pLSA as it can easily generalize to new documents. If we haven't previously seen a document

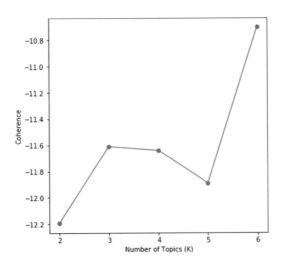

FIGURE 8.9   Evaluating a topic model according to coherence.

in the corpus, we don't have that data point. To resolve this, LDA uses the corpus as training data to estimate the *Dirichlet* distribution of document-topic distributions, and then proceed from there.

8.5 SUMMARY

There are several approaches to clustering words or documents. However, some of them don't account for the data distribution which can be associated with these clusters. One way to tackle this problem is by creating topic models, which are clearer to interpret than traditional methods. There are several techniques for modeling topics including LSA Probabilistic Variants (pLSA) and LDA. One of the most popular is the LDA because it has a robust model in the way of how textual data can be sampled in order to generate efficiently the distributions of topics associated with documents and words associated with topics.

8.6 EXERCISES

This section shows an example of applying the LDA method for topic modeling.

8.6.1 Modeling Topics with LDA

For this example, you must download the "lda.py" program from the book site. We'll need to import some functions already defined in our "utils.py" program and install the paramiko[1] packages, which allows to connect to a display server, and pyLDAvis[2] packages, which allows you to view topic template results:

pip install paramiko

pip install pyLDAvis

Then we imported the previously defined GenSim package for the management of the corpus and evaluation of the coherence of the models as well as the pyLDAvis package for topic visualization:

```
import gensim
from gensim import corpora
from gensim.models.coherencemodel import CoherenceModel
import pyLDAvis
import pyLDAvis.gensim as gensimvis
```

---

[1] http://www.paramiko.org/.
[2] https://pyldavis.readthedocs.io/en/latest/.

Then we need to reuse functions defined in "utils.py", so we load them into our program:

```
from past.builtins import execfile
execfile('utils.py')
```

We need to define a function to preprocess the content of the corpus (PreProcessingWithNouns(..)), which was previously defined to work only with proper names (PROPN) or common names (NOUN) of texts. However, we'll slightly adapt it so that once you perform all the cleaning tasks for each text, you separate each line in a token list with our Tokenize(..) function:

```
def PreProcessingWithNouns(texts):
    cleanText = []
    pattern = r'(\w+)/(PROPN|NOUN)'
    for text in texts:
        text = List_to_Sentence(ExtractNounsFromLine(pattern,text))
        text = RemoveStopwords(text)
        text = Lematize(text)
        text = RemoveNumbers_Puntuactions(text)
        if len(text)!=0:
            text = regex.sub(' +', ' ', text)
            tokens = Tokenize(text)
            cleanText.append(tokens)
    return(cleanText)
```

Furthermore, in this function we'll reuse the same function "ExtractNounsFromLine(..)", also defined in the exercise in Chapter 5, to extract nouns from POS tagged lines.

Now we need a function that allows us to view in an accessible way a generated topic model (model) for a corpus and its dictionary. This function prepares the data for visualization (gensimvis.prepare(..)), generating the vis_data structure, which is then visualized with the pyLDAvis. show(..) method:

```
def VisualizeLDA(model,corpus,dictionary):
    vis_data = gensimvis.prepare(model, corpus, dictionary)
    pyLDAvis.show(vis_data)
```

Finally, we need to define a function to visually evaluate the quality of the model depending on the number of topics to choose from. This takes as input the corpus, its dictionary, the maximum number of topics to evaluate (i.e., number of documents in the corpus), and the metric to evaluate (by default, *Perplexity*). Two steps are required:

1. Several values of K are iterated (i.e., number of topics) to create a list with the values of the evaluation metric.

   a. For each value of K, the topic model is executed (gensim.models. ldamodel.LdaModel(..)) given the corpus K and the dictionary (dicc).

   b. Depending on the chosen metric, the value of its Perplexity (model.log_perplexity(..)) or its Coherence (CoherenceModel(..)) is determined and stored in a list.

2. From the list of metric values, the values of each K are plotted versus the values of the corresponding metric.

```python
def ShowLDAMetricEvolution(corpus,dic,MaxDoc,metric="perp"):
    descrip = {"perp":"Perplexity",
               "u_mass":"Coherence"}
    score = []
    list_k = list(range(2, MaxDoc))
    for K in list_k:
        model = gensim.models.ldamodel.LdaModel(corpus, num_topics=K,
                                                id2word = dic)
        if (metric =="perp"):
            value = model.log_perplexity(corpus)
        else:
            coherence = CoherenceModel(model=model, corpus=corpus,
                                       dictionary=dic, coherence="u_mass")
            value = coherence.get_coherence()
        score.append(value)
    plt.figure(figsize=(6, 6))
    plt.plot(list_k, score, '-o')
    plt.xticks(list_k)
    plt.xlabel(r'Number of Topics (K)')
    plt.ylabel(descrip[metric])
```

Finally, our program loads the language model, creates and preprocesses the corpus, assigns the maximum number of documents, and the preliminary number of topics to generate:

```python
nlp = en_core_web_sm.load()

texts, _doc_id  = CreateCorpus(PATH)
texts   = PreProcessingWithNouns(texts)
MaxDoc = 7
K=3
```

However, the preprocessed corpus (texts) needs to be converted into a suitable format for the topic generation method[3]. For that, we must follow these steps:

1. Build a dictionary (corpora.Dictionary(..)), a list of words indexed from the corpus of the type *(word, index)*.

---

[3] https://radimrehurek.com/gensim/corpora/dictionary.html.

2. Convert the document corpus to a BoW representation (doc2bow(text)) as a list of pairs *(word index, frequency)*.

This can be seen as follows:

```
dictionary = corpora.Dictionary(texts)
corpus = [dictionary.doc2bow(text) for text in texts]
```

Once we have the reformatted corpus, we can generate the topic model using the gensim.models.ldamodel.LdaModel(..) method from this corpus, the number of topics *K*, and the indexed dictionary of words. Using the generated model (modelLDA), we can then show the *K* topics, with the best four words for each topic:

```
modelLDA = gensim.models.ldamodel.LdaModel(corpus, num_topics=K,
                                           id2word = dictionary)

print(modelLDA.print_topics(num_topics=K, num_words=4))
```

The result shows the following topic distribution and their probabilities estimated for each of the four topics (0–3):

```
In [189]: print(modelLDA.print_topics(num_topics=K, num_words=4))
[(0, '0.014*"England" + 0.012*"Irons" + 0.010*"Stewart" + 0.010*"Moore"'),
 (1, '0.011*"season" + 0.010*"Klopp" + 0.009*"Flamengo" + 0.009*"slalom"'),
 (2, '0.017*"Leslie" + 0.016*"year" + 0.013*"England" + 0.011*"time"')]
```

Note that we previously made an assumption that $k=4$. However, we aren't sure if that's the optimal number of topics. In order to visually evaluate the quality of the model with respect to the Perplexity or Coherence metrics, we can simply invoke our function to visualize the evolution of the values of both metrics:

```
ShowLDAMetricEvolution(corpus,dictionary,MaxDoc,"perp")
ShowLDAMetricEvolution(corpus,dictionary,MaxDoc,"u_mass")
```

Therefore, the following graphs are displayed:

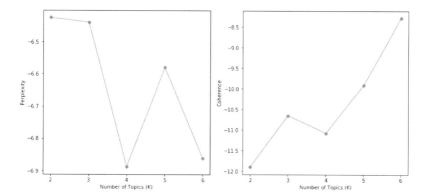

You could use any of the two metrics that you consider convenient. The graphs show that the minimum Perplexity is reached when K=4, whereas the highest Coherence is reached when K=6.

On the other hand, we could visualize our topic model for visual inspection purposes in a more accessible way, so with our model (modelLDA) we use our visualization function on pyLDAvis:

```
VisualizeLDA(modelLDA,corpus,dictionary)
```

Showing the following graphical interface:

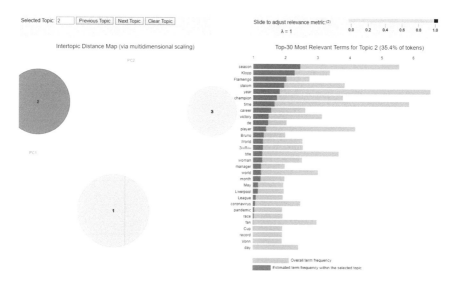

On the left side, you can see the topics displayed at a certain distance through multidimensional scaling (MDS), having the possibility of choosing the topic to be displayed (in red). On the right side is displayed the frequency of the best 30 words associated with each topic (in red) out of the total frequency (light blue).

Note that when LDA is run on a corpus, some words will be frequent throughout the corpus, and therefore they'll be identified as the best words by their frequency p(w|k) in various topics. By their transversality, they won't have much relevance. To solve this aspect, usually this relative frequency can be multiplied by a relevance factor λ that's associated with an exponential of entropy. In this way, when $\lambda=1$, the best words are simply those with a frequency of $p(w|k)$; while when $\lambda<1$ it means that the best words which are very frequent will be penalized, so their frequency will be: $p(w|k)*\lambda$.

CHAPTER 9

Document Categorization

9.1 INTRODUCTION

Organizations, companies, and public bodies use a lot of textual information that they need to structure, efficiently categorizing them in certain previously defined classes. Examples of this type of task include the categorization of emails, classification of sentiment expressed in social network messages, categorization of news, classification of legal documents, classification of frequently asked questions, etc. (Atkinson et al., 2015; Figueroa & Atkinson, 2016). This allows organizations to save considerable time on analyzing data, helps inform business decisions, and efficiently automates business processes, among other benefits.

Suppose the following examples of user messages on Twitter:

User 1:

> *@ATT great now and always, amazing service and coverage in all US, great work @ATT, thanks for all.*

User 2:

> *I've 30 minutes trying to unsubscribe from @ATT services. Many times, they leave me waiting just to send me to three different people. It's not acceptable.*

You work in the customer services area of the communications company called ATT, mentioned in the messages, and you want to have a real-time

DOI: 10.1201/9781003280996-9

report on the user's opinions about the company's services. This would imply that you must determine those messages that speak well of the service (i.e., positive sentiment) and those that speak badly about it (i.e., negative sentiment) and then account for them and deliver them to a *dashboard* for decision-making.

Given the number of messages that are received every day, this task cannot be performed manually, so it requires some method of textual analysis. You could use some method of document clustering (Chapter 7), but this would only serve to group messages with similar characteristics, and not necessarily for those that represent the same sentiment. On the other hand, topic models could be generated to identify terms associated with latent or topic variables (Chapter 8). However, there's linguistic information that a topic model doesn't account for (i.e. deterministic elements in an opinion such as an adjective, noun, etc.), and, on the other hand, the topics that are generated don't have a predefined interpretation.

Thus, for the *Message* 1 in the example, it's relatively simple to determine that it expresses a positive sentiment about the company, since there are certain words and roles (i.e., adjectives) that are explicit and characteristic of that sentiment. In this case, the solution of the problem would be quite simple since we could create two word lists: one that contains characteristic words of the positive polarity and another that contains those of negative polarity. Then, a method should take each message and determine in what proportion it contains words of positive or negative polarity and then decide the sentiment with the greatest weight.

As users express their opinions freely, soon you'll realize that this strategy isn't very robust because explicit trigger words won't always be found; so you should, strictly speaking, try to understand the complete language with some Natural-Language Processing (NLP) technique (Chapter 2). In fact, if you look at the opinion of *user* 2, you'll notice that the sentiment about the service is negative; however, our previous strategy has no way to discriminate this. Perhaps, a topic model could be generated to group words associated with topics; however, apart from statistical distributions that underlie topics, in principle you don't have to realize that there are some words that are more associated with a polarity than with another.

As the number of messages you receive increases, the task becomes more complicated. Definitively, NLP techniques are required to understand the complete sentences and therefore their sentiment. However, you may notice that the social media messages form the example aren't only quite informal, but they mix natural language with many special purpose symbols, being also very short. As a consequence, the exhaustive use of NLP methods per se is not always efficient, so we need intermediate approaches.

Intuitively, a human could tag or classify such messages based on their experience. Unfortunately, as the number of messages grows, this task would become more complex in terms of the patterns to be detected in the messages and the time required to analyze them. However, we could try to computationally reproduce a strategy similar to that of humans: Provide messages that were previously tagged by humans, train a computational method to learn the hidden patterns in past decisions, and then use these patterns or models to tag messages that the method has never seen before.

9.2 CATEGORIZATION MODELS

The task of automatically labeling documents from a set of predefined categories or labels is usually called *Text Categorization*. In general, a text categorizer can be used to organize, structure, and classify textual information. Typically, categorization can be approached from three lanes:

- *Rule-Based Systems*: This type of approach applies a system based on classification rules. For this, linguistic rules constructed manually by human experts, based on the content of the documents, are directly programmed. Then an algorithm takes these rules and classifies topics, detecting semantically relevant elements of a text. Each rule is constructed of a pattern that must be triggered and a class label that must be assigned.

For example, suppose we want to classify news articles into two classes, labeled *sports* and *politics*. First, two sets of words that characterize each group should be defined (i.e. words related to *sports* such as soccer, basketball, etc.). Then when you want to classify a new text, you will need to count the number of words related to *sports* (or *politics*) that appear in the text. If the number of occurrences of *words* in the *sports* topic is greater than that of the *political* topic, then the text will be classified as *sports* and vice versa.

The classification system can be improved by refining existing rules and adding new ones. However, building these rules can be very complex for someone without expert knowledge, and it requires constant analysis and testing to make sure it works the right way. Also, by adding new rules existing ones can be altered or cause conflicts, so systems like these require a lot of maintenance and aren't scalable.

- *Machine Learning Systems*: This type of approach uses supervised machine learning techniques and automatically builds a categorization model from a *training corpus*, consisting of texts and their historical class labels (Aggarwal, 2018; Srivastava & Sahami, 2009). However, machine learning models cannot understand a text directly, so it's necessary first to generate efficient representations of them before they can recognize patterns, extract relevant features, and categorize them. Usually, the training corpus is prepared by humans, so that a categorization algorithm can create a textual classification model, as shown in Figure 9.1.

Once the model has been created, the classification method is capable of categorizing new texts (*test dataset*) because it has learned to make predictions automatically (Figure 9.2).

The advantage of this approach is that if the method is required to increase its predictive power, more training corpuses *annotated* (i.e., labeled) by humans must be prepared, and the model is then re-trained without the need to generate complex procedures.

- *Hybrid Systems*: These methods are simply combinations of rule-based systems and classifiers that use machine learning, which improves results as the rules are refined. This type of approach can be used to "touch up" categories that were incorrectly modeled by the Auto Sorter.

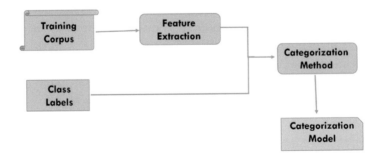

FIGURE 9.1   Testing a text classification model.

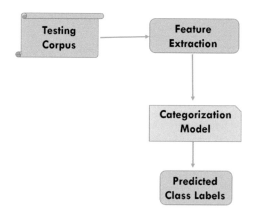

FIGURE 9.2   Training a text classification model.

Text classification, using supervised machine learning, is usually much more accurate than human-written rule-based systems, especially for complex classification tasks. Also, an automatic categorizer is easier to maintain and you can always tag new examples to learn new tasks.

Formally, a finite set of n class labels is required to build a classification model $C=\{c_1, c_2,..., c_n\}$, a set of m training documents D with their corresponding class labels labeled by hand, in the form of pairs $(d_1,c_1),... (d_m,c_m)$. As a result, an *M classification method* will learn a model f that's capable of transforming new text t into a class label in C.

To approach this task, a method must learn to generate a model that accounts for the hidden patterns underlying the classification. In general, there are two types of models that a supervised classification method can produce: *discriminative models* and *generative models* (Bishop, 2006; Flach, 2012). To understand the idea intuitively, consider the task of automatically classifying animal photographs. A generative model could generate new photographs of animals that look like real animals, while a discriminative model could discriminate a dog from a cat. Given a set of X data instances and a set of class Y labels, these types of models operate as follows:

- *Discriminatory Model*: This type discriminates (*separates*) different types of class instances, capturing the conditional probability $P(Y|X)$; that is, it learns the decision limit between classes, reporting how likely it is that a class tag will be assigned to an instance.

The parameters of P(Y|X) are estimated directly from the training data. Some examples of discriminatory models include decision trees, logistic regression, maximum entropy classification, support vector machines, traditional neural networks (i.e., feed-forward), closest neighbors, conditional random fields, etc. (Flach, 2012).

- *Generative Model:* This type generates new data instances, capturing the joint probability P(X, Y) or only P(X) if there are no labels; that is, it models the way (i.e., distribution) in which the data is generated into the classes. Thus, a generative model considers the distribution of the data itself and reports how likely a given example is. Some methods that predict a word or the context of a word, such as in Word2Vec (Chapter 6), usually produce generative models since they can assign a probability to a sequence of words. In this type of model, the parameters of P(X|Y) and P(X) are estimated directly from the training data, and the Bayes rule is used to calculate P(Y|X). Some examples of generative models include Bayesian Networks, Hidden Markov Models (HMM), Bayesian Naïve classifiers, Generative Adversarial Networks (GAN), etc. (Sherstinsky, 2020; Foster, 2019).

Generative models usually outperform discriminative models in small datasets because generative assumptions impose a certain model structure to prevent overfitting. For example, the *Naïve assumption* in Bayesian classifiers is rarely fulfilled, so models like *Maximum Entropy* (or Logistic Regression) will tend to be superior to *Naïve Bayes* as the dataset grows. This is because the *Maximum Entropy* methods capture dependencies that *Naïve Bayes* cannot capture. However, when a small dataset is available, methods like Maximum Entropy could capture false patterns that don't really exist. Thus, a Naïve Bayes classifier can act as a model *regularizer,* preventing overfitting (Bishop, 2006).

In the case of document categorization, both generative models (i.e., Bayesian Classification) and discriminative models (i.e., Maximum Entropy) generate very good results. Generative models can learn the underlying structure of the data if the model is *properly* specified and in case it's valid. On the other hand, discriminatory models can be more effective when generative assumptions aren't met. This is because discriminatory models are less dependent on a particular structure and the real world is *dirty*, so assumptions are rarely fully satisfied.

9.3 BAYESIAN TEXT CATEGORIZATION

A Bayesian classifier is a family of simple multinomial probabilistic classification methods, the simplest being the so-called *Naïve* Bayesian classifier
or Naïve Bayes. The fundamental assumption is that there's a certain correlation between the probability of the occurrence of the words contained
in a text and the probability that the text belongs to a certain category.
This correlation can be modeled probabilistically if certain assumptions
are made.

The *Naïve Bayes* classifier uses Bayes' theory to decide the most likely
class to which an input text belongs. Its naïve property comes from the
assumption that the characteristics of a text are mutually independent. In
practice, this assumption is generally not met but still produces classifiers
with good performance in many cases, especially when the corpuses are
small.

For this, a training corpus consisting of pairs of n documents with their
respective class labels is available: $(d_1,c_1),...(d_n,c_n)$, where each class label
belongs to a defined set of *m* lessons. In addition, each d_i document is represented by its corresponding set of characteristics x_i. Then, the objective
of the classifier is to learn a model that's capable of predicting the class of
a document that wasn't previously seen.

To find the best model that fits new documents, you must maximize the
posterior probability (MAP) that a document belongs to a certain class,
defined in Equation 9.1 as:

$$P(\text{Class}|\text{Document}) = \frac{P(\text{Document}|\text{Class}) * P(\text{Class})}{P(\text{Document})} \qquad (9.1)$$

Equation 9.1 *A Posteriori* Probability Using Bayesian Classification.

where *P(Document|Class)* is the normal (or *Gaussian*) distribution of
the characteristics of a document given a class or the probability of observing the characteristics of a given Document that belongs to a class (i.e.,
conditional class probability), *P(Class)* is the *a priori* belief of the class (i.e.,
a priori probability), and *P(Document)* is the *evidence* or probability of
observing the characteristics of the document.

Suppose documents that represent opinions on a social network and
that can express two types of sentiment: *positive* or *negative*. Given a document (opinion) represented by a set of characteristics *x = [liked, much]*, we
want to determine which class that document belongs to. For this, we must
find a class for which the posterior probability is, given such a document.

In this case, we have two possible classes. Therefore, we must estimate *P(positive/x)* and *P(negative/x)*. Then the document belongs to the *positive* class if it is that *P(positive/x)> P(negative/x)*, otherwise it is classified as *negative*.

To estimate these probabilities, the other components of the classification in Equation 9.1 must be calculated, that is, the class conditional probability, the *a priori* probability, and the evidence.

From a computational point of view, the computation of the *P(Document)* evidence is not very efficient, since it forces us to count all the sequences of characteristics of the Document throughout the corpus. To solve this, a *Naïve Bayes* classifier makes two fundamental assumptions (Baron, 2019):

1. Data samples are independent and identically distributed; that is, the random variables are independent of each other and are generated from a similar probability distribution. This independence means that the probability of one observation does not affect the probability of another observation.

2. The *features* are conditionally independent. Under this *naïve* assumption, the conditional probabilities (*likelihood*) of the samples can be estimated directly from the training data, instead of evaluating all the possibilities of *x*.

9.3.1 Conditional Class Probability

Given a document represented with a set of features x of r dimensions, and making our Naïve assumptions, the conditional probability of the class can be calculated as:

$$P(x \mid \text{Class}) = P(x_1 \mid \text{Class}) * P(x_2 \mid \text{Class}) * P(x_r \mid \text{Class})$$

$$= \prod_{k=1}^{r} P(x_k \mid \text{Class})$$

This can be seen in simple terms such as how likely it is to observe a particular pattern x given that it belongs to a certain class. The individual probability of each characteristic $P(x_k \mid \text{Class})$ can be determined using the MLE estimator, such as:

$$P(x_k \mid \text{Class}) = \frac{N_{x_k, \text{Class}}}{s}$$

where

- $N_{x_k,\text{Class}}$ is the frequency of x_k in class samples.

- N_{Class} is the total number of samples in the class.

Let's assume that we have a training corpus that contains 500 opinions from social networks, of which 100 correspond to opinions that express positive sentiments and the rest are negative sentiments.

We want to compute the class conditional probability that a new *I really like* message belongs to the positive class. The pattern consists of two relevant characteristics (discarding *stopwords*): [really, like], and the class probability is the product of the "probability of finding the word *really* since the message is of the positive class" by the "probability to find the word *like* since the message is of the negative class", so the estimate remains as:

$$P\big([\text{really},\text{like}]\,|\,\text{positive}\big)=P\big(\text{really}\,|\,\text{positive}\big)*P\big(\text{like}\,|\,\text{positive}\big)$$

Using the training corpus, we can estimate these individual probabilities using MLE. For this, we simply calculate the frequency of these words in the corpus for the positive class, assuming that the frequency of like is 20 and the frequency of lot is 2, the estimate is as follows:

$$P\big([\text{really},\text{like}]\,|\,\text{positive}\big)=\frac{20}{100}*\frac{2}{100}=0,004$$

9.3.2 *A Priori* Probability

Our Bayesian Naïve classification model formulated from Equation 9.1 also needs to represent the *a priori beliefs* of the classification, usually called priors or *a priori probability*. A **prior** describes the probability of occurrence of a particular class in the training corpus.

If the *priors* follow a uniform distribution, the posterior probabilities will be completely determined by the conditional class probabilities and the evidence. Since the evidence is constant, the decision rule will depend only on the class conditional probabilities. Thus, the MLE can be estimated as:

$$P(\text{Class})=\frac{N_{\text{Class}}}{N}$$

where

- N_{Class} is the frequency of the samples that belong to the class.
- N is the total number of samples.

In our example, $P(\text{Class} = \text{positive})$ can be calculated as:

$$P(\text{Class} = \text{positive}) = \frac{\text{No.of positive opinions}}{\text{No.of total opinions}} = \frac{100}{500} = 0.2$$

9.3.3 Evidence

Evidence P(document) can be expressed as the probability of finding a particular pattern or characteristics x of the document, independent of the class label, and can be estimated as:

$$P(x) = P(x|\text{Class}_1) * P(\text{Class}_1) + P(x|\text{Class}_2) + P(x|\text{Class}_2)$$

However, although evidence is required to calculate the posterior probabilities, it can be removed from the decision rule since it's only a scalar factor. Thus, the decision can be approximated to determine if:

$$P(x|\text{Class}_1) * P(\text{Class}_1) > P(x|\text{Class}_2) * P(\text{Class}_2)$$

9.3.4 Classification

Once *a priori* probabilities, *a posteriori* probabilities, and evidence are estimated, a new sample can be classified as one class or another, simply by applying the rule:

$$\text{SI } P(\text{Class}_1|x) \geq P(\text{Class}_2|x) \text{ THEN Classify as Class}_1 \text{ otherwise as Class}_2$$

Note that when trying to classify a new text, there could be characteristics that weren't in the training corpus; so the conditional class probability will be 0, and as a consequence, the posterior probability will also be 0. In order to avoid this 0-probability problem, values can be smoothed by adding a term to the Bayes model. One of the most common correction factors is the *Laplace* smoothing (Baron, 2019), which is estimated as:

$$P(x_k|\text{Class}) = \frac{N_{x_k,\text{Class}} + \infty}{N_{\text{Class}} + \infty d}$$

where

- $N_{x_k,\text{Class}}$ is the frequency of the feature x_k in the *class* samples.

- $\propto$ is the smoothing parameter greater than zero, usually $\propto = 1$ ($\propto$ should be 0, if there is no smoothing).

- N_{Class} is the total number of samples in the *Class*.

- d is the size of the feature vector.

Although a *Naïve Bayes* categorization model generally performs well on small corpuses, it can easily degrade if documents contain strongly correlated features. Because of this, we need classification models that are based on fewer assumptions.

9.4 MAXIMUM ENTROPY CATEGORIZATION

Suppose a document contains the word coronavirus; it's highly likely that it also contains the word pandemic, so these words are correlated and should affect the final decision class. In these cases, not only is the Naïve assumption breached but the model loses its ability to exploit the interaction between these characteristics. Hence, we need other categorization methods that don't make as many assumptions in the distributions.

One way to tackle the above problem is to find, by means of some optimization strategy, the best *weights* for these characteristics in such a way as to maximize the probability that the training data belongs to a certain category (Figueroa & Atkinson, 2011). A typical discriminative textual categorization model that's capable of performing this task is called the *Maximum Entropy* (*MaxEnt*) classification model (Baron, 2019; Srivastava & Sahami, 2009).

Compared to a Bayesian classifier, there are two fundamental differences:

1. *MaxEnt* doesn't make assumptions about the independence of the characteristics of a text, so it can be used when this assumption is breached.

2. Since *MaxEnt* makes minimal assumptions, it can be used when we don't know anything about the *a priori* distribution and/or when we're not sure of it.

MaxEnt is a probabilistic classifier that belongs to the family of exponential models and is based on the *Principle of Maximum Entropy* (Karmeshu, 2003). This establishes that from the training data, the model that best represents the current state of knowledge expressed by those data is the one with the highest *Entropy*. In information theory, the entropy of an information source or random variable X is a measure of its information *uncertainty* (Bishop, 2006) and is usually defined as:

$$H(X) = -\sum_i P(x_i) \log_2 P(x_i)$$

where $P(x_i)$ is the probability of one of the states (values) of the variable X, so the final entropy is the weighted sum of the amount of information from the different variable stages. The distribution of entropy values for different probability values of X can be seen in Figure 9.3. As the probability of the variable taking a certain value approaches 0.5, there's uncertainty about whether to take one value or another (for example, an unpredictable result), and entropy reaches its maximum value (1.0). However, as the probability of the variable approaches 1 (i.e., total certainty or completely predictable result), the entropy reaches its minimum value (0.0).

Usually, in a decision-making process, one would look for variable distributions associated with a class that minimizes entropy. However, this assumes that there's a compromise of one class over the other. It's reasonable then to think that maximizing entropy can be advantageous since:

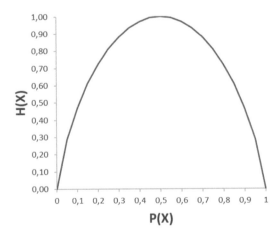

FIGURE 9.3   Entropy for probability distribution of X.

1. Data commitments are minimized.

2. Everything that's known is modeled and nothing is assumed for the unknown.

Because of this, *MaxEnt* must build a stochastic model that best represents the behavior of a random process, without many prior assumptions: taking a contextual information x input from a document (i.e., characteristics) and producing the resulting class y. For this, data must be collected from a training corpus of size N, with a number of predefined class labels, containing documents represented as pairs (x_i, y_j) of characteristics and the respective classes, and then summarize the training sample according to its probability distribution: $P(x_i, y_j) = \dfrac{1}{N} * n(x_i, y_j)$, where n is the number of times where (x_i, y_j) occurs in the document sample.

This is used to build the statistical model of the random process that assigns a text to a specific class, considering the contextual information. In its most basic form, this context takes the form of an *indicator function* or binary feature f defined as:

$$f_j(x, y) = \begin{cases} 1, \text{ if } y = c_i \text{ and } x \text{ has } w_k \\ 0, \text{ otherwise} \end{cases}$$

The function returns 1 only when the class of a document is c_i and the document contains the word w_k. Because of this, a training document can be represented as a set of f_j indicator functions. In this way, the expected value of a characteristic f_j can be estimated as:

$$P(f_j) = \sum_{x,y} p(x, y) f_j(x, y)$$

If each sample (x, y) occurs once in the training set, then $P(x, y)$ equals $1/N$. Then we restrict the expected value assigned by the model to the expected value of the function f_j, with respect to the model $p(y|x)$, and that corresponds to:

$$P(f_j) = \sum_{x,y} P(x) P(y|x) f_j(x, y)$$

There $P(x)$ is the distribution of x in the training corpus. Restricting the expected value so it's the same as the empirical value, it can be found that:

$$\sum_{x,y} P(x)P(yx)f_j(x,y) = \sum_{x,y} P(x,y)f_j(x,y)$$

Then we can find as many constraints as the number of indicator functions f, which can be satisfied using an infinite number of models. To build a model, the best candidate model must then be selected based on specific criteria. According to the principle of *Maximum Entropy*, models selected should be as close as possible to the uniform distribution; that is, $p*$ inside models should have maximum entropy:

$$p^* = \text{argmax}_{p \in C} - \sum_{x,y} P(x)P(yx)\log P(y \mid x)$$

So,

$$P(yx) \geq 0 \text{ for all } x, y$$

$$\sum_y P(yx) = 1 \text{ for all } x$$

$$\sum_{x,y} P(x)P(yx)f_j(x,y) = \sum_{x,y} P(x,y)f_j(x,y) \text{ for } j \in \{1,2,...,n\}$$

To solve this optimization problem, *Lagrange* multipliers (Klein, 2015) are used in order to transform it into a dual problem without restrictions. Weights or lambda variables $\{\lambda_1,..., \lambda_n\}$ are then estimated applying some estimation method such as MLE, iterative scaling techniques such as GIS (Generalized Iterative Scaling) or IIS (Improved Iterative Scaling) (Baron, 2019).

It can be shown that if we find the weights $\{\lambda_1,..., \lambda_n\}$ that maximize the optimization problem, the probability that a given document x is classified as y can be defined as a logistic regression task (exp); therefore, it can be estimated as shown in Equation 9.2:

$$p^*(yx) = \frac{\exp\left(\sum_i \lambda_i f_i(x,y)\right)}{\sum_y \exp\left(\sum_i \lambda_i f_i(x,y)\right)} \tag{9.2}$$

Equation 9.2: MAP classification using MaxEnt

Note that after the optimization process, weight values will be obtained for each of the indicator functions (or *features*). Because of this, to classify a new document it's only necessary to apply the decision rule of *Maximum A Posteriori* (MAP) and select the highest probability category, considering the weights corresponding to the *features* of that document.

Then *training* of a *MaxEnt* classifier is carried out with the following steps:

1. Define a set of class labels *y*.

2. Identify a set of indicator functions *f* from the input document corpus.

3. Iteratively find the weight parameter (λ) values that satisfy the constraints while maximizing the entropy of the distribution.

Finally, to categorize an unknown document *x*:

- Identify a set of indicator features from document x.

- Given the previously learned weights (λ), determine MAP (Equation 9.2) to obtain the greatest probability class for document *x* on its *f* features and corresponding λ weights.

For example, consider the following Twitter message: "@att's service is not good for people, they leave me waiting", which should be classified into one of two sentiments: *positive* (+) or *negative* (−). To do this, the vector *x* of the input message is represented with relevant words such as [service, att, not, good, people, waiting]. Also, assume that you've a training corpus made up of two sentences with their respective sentiments:

Sentiment (+): @ATT great now and always, amazing service and coverage in all US, great work @att, thanks for all.

Sentiment (−): I've 30 minutes trying to unsubscribe from @ATT services. Many times, they leave me waiting just to send me to three different people. It's not acceptable.

Then, to estimate the most likely class to which the new message belongs, we determined the functions *f* only for a subset of seven words from the training corpus with their respective absence (0) or presence (1) in the positive and negative opinions, as shown in Figure 9.4.

Furthermore, let's assume that an optimization method has already determined the best weights λ for each indicator function *f*. Then we determine the probability that the message *x* belongs to (sentiment) class

Indicator functions f

	ATT	good	waiting	not	service	always	people	p(y|x)
y=+	1	1	0	0	1	1	0	0,19
y=-	1	0	1	1	1	0	1	0,81

λ		0	0,78	0,64	0,95	0,35	0,23	0,85	

									exp(Σ)
λ $f+$	0	0,78	0	0	0,35	0,23	0		3,90
λ $f-$	0	0	0,64	0,95	0,35	0	0,85		16,28

Total   20,18

FIGURE 9.4   Computing indicator functions and probability of classes.

(+) and class (−) based on the proportions of the exponentials of the sum of the factors of the weights and the indicator functions (Equation 9.2). Finally, the values for the probability of the class (+) and (−) correspond to 0.19 and 0.81, respectively. Therefore, the original message is classified as negative sentiment.

9.5 EVALUATION

Given the nature, assumptions, and strategies that categorization methods use, it's reasonable to think that they have a different performance over a training corpus. To determine how well they learn to categorize a method or how they compare to others, we must assess the quality of the models produced. For this, there're some usual performance metrics, depending on the categorization scenario:

- *Model Performance:* It allows to determine how well document instances are categorized, given a learned model. For example, a classifier can take customer complaints and categorize them with an *Accuracy* of 90%. What does this mean? (Chapter 3)

- *Classification Cost:* It allows determining the classification cost on a set of documents. For example, the pre-classifier might wrongly categorize complaints into the wrong class. What impact does that have for customers or the company?

- *Corpus Size:* It allows determining the performance of the classification model as the training and/or test corpus varies. For example, the pre-sorter might work very well for a certain training corpus size. However, I's not sustainable over time to classify new complaint documents.

It's common to evaluate *binary categorization* tasks, that is, tasks where the result of the classification can be one of two possible classes. Examples of this include detecting spam (spam/non-spam), predicting credit card fraud (fraud/non-fraud), etc. However, in many real applications, a text can belong to more than one class (aka multiclass categorization). For example, a news text on climate change could be associated with the *environment* class and also with *politics*, etc.

The usual way to evaluate a text categorizer performance is to use *cross validation* methods (Baron, 2019). This consists of separating the corpus into a training set of fixed-length random samples (i.e. 4 sets with 25% of the data). For each set, the classifier is trained with the rest of the samples (i.e. 75%). The classifier then performs the classification on its respective sets and the results are compared to the actual class labels generated by human scorers. This allows to determine when a classification was correct.

The evaluation result can be generated by calculating the usual metrics such as Accuracy, Precision, Recall, and F1-Score (Chapter 3). However, there are moments when these metrics alone aren't enough to analyze the behavior of a classifier, since they only evaluate a specific instant of time with a certain distribution of the data.

On the other hand, many of the categorization methods are probabilistic, so their output is compared to some cutoff threshold to determine whether one class or the other is predicted.

The example model predicts two classes with the following exit probabilities for four sample documents: [0.45, 0.6, 0.7, 0.3]. Depending on the cut thresholds, different class labels would be obtained:

$$\text{Cut} = 0.5: \text{redicted-classes} = [0,1,1,0]$$

$$\text{Cut} = 0.2: \text{Predicted-classes} = [1,1,1,1]$$

$$\text{Cut} = 0.8: \text{Predicted-classes} = [0,0,0,0]$$

This shows that by varying the threshold values completely, different classes are obtained. As a consequence, each of these cases would produce different *Precision* and *Recall* rates. Due to this, it's required to have a systematic way of finding the cutoff thresholds in order to obtain more representative values of the metrics.

One of the popular analysis methods is called a *Receiver Operating Characteristic* (ROC) curve that corresponds to a graphical representation of Recall versus Precision for a binary classifier, as the discrimination threshold varies (Zou et al., 2016). An ROC curve plots two parameters: (1) The TP rate (or TPR) that corresponds to *Recall* and (2) the FP rate (or FPR) that corresponds to Precision, where FPR is calculated as FP/ (FP+TN). Note that by lowering the threshold for the positive class more samples are classified as positive, increasing both the FP rate and the TP rate, as shown in the curve in Figure 9.5, with an area under the ROC curve of 0.85.

The graph shows that there's a tradeoff between how high Recall should be versus how much we want to limit errors (FPR). Thus, an ROC curve allows observing the general performance of the model and selecting a good cut threshold for it.

To calculate the points on an ROC curve, some probabilistic classification model must be evaluated many times with different thresholds, which would be very inefficient. One solution is to use an algorithm based on ordering that gives us this information, calculating the *Area Under the Curve* (AUC)

In simple terms, the AUC measures the complete 2-dimensional area under the ROC curve (between 0 and 1) from the coordinates (0,0) to (1,1). One way to interpret AUC is as the probability that a model orders a positive random sample much better than a negative random sample. Therefore, a model whose predictions are 100% incorrect will have an AUC of 0.0 while one whose predictions are 100% correct will have an AUC of 1.0.

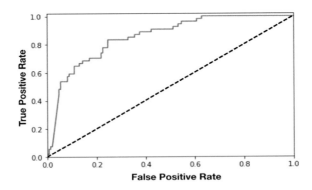

FIGURE 9.5   An example of a Receiver Operating Characteristic (ROC) curve.

9.6 SUMMARY

Document categorization is the text mining task that consists of assigning a predefined class label to a document from models generated from training corpuses. The categorization task is present in many business, industrial, and scientific applications such as sentiment analysis, email classification, document filtering, client profile categorization, relationship identification in scientific literature, etc. There are several categorization methods based on Bayesian models, neural network models, maximum entropy methods, etc. Some of those make many assumptions about the distribution of the data (i.e., Bayesian approaches), while others minimize compromise on the data (i.e., maximum entropy). The standard evaluation considers Accuracy, Precision, and Recall measures, which allow evaluating the performance of classifiers but compare them in the analysis of large corpuses.

9.7 EXERCISES

This section shows two practical examples of applying text categorization:

1. Sentiment categorization based on a Naïve Bayes Classifier.

2. News classification based on MaxEnt.

9.7.1 Naïve Bayes Categorization

For this example you must download the program "bayes.py" from the book site. We'll need to import functions already defined in our "utils.py" program and install the textblob package[1] for Bayesian classification:

    conda install -c conda-forge/label/gcc7 textblob

We will use the classifier to determine the sentiments that opinions are expressing in different media (i.e., social networks, reviews, forums, etc.), which we'll catalog in two polarities for simplicity, positive (pos) or negative (neg), to then visualize them in a simple graph as a function of time. There are several ways to obtain opinion messages from different media, applying scrapping[2] methods or using available data sets with opinions and their polarities. To simplify the example, we'll use the last approach;

---

[1] https://textblob.readthedocs.io/en/dev/.
[2] https://realpython.com/beautiful-soup-web-scraper-python/.

we'll need three CSV (comma separated content) files available on the book site:

1. "training.csv": This has examples of opinions for classifier training in the format, "message, polarity".

2. "testing.csv": This has examples of opinions for the classifier test with the same previous format.

3. "nuevos.csv": This has examples of opinions without polarity in sentiment but with their issue date, so the format is "message, date".

Then, we import a few libraries from TextBlob, NumPy, and others to handle files in the CSV format:

```
from textblob.classifiers import NaiveBayesClassifier
from numpy import unique
import csv
from pylab import *
```

First, we define a function in charge of loading a CSV file into a list of feedback messages. Note that the format of the files with the training and testing examples have the same format while that of the new messages only differs in that they contain the date instead of polarity. Because of this, we use a single function (LoadCSVFile(..)) for these purposes, which is given the name of the file to load, and a boolean "flag" (IsNewText, which by default is set as False) that indicates that you can upload a new file (opinion and date) or a training/test file (opinion and polarity). Therefore, when opening a file, if the text is indicated as new, it creates a list of pairs (sentence, date), whereas it creates a list with all the pairs (sentence, sentiment) if the file is not new (training/testing):

```
def LoadCSV(FileName, IsNewText=False):
    fileID = open(FileName)
    text   = csv.reader(fileID, delimiter=',')
    if (IsNewText):
        Opinions = [(sentence,date.strip()) for (sentence,date) in text]
    else:
        Opinions = [(sentence,senti.strip()) for (sentence,senti) in text]
    return(Opinions)
```

To classify the opinions of the test texts, we need a function (ClassifyOpinions(..)) that takes the model previously learned in the training (model) and the list of new sentences to classify (i.e., pairs of (sentence, date)). This then creates a list (SentiList) with the result of the classification for each sentence along with its date. From this, a list is generated (CountList) containing the positive and negative sentiment counters for each date:

```
def ClassifyOpinions(model,TestList):
    SentiList = [ (model.classify(sent),date)
                            for (sent,date) in TestList]
    CountList = CountOpinions(SentiList)
    return(CountList)
```

The counting of options classified as positive or negative by date is carried out by the CountOpinions(..) function, which takes the list (SentiList) of the classification results (i.e., pairs of (sentiment, date)). This then creates a list of frequencies (FreqList) with triplets of the form (date, pos count, and neg count) that contains the positive and negative sentiment counters, respectively, for each date (i.e., on a certain date, there may be several opinions):

```
def CountOpinions(SentiList):
    DateList = unique([date  for (sent,date) in SentiList])
    FreqList = []
    for date in DateList:
        countPOS = 0
        countNEG = 0
        for (s,d) in SentiList:
            if (d == date):
                if (s == "neg"):
                    countNEG += 1
                else:
                    countPOS += 1
        FreqList.append((date,countPOS,countNEG))
    return(FreqList)
```

Once the list with the positive and negative ratings has been generated, we define a function to display in a simple line chart, the frequency of positive and negative sentiments ordered by date:

```
def ShowSentimentEvolution(DateList,CountPOSList,CountNEGList):
    ax = figure().gca()
    ax.plot(DateList,CountPOSList,"o-" "r",DateList,CountNEGList,"o-")
    ax.yaxis.set_major_locator(MaxNLocator(integer=True))
    title("Sentiments Evolution")
    legend(('Positive', 'Negative'), loc = 'upper right')
    xlabel('Date')
    ylabel('No. of Opinions')
    show()
```

As usual, our main program initializes our language model, loads the training and test files, respectively, which are located in the directory indicated by PATH:

```
PATH = "./"

nlp = en_core_web_sm.load()

training    = LoadCSV(PATH+"training.csv")
testing     = LoadCSV(PATH+"testing.csv")
```

Now we must train our Bayesian classifier (NaïveBayesClassifier(..)) with the training data and load the new texts (IsNewText=True) to further classify new opinions, with our learned model:

```
model = NaiveBayesClassifier(training)
NewTexts    = LoadCSV(PATH+'new.csv',True)
DateList = ClassifyOpinions(model,NewTexts)
```

At this point, we could already display a list that contains the result of the classification for each of the new sentences for each date and polarity:

```
In [196]: print(DateList)
[('10/03/19', 1, 2), ('16/03/19', 0, 2), ('20/03/19', 2, 0), ('25/04/19', 0,
2)]
```

This shows that, for example, on 10/03/19 we classified 1 positive sentiment opinions and 2 negative sentiment opinions, and so on.

Once we get this list of rankings, we separate it into three lists that we need to view: a list with the dates (Dates), a list with the number of positive sentiments for each date (CountPOS), and another with the number of negatives sentiments for each date (CountNEG). We then show the resulting variables:

```
Dates = [d for (d,_,_) in DateList]
CountPOS = [cpos for (_,cpos,_) in DateList]
CountNEG = [cneg for (_,_,cneg) in DateList]

ShowSentimentEvolution(Dates,CountPOS,CountNEG)
```

So we get the following, where the red and blue lines represent the positive and negative sentiments, respectively:

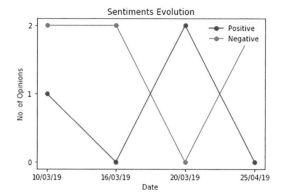

This analysis result allows us to make future decisions about the preferences of users, customers, or others, in terms of sentiment trends for certain users, peaks times, etc.

But how do we know how well our classifier did? For this, we can evaluate metrics such as Accuracy, using the accuracy(..) method of the learned model:

```
TrainAccuracy = round(model.accuracy(training),2)
TestAccuracy  = round(model.accuracy(testing),2)
```

Next, we can determine the accuracy on training and test data:

```
In [13]: print(TrainAccuracy)
0.89

In [14]: print(TestAccuracy)
0.67
```

Since we are using small datasets, results are not high. However, as the size of the training and test datasets increase the overall performance should reach much better results. On the other hand, if you want to classify a particular text, we can use the classify method associated with the model, with an input text, or the prob_classify(..) method to obtain the classification probability in any of the possible categories:

```
In [49]: model.classify("i like the console")
Out[49]: 'pos'

In [50]: decision = model.prob_classify("i like the console")

In [51]: decision.prob("pos")
Out[51]: 0.5402472613917071
```

9.7.2 MaxEnt Categorization

For this example of MaxEnt categorization, you must download the program "maxent.py" from the book site. We will need to import some functions already defined in our "utils.py" program and some available for frequency classification and analysis available in the NLTK library:

```
import nltk, nltk.classify.util, nltk.metrics
from nltk.classify import MaxentClassifier
from nltk.probability import FreqDist
```

We'll use the *MaxEnt* classifier to categorize news from two corpuses of different types: sports and coronavirus. So, we'll need to create dictionaries, feature lists, training/test data, and normalize our corpuses. First, we need to define a function (CreateDictionary(..)) to create a dictionary with the most frequent words. For this, we take the tokens of the corpus of both kinds of news, and a maximum number of terms for that dictionary (MaxTerms). We then join the token lists into a single list (WordList), from which we calculate the frequency distribution of each of the words and generate an ordered dictionary with pairs of the form: {*word: frequency*}. Next, we extract the keys of that dictionary into a list (.kets()), we then return the MaxTerms words from that list:

```
def CreateDictionary(Tokens_class1,Tokens_class2,MaxTerms):
    WordList      = Tokens_class1 + Tokens_class2
    WordFreq      = FreqDist(WordList)
    my_keys       = list(WordFreq.keys())
    return (set(my_keys[:MaxTerms]))
```

We need to define a function that creates the *feature* sets for each of the tokens in each class. For this, we generate and return a list of *features* for each class from each t token, where each feature is a pair of the form: ({*t:True*},*Class*):

```
def CreateFeatureSets(Tokens_class1,Tokens_class2):
    Features_class1 = [({t:True},class1) for t in Tokens_class1]
    Features_class2 = [({t:True},class2) for t in Tokens_class2]
    return((Features_class1,Features_class2))
```

Now we need to build the training data sets and the testing data sets for the categorizer, so we must divide the total set of *features* of both classes into a proportion of the training data (PropTraining) and the difference for test. To do this, we define two functions, one that creates the list of training *features* (CreateTrainingFeatures(..)) and another that creates the list of test features (CreateTestFeatures(..)). The first returns the list of features from the first position to one given by a cutoff threshold per class (class1cutoff and class2cutoff) while the second returns the list of *features* from the position of the cutoff threshold of each class (class1cutoff and class2cutoff) to the final position, that is, the difference between the total length of each list and the cutoff threshold:

```
def CreateTrainingFeatures(Features_class1,Features_class2,PropTraining):
    (class1cutoff,class2cutoff) = CalculateCutoff(Features_class1,
                                                  Features_class2,
                                                  PropTraining)
    return (Features_class1[:class1cutoff]+Features_class2[:class2cutoff])


def CreateTestingFeatures(Features_class1,Features_class2,PropTraining):
    (class1cutoff,class2cutoff) = CalculateCutoff(Features_class1,
                                                  Features_class2,
                                                  PropTraining)
    test_class1 = int(len(Features_class1)-class1cutoff)
    test_class2 = int(len(Features_class2)-class2cutoff)
    return(Features_class1[-test_class1:] + Features_class2[-test_class2:])


def CalculateCutoff(Features_class1,Features_class2,PropTraining):
    class1cutoff = int(len(Features_class1)*PropTraining)
    class2cutoff = int(len(Features_class2)*PropTraining)
    return(class1cutoff,class2cutoff)
```

To determine the cutoff threshold, we define the function CalculateCutoff(..), which simply takes each list of *features* and calculates their length relative to the data proportion in the specified training set (PropTraining).

Now we must define the function that allows us to train the MaxEnt classification model. For this, the function (TrainModel(..)) receives the set of training features (trainingFeatures) and trains our model (MaxentClassifier) based on three parameters: the training set itself, the iterative scaling algorithm that we'll use to create the *feature* weights, and the number of iterations of such an algorithm. In our case, we have chosen the GIS method:

```
def TrainModel(trainingFeatures):
    model = MaxentClassifier.train(trainingFeatures,
                                   algorithm="GIS",max_iter=4,trace=0)
    return(model)
```

We must reuse a function to preprocess a corpus already defined in the exercises in Chapter 5, because, apart from cleaning and normalization, we'll only use the nouns extracted from each sentence, as *features*:

```
def PreProcessingWithNouns(texts):
    cleanText = []
    pattern = r'(\w+)/(PROPN|NOUN)'
    for text in texts:
        text = List_to_Sentence(ExtractNounsFromLine(pattern,text))
        text = RemoveStopwords(text.lower())
        text = Lematize(text)
        text = RemoveNumbers_Puntuactions(text)
        if len(text)!=0:
            text = regex.sub(' +', ' ', text)
            cleanText.append(text)
    return(cleanText)

def ExtractNounsFromLine(pattern,line):
    text      = line.rstrip()
    taggedText = POS_tagger(text)
    WordList   = [w for (w,t) in regex.findall(pattern,taggedText)]
    return(WordList)
```

After preprocessing the corpus, we must generate the list of tokens for each document, so we add a function that simply takes a set of texts from a document, separates them into tokens (Tokenize(..)), and then creates a list with those tokens:

```
def TokenizeDocuments(texts):
    Tok_list = []
    for t in texts:
        tokens = Tokenize(t)
        for tok in tokens:
            Tok_list.append(tok)
    return(Tok_list)
```

One of the tasks that you can do with the trained classification model is just to take any string or text and classify it. This text must go through stages similar to those used for complete documents, so a function is needed to create the features to classify that text. For this, we define a function (CreateFeatures(..)) that takes a text, lemmatizes it, generates its tokens, and then returns its list of *features*:

```
def CreateFeatures(text):
    l = Lematize(text.lower())
    t = Tokenize(l)
    f = GenerateWordFeatures(t)
    return(f)

def GenerateWordFeatures(words):
    return {word:True for word in words if word in top_words}
```

The function used to create the list of *features* from words (GenerateWordFeatures(..)) takes a word list and generates a list in dictionary format ({..}) which contains the words that are only included in the vocabulary initially built for the corpus (top_words). In this case, every word that exists is included in the dictionary in the format: *word: True*.

The main program initializes the language model, loads the corpus for each class, preprocesses them, and generates the list of tokens for each one. Note that the class names must match the directory names where our sample documents are located, in the path specified by PATH:

```
PATH = "E:/JOHN/BOOK/ENGLISH/TextAnalytics-Examples/CORPUS/"
nlp = en_core_web_sm.load()
class1 = "sports"
class2 = "coronavirus"

corpus_class1,_ = CreateCorpus(PATH+class1+"/")
corpus_class2,_ = CreateCorpus(PATH+class2+"/")
corpus_class1 = PreProcessingWithNouns(corpus_class1)
corpus_class2 = PreProcessingWithNouns(corpus_class2)

Tokens_class1 = TokenizeDocuments(corpus_class1)
Tokens_class2 = TokenizeDocuments(corpus_class2)
```

Then we adjust the maximum number of terms for our dictionary, create a dictionary generating the top_words list, and create the *feature* sets for both classes (features_class1 and features_class2):

```
MAXTERMS = 400
top_words = CreateDictionary(Tokens_class1,Tokens_class2,MAXTERMS)
(Features_class1,Features_class2) = CreateFeatureSets(Tokens_class1,
                                                      Tokens_class2)
```

From these *feature* lists for each class, we create the training and test *feature* lists for each of them, assuming a training ratio of 70% (0.7):

```
training_features = CrearTrainingFeatures(Features_clase1,Features_clase2,0.7)
testing_features  = CrearTestingFeatures(Features_clase1,Features_clase2,0.7)
```

Then we can train our *MaxEnt* model with the training data:

```
Clasificador = EntrenarModelo(training_features)
```

Once trained, we could show the ten best *features* (lemmatized) and their weights that the classifier learned for both classes (i.e., coronavirus and sports):

```
In [57]: model.show_most_informative_features(10)
   -0.012 death==True and label is 'sports'
   -0.012 voice==True and label is 'sports'
   -0.011 pandemic==True and label is 'sports'
   -0.010 england==True and label is 'coronavirus'
   -0.009 virus==True and label is 'sports'
   -0.008 city==True and label is 'sports'
   -0.008 number==True and label is 'sports'
   -0.008 coronavirus==True and label is 'sports'
   -0.007 year==True and label is 'coronavirus'
    0.005 people==True and label is 'coronavirus'
```

Where the weights that the method gives to each feature (ie, "death = True") in each class (i.e, sports) are shown. At this time, we can already determine the model accuracy for both the training and testing *features*, using the classify.accuracy(..) method of the NLTK library for our model (Classifier):

```
Terminal 1/A ×

In [58]: print("Training Accuracy: ")
    ...: print(nltk.classify.accuracy(model, training_features))
    ...: print("Testing Accuracy: ")
    ...: print(nltk.classify.accuracy(model, testing_features))
Training Accuracy:
0.9343780607247796
Testing Accuracy:
0.576309794988105
```

Note that we are using small test datasets so the performance should be higher as the size of data increases. Furthermore, when evaluating the method with the test *features*, the prediction detail for each sample example isn't shown. In order to classify a simple test text we must use the classify(..) method of our model (model) from an input of *features*. Since the input is usually pure text which can't be directly classified, we must take the text and create the corresponding list of *features* using our CreateFeatures(..) function:

```
category = model.classify(
                 CreateFeatures("victims of covid in the world"))

print("Text Label: " + category)
```

Finally, the result when applying the classifier is:

```
In [59]: category = model.classify(
    ...:                 CreateFeatures("victims of covid in the
world"))
    ...:
    ...: print("Text Label: " + category)
Text label: coronavirus
```

This coincides with our intuition that the input text is more related to the coronavirus category than to sports.

Concluding Remarks

In today's world, the amount of stored information has been enormously increasing in the unstructured form and cannot be used for any processing to extract useful information, so unstructured data analysis techniques known as text analytics or text mining must be applied. These include summarization, classification, clustering, information extraction, and visualization. Text Analytics can be defined as a technique which is used to extract interesting information or knowledge from the text documents. Hence text mining refers to the process of extracting interesting and nontrivial patterns or knowledge from text documents aiming to discover insights with very high commercial values.

The terms *text mining* and *text analytics* are largely synonymous in meaning in conversation, but they can have a more nuanced meaning. Both of them extract textual patterns and trends within unstructured data through the use of machine learning, statistics, and Natural-Language Processing (NLP). By transforming the data into a more structured format, more quantitative insights can be found through text analytics. Data visualization techniques can then be harnessed to communicate findings to wider audiences. Text mining is therefore important as it helps in fetching the information from an unstructured or semi-structured text that is stored in natural language using advanced analytics and statistical algorithms.

The increasing popularity of text analytics technology is credited by the growing adoption of social media platforms and a rising preference toward cloud technology for data storing. There is a worldwide shift among companies to accept cloud technology. The capability to control fraud, supervise risk, and plan successful marketing campaigns are the key factors for the adoption of text analytics across industries. The global text analytics market is also bound to certain limitations such as lack of awareness among end users for software management, high operation cost, and agreement issue with current IT infrastructure.

TEXT ANALYTICS TECHNIQUES

The process of text mining comprises several activities that enable users to uncover information from unstructured text data. Before you can apply different text mining techniques, one must start with text pre-processing, which is the practice of cleaning and transforming text data into a usable format. This practice is a core aspect of NLP and it usually involves the use of techniques such as language identification, tokeni-zation, part-of-speech tagging, chunking, and syntax parsing to format data appropriately for analysis. When text preprocessing is complete, you can apply text mining algorithms to derive insights from the data. Some of these common text mining techniques include information retrieval (i.e., tokenization, stemming), Natural-Language Processing (i.e., part-of-speech tagging, summarization, categorization, sentiment analysis), and information extraction (i.e., named-entity recognition, feature selection and extraction).

TEXT ANALYTICS APPLICATIONS

Industry-specific text analytics technology is used across sectors such as banking and insurance firms, law enforcement and civil litiga-tion, government enterprise, IT sector, publishing firms and media, pharmaceuticals-based research companies, and others for varied appli-cations such as fraud detection, analysis of warranty, medical research, and e-discovery. Companies such as IBM, SAP SE, and Microsoft have assessed the market requirements and provide the services to develop industry-specific text analytics tools.

Thus, text analytics has impacted the way that industries work, allow-ing them to improve product user experiences as well as make faster and better business decisions. Some applications include:

- **Customer service:** when combined with text analytics tools, feed-back systems, such as customer surveys, online reviews, support tickets, and social media profiles, enable companies to improve their customer experience with speed. Text mining and sentiment analysis can provide a mechanism for companies to prioritize key pain points for their customers, allowing businesses to respond to urgent issues in real time and increase customer satisfaction.

- **Healthcare:** Text mining techniques have been increasingly valuable to researchers in the biomedical field, particularly for clustering information. Manual investigation of medical research can be costly and time consuming; text mining provides an automation method for extracting valuable information from medical literature.

- **Risk management:** Text analytics also has applications in risk management, where it can provide insights around industry trends and financial markets by monitoring shifts in sentiment and by extracting information from analyst reports and whitepapers. This is particularly valuable to banking and financial institutions as this text data provides more confidence when considering business investments across various sectors.

- **Maintenance:** Text mining provides a rich and complete picture of the operation and functionality of products and machinery. Over time, text mining automates decision-making by revealing patterns that correlate with problems and preventive and reactive maintenance procedures. Text analytics helps maintenance professionals unearth the root cause of challenges and failures faster.

- **Business Intelligence**: Many companies are using text mining for analysis that supports their key decision-making. Text mining makes the whole analysis process lot more efficient by cutting down the time spent on analysis with accurate insights.

- **Fraud Detection**: Text mining has been helping in highlighting the fraud claims and helping the insurance companies at large. Companies can now process the claims at a much faster pace without falling for fraudulent claims with the help of text mining.

- **Contextual Advertising**: The online advertising industry has been targeting the mass audience that is present on different online platforms, furthering the reach of the enterprises. Text mining makes it efficient by several folds by placing advertisements that are relevant laying a better impact.

THE FUTURE OF TEXT ANALYTICS

Text analytics is already developing a solid foothold, and it will continue to be a necessity in the future. Text analytics implementation was originally slow to gain traction, as there were only loosely integrated, stand-alone solutions available and in many cases it took some time for various industries to realize the true value behind the sophisticated analytical solution. Over the past years, however, adoption rates are increased, and this is expected to continue through 2022 and beyond.

This is partially due to the increase in the sheer quantity of free-form text data available. Furthermore, text analytics can now find value in this data as part of an enterprise-ready, integrated solution. Humans analyzing text by hand, although sometimes very accurate, can be highly variable; some text analytics solutions are more than 90 percent accurate and the speed is exponentially faster.

The exponential rise in text data means that it can no longer be ignored if companies want to stay competitive. Text is, after all, the primary method used for recording thoughts and feelings, and for expressing ideas and reasoning. More than ever before, customers are finding they have a voice.

As organizations take on text analytics, they should utilize tools that allow them to mine the text data for relevant categories of content, automatically determine sentiment by category, and correlate insights using the same categorization and sentiment model across all feedback channels.

Using text analytics, businesses can reach a whole new level of insight into what is being said about them. These tools allow organizations to match sentiment from both positive and negative feedback, analyze sentiment across categories that suit their business, receive timely alerts about sentiment changes, and align those insights with key customer metrics.

Recently, research on deep-learning techniques has brought novel NLP models for NLP and so for text analytics tasks. This includes transformer-based language models such as BERT, GPT, and ELMO, which may improve the text mining adaptability to different domains and languages, accelerate initial configuration, reduce maintenance, and improve accuracy. Transformer-based language models can automatically determine the meaning of words and their association with other words, which can help to categorize sentences into topics and determine the sentiment associated with that topic.

There has been great buzz around these transformer models and the reason is simple: Traditional NLP approaches are getting disrupted by state-of-the-art deep-learning methods built on the latest breakthroughs in research. These breakthroughs are not only revolutionizing the way computers process text data but can also democratize access to high-quality text analysis within an organization.

Bibliography

Agarwal, B., Nayak, R., Mittal, N. & Patnaik, S., 2020. *Deep Learning-Based Approaches for Sentiment Analysis*. Singapore: Springer.

Aggarwal, C., 2013. *Data Clustering: Algorithms and Applications*. Boca Raton, FL: Chapman and Hall/CRC.

Aggarwal, C., 2018. *Machine Learning for text*. Cham: Springer.

Aho, A., Lam, M., Sethi, R. & Ullman, J., 2013. *Compilers: Principles, Techniques, and Tools*. London: Pearson.

Atkinson, J., 2006. Intelligent text mining. In: Zha, X.F. (ed.) *Artificial Intelligence and Integrated Intelligent Information Systems: Emerging Technologies and Applications*. Loveland, CO: Group Publishing.

Atkinson, J., 2007. Evolving explanatory novel patterns for semantically-based text mining. In: Kao, A., and Poteet, S.R. (eds.) *Natural Language Processing and Text Mining*. London: Springer.

Atkinson, J., 2007. Interactive explanatory and descriptive natural-language based dialogue for intelligent information filtering. *Advances in Computers*, 70, pp. 61–103.

Atkinson, J., 2008. Intelligent text mining: Putting evolutionary methods and language technologies together. In: Song, M., and Wu, Y.-F.B. (eds.) *Handbook of Research on Text and Web Mining Technologies*. Hershey, PA: Information Science Reference.

Atkinson, J. & Andrade, C. F. A., 2013. Evolutionary optimization for ranking how-to questions based on user-generated contents. *Expert Systems with Applications*, 40(17), pp. 7060–7068.

Atkinson, J. & Aravena, E., 2009. Discovering Implicit Intention-Level Knowledge from Natural-Language Text. *International Journal of Knowledge-Based Systems*, 22, pp. 502–508.

Atkinson, J. & Bull, V., 2012. A multi-strategy approach to biological named entity recognition. *Expert Systems with Applications*, 39(17), pp. 12968–12974.

Atkinson, J., Curtis, D. & Montecinos, G., 2016. Question-driven topic-based extraction of protein-protein interaction methods from biomedical literature. *Information Sciences*, 360, pp. 170–180.

Atkinson, J., Gonzalez, A., Muñoz, M. & Astudillo, H., 2014. Web metadata extraction and semantic indexing for learning objects extraction. *Applied Intelligence*, 41(2), pp. 649–664.

Atkinson, J. & Matamala, A., 2012. Evolutionary shallow natural language parsing. *Computational Intelligence*, 28(2), pp. 156–175.

Atkinson, J. & Munoz, R., 2013. Rhetorics-based multi-document summarization. *Expert Systems with Applications*, 40(11), pp. 4346–4352.

Atkinson, J. & Palma, D., 2018. Coherence-based automatic essay assessment. *IEEE Intelligent Systems*, 33(5), pp. 26–36.

Atkinson, J. & Pérez, C., 2013. A semantically-based lattice approach for assessing patterns. *Computación y Sistemas*, 17, pp. 467–476.

Atkinson, J. & Rivas, A., 2008. Discovering novel causal patterns from biomedical natural-language texts using bayesian nets. *IEEE Transactions on Information Technology in Biomedicine*, 12, pp. 714–722.

Atkinson, J., Salas, G. & Figueroa, A., 2015. Improving opinion retrieval in social media by combining features -based coreferencing and memory-based learning. *Information Sciences*, 299, pp. 20–31.

Baron, M., 2019. *Probability and Statistics for Computer Scientists*. Boca Raton, FL: Chapman and Hall/CRC.

Beaujean, A., 2014. *Latent Variable Modeling Using R: A Step-by-Step Guide*. Abingdon: Routledge.

Bengfort, B. & Bilbro, R. O. T., 2018. *Applied Text Analysis with Python: Enabling Language-Aware Data Products with Machine Learning* . Newton, MA: O'Reilly Media.

Bermúdez, J., 2020. *Cognitive Science: An Introduction to the Science of the Mind*. Cambridge: Cambridge University Press.

Bird, S., Klein, E, & Loper, E., 2009. *Natural Language Processing with Python: Analyzing Text with the Natural Language Toolkit*. Newton, MA: O'Reilly Media.

Bishop, C., 2006. *Pattern Recognition and Machine Learning* . New York: Springer.

Bohnet, B., et al., 2018. *Morphosyntactic Tagging with a Meta-BiLSTM Model over Context Sensitive Token Encodings*. Melbourne, Australia, s.n.

Bokka, K., Hora, S. & Jain, T., 2019. *Deep Learning for Natural Language Processing: Solve Your Natural Language Processing Problems with Smart Deep Neural Networks*. Birmingham: Packt Publishing.

Burns, S., 2019. *Natural Language Processing: A Quick Introduction to NLP with Python and NLTK*. Seattle, WA: Amazon.com Services.

Büttcher, S., Clarke, C. & Cormack, G., 2010. *Information Retrieval: Implementing and Evaluating Search Engines*. Cambridge, MA: MIT Press.

De Swart, H., 2015. *Introduction to Natural Language Semantics*. Stanford, CA: Center for the Study of Language and Information.

Devlin, J., Wei, M., Kenton, C. & Toutanova, L., 2019. BERT: Pre-training of Deep Bidirectional Transformers for Language Understanding. *Proceedings of NAACL-HLT*, 2019, pp. 4171–4186.

Eisenstein, J., 2019. *Introduction to Natural Language Processing*. Cambridge, MA: The MIT Press.

Figueroa, A. & Atkinson, J., 2011. Maximum entropy context models for ranking biographical answers to open-domain definition questions. *AAAI*.

Figueroa, A. & Atkinson, J., 2016. Ensembling Classifiers for Detecting User Intentions behind Web Queries. *IEEE Internet Computing*, 20, pp. 8–16.

Flach, P., 2012. *Machine Learning : The Art and Science of Algorithms that Make Sense of Data*. Cambridge: Cambridge University Press.

Foster, D., 2019. *Generative Deep Learning: Teaching Machines to Paint, Write, Compose, and Play*. Newton, MA: O'Reilly Media.

Friedl, J., 2006. *Mastering Regular Expressions : Understand Your Data and Be More Productive*. Newton, MA: O'Reilly Media.

Ghosh, S. & Gunning, D., 2019. *Natural Language Processing Fundamentals: Build Intelligent Applications that Can Interpret the Human Language to Deliver Impactful Results*. Birmingham: Packt Publishing.

Gillon, B., 2019. *Natural Language Semantics: Formation and Valuation*. Cambridge, MA: The MIT Press.

Goldberg, Y., 2017. *Neural Network Methods for Natural Language Processing*. San Rafael, CA: Morgan & Claypool Publishers.

Graves, A., 2012. *Supervised Sequence Labelling with Recurrent Neural Networks*. Heidelberg: Springer.

Hearst, M., 1998. Automated discovery of WordNet relations. In: Fellbaum, C. (ed.) *WordNet: An Electronic Lexical Database and Some of its Applications*. Cambridge, MA: The MIT Press.

Huang, T., Hsieh, C. & Wang, H., 2018. Automatic meeting summarization and topic detection system. *Data Technologies and Applications*, 52, pp. 351–365.

Ignatow, G. & Mihalcea, R., 2017. *An Introduction to Text Mining: Research Design, Data Collection, and Analysis*. New York: SAGE Publications.

Jurafsky, D., Martin, J., Norvig, P. & Russell, S., 2014. *Speech and Language Processing*. London: Pearson.

Kamath, U., Liu, J. & Whitaker, J., 2019. *Deep Learning for NLP and Speech Recognition*. Berlin: Springer.

Karmeshu, 2003. *Entropy Measures, Maximum Entropy Principle and Emerging Applications (Studies in Fuzziness and Soft Computing)*. Berlin: Springer.

Kendall, E. & McGuinness, D., 2019. *Ontology Engineering*. San Rafael, CA: Morgan & Claypool Publishers.

Klein, P., 2015. *Coding the Matrix: Linear Algebra through Computer Science Applications*. London: Newtonian Press.

Kuhn, M. & Johnson, K., 2019. *Feature Engineering and Selection: A Practical Approach for Predictive Models*. Boca Raton, FL: CRC Press.

Landauer, T., McNamara, D., Dennis, S. & Kintsch, W., 2014. *Handbook of Latent Semantic Analysis* . Abingdon: Routledge.

Liu, B., 2015. *Sentiment Analysis: Mining Opinions, Sentiments, and Emotions*. Cambridge: Cambridge University Press.

Mohri, M., Rostamizadeh, A. & Talwalkar, A., 2018. *Foundations of Machine Learning* . Cambridge, MA: The MIT Press.

Pozzi, F., Fersini, E., Messina, E. & Liu, B., 2016. *Sentiment Analysis in Social Networks*. Burlington, MA: Morgan Kaufmann.

Rabiner, L. & Schafer, R., 2011. *Theory and Applications of Digital Speech Processing.* London: Pearson.

Russell, S. & Norvig, P., 2016. *Artificial Intelligence: A Modern Approach.* London: Pearson.

Sankar, C., et al., 2019. *Do Neural Dialog Systems Use the Conversation History Effectively? An Empirical Study.* Florence, Italy: ACL (Association for Computational Linguistics).

Sarkar, D., 2016. *Text Analytics with Python: A Practical Real-World Approach to Gaining Actionable Insights from your Data.* New York: Apress.

Schmidt, J., 2019. *Self-organizing Neural Maps: The Retinotectal Map and Mechanisms of Neural Development: From Retina to Tectum.* Cambridge, MA: Academic Press.

Sherstinsky, A., 2020. Fundamentals of Recurrent Neural Network (RNN) and Long Short-Term Memory (LSTM) network. *Physica D: Nonlinear Phenomena,* 404, p. 132306.

Sipser, M., 2012. *Introduction to the Theory of Computation.* Boston, MA: Cengage Learning.

Srivastava, A. & Sahami, M., 2009. *Text Mining: Classification, Clustering, and Applications.* Boca Raton, FL: Chapman and Hall/CRC.

Stede, M., 2011. *Discourse Processing.* San Rafael, CA: Morgan & Claypool Publishers.

Struhl, S., 2015. *Practical Text Analytics: Interpreting Text and Unstructured Data for Business Intelligence.* London: Kogan Page.

Tan, P.-N., Steinbach, M., Karpatne, A. & Kumar, V., 2018. *Introduction to Data Mining.* London: Pearson.

Vasiliev, Y., 2020. *Natural Language Processing with Python and SpaCy: A Practical Introduction.* San Francisco, CA: No Starch Press.

Wilmott, P., 2020. *Machine Learning : An Applied Mathematics Introduction.* Oxford: Panda Ohana Publishing.

Wu, C.-S., et al., 2019. *Transferable Multi-Domain State Generator for Task-Oriented Dialogue Systems.* Florence, Italy: ACL (Association for Computational Linguistics)..

Yang, Q., Zhang, Y., Dai, W. & Pan, S., 2020. *Transfer Learning.* Cambridge: Cambridge University Press.

Zhai, C. & Massung, S., 2016. *Text Data Management and Analysis: A Practical Introduction to Information Retrieval and Text Mining.* San Rafael, CA: ACM and Morgan & Claypool Publishers.

Zou, K., et al. 2016. *Statistical Evaluation of Diagnostic Performance: Topics in ROC Analysis.* Boca Raton, FL: Chapman and Hall/CRC.

Glossary

Annotation Practice and result of adding "notes" or electronic glosses to a text, which may include highlights, linguistic purpose tags, links, etc.

Machine Learning Artificial intelligence area that studies computational algorithms that improve their performance as they gain more experience. Machine learning algorithms build mathematical models from sample data, known as "training data," in order to make predictions or decisions without being explicitly programmed.

Unsupervised Learning A machine learning task that searches for patterns that haven't been previously detected in a dataset without preexisting exit tags and with minimal human supervision.

Supervised Learning Machine learning task that transforms an input into an output based on examples of desired input–output pairs labeled by humans.

Centroid Position of the arithmetic mean or center of all points in a geometric figure. That is, the point at which a cut in the figure could be perfectly balanced at the "point of a pin". This extends to any target in n-dimensional space: Centroids are the average position of all points in all coordinate directions.

Class Set of individuals or objects. A class can be defined either by extension or by intention, using some ontological language. In other words, a class is a taxonomic unit that can group instances of objects.

Corpus Linguistic resource consisting of a large set of texts or documents, which are used to perform statistical analysis, hypothesis testing, revision of the occurrence of linguistic rules, etc.

Dataset Dataset on a particular topic. In the case of having a table structure, each column represents a particular variable, and each row corresponds to a data record.

Categorical Data Variable that can take one of a limited and fixed number of possible values (for example, enumerated data type) and assigning each one to a particular group or nominal category based on some qualitative property.

Dimension The dimension of a space or mathematical object is defined as the minimum number of coordinates necessary to specify any point within it.

Euclidean Distance Ordinary distance in a straight line between two points in a Euclidean space.

Probability Distribution Mathematical function that gives the occurrence probabilities of different possible results of a random experiment.

Entropy The basic amount of information that can be associated with any random variable, which can be interpreted as the average level of "surprise" or "uncertainty" inherent in the possible results of the variable.

Vector Space Set of objects called vectors that can be added or multiplied by numbers, called scalars.

Tag Keyword or term that's assigned to a piece of linguistic information, which allows describing and searching for an item. Tags are usually chosen from a controlled language vocabulary.

Feature Individually measurable property or characteristic of an observed phenomenon. Choosing informative, discriminatory, and independent features is a fundamental task to produce effective algorithms in classification, prediction, or other tasks.

Curse of Dimensionality Type of phenomenon that arises when data is analyzed and organized in highly dimensional spaces that don't occur in low-dimensional environments. In particular, as the dimensionality of the data increases, the volume of the space increases so rapidly that the available data becomes more dispersed.

Bag of Words Model Simplified representation used in natural language processing and information retrieval, in which a text is represented as a "bag" (multi set) of its words, without considering grammatical aspects or word order.

Artificial Neural Network System inspired by biological neural networks, which automatically learn to perform tasks considering examples, and generally without being programmed with task-specific rules.

Overfit Effect of overtraining a machine learning algorithm with certain data for which the desired result is known. In other words, when over-trained, an algorithm can be adjusted to very specific characteristics of the training data that don't have a causal relationship with the objective function.

Token Particular instance of a class language object. A linguistic element, such as a phrase, can have multiple tokens.

Topic Subject of a sentence or text about what is being talked about. Therefore, a topic has pragmatic and not grammatical considerations.

Topology Set of properties of a geometric object that are preserved against continuous deformations. A topological space has an associated structure, called a topology, which allows defining continuous deformations of subspaces.

Latent Variable Variable type that's not directly observable but can be inferred using a mathematical model from other variables that are observable.

Index